Perth:
a Place in His

Edited by
David Strachan

Published by Perth and Kinross Heritage Trust 2011

Printed and Bound by Farquhar and Son Ltd., Perth

ISBN 978-0-9564427-5-8

Perth and Kinross
Heritage Trust
Archaeology | Architecture | Conservation

Front Cover illustrations: *A reconstruction painting showing the plundering of the friaries following John Knox's sermon at St John's on 11 May 1559 (artist: David Simon/© Perth and Kinross Heritage Trust)*

Back cover illustrations: *The King William the Lion charter of 2010 (Perth and Kinross Council Archives) and (top-left) Magnus Jackson's photograph of the harbour in the 1880s; (top-right) Perth High Street c1905; (bottom-right)* View of Perth from Boatland *by David Octavius Hill in 1826 (all courtesy of Perth Museum and Art Gallery); and (bottom-left) a print by J Stewart and J Swan from the early 1840s showing Perth bridge and the North Inch (AK Bell Library, Local Studies).*

Acknowledgements

My foremost debt in preparing this volume is to the authors who have provided such a wealth of information with such imagination and insight. I would also like to acknowledge Steve Connelly, Sara Ann Kelly and Sue Payne who were instrumental in organising the conference on which the publication is based.

Finally, both the conference and publication were made possible as result of generous funding from Perth Common Good Fund; Perth Civic Trust; The Guildry Incorporation of Perth; and The Glover Incorporation of Perth.

Contents

Preface

Perth: a Place in History was a remarkably successful two-day conference held last year in Perth Concert Hall. It was an important element in the year-long celebrations with which Perth marked the 800th anniversary of the Royal Charter granted to the city by King William the Lion in 1210. In my opening address I expressed the hope that the conference would add intellectual gravitas to the celebrations, and I was not disappointed. I also said that a vital component of the event would be the publication of the proceedings. That has now come to pass, and so it gives me great pleasure to write this introduction.

The actual date of King William's charter is a matter of some uncertainty. Since the 1600s both Crown and Council have assumed it was in 1210, but recently historians have revised the probable date backwards to 1209. However, in 1960 Perth celebrated its 750th anniversary with a visit by H.M. The Queen, and the opening of the Queen's bridge, and so 2010 was still the obvious date to celebrate the anniversary. Furthermore, although King William granted the earliest charter that still survives, Perth's first royal charter (now sadly lost) was bestowed by King David I in the 1120s.

The Perth800 celebrations were part of the Council's strategy to stimulate Perth's economy and raise its international profile as it prepared to launch a bid to restore Perth's ancient city status during the Queen's Diamond Jubilee Year in 2012.

The idea for the conference was developed by a group of Council officers with a keen interest in fostering the study of the history of Perth & Kinross: Sara Ann Kelly, Local Studies Librarian; Sue Payne, Museum Principal Officer (History) and Steve Connelly, Archivist. Perth & Kinross Heritage Trust aided in fund-raising and presenting the conference. From the start the ambition was to bring high calibre speakers from near and far to explore different aspects of Perth's archaeology and history.

The conference attracted generous sponsorship from the Glover Incorporation of Perth, The Guildry Incorporation of Perth, Perth Common Good Fund and Perth Civic Trust, all of which allowed the conference to be held in the main auditorium of Perth Concert Hall, attracting an excellent audience of around 500 on each day.

Everyone who was there agreed that it was an excellent event and we were very grateful to the contributors for sharing their expertise and insights into Perth's past. These published proceedings will bring those observations to the wider audience that they deserve. We are very grateful to our speakers for taking the extra effort to convert their oral contributions into written articles.

Great credit goes to David Strachan of the Heritage Trust for taking on the considerable task of editing and publishing the proceedings within one year of the event.

Dr John Hulbert
Provost of Perth & Kinross
August 2011

Introduction

Despite the pioneering article by Professor A.A.M.Duncan in 1974[1], and the programme of rescue archaeology in the 1970s and 80s, which at that time brought Perth to the forefront of Scottish medieval urban studies, the city has not seen as much work published on its history in recent decades as other ancient burghs, such as Edinburgh, Glasgow or Dundee. In 2010 occurred the eight hundredth anniversary of the grant of a royal charter to Perth by William the Lion. It was a wonderful notion to embody in the civic celebrations of this event, a major historical conference that would bring together recent historical scholarship on the city, from earliest times to the present day. The papers from those two days of meeting and discussion form the present volume.

The twelve authors represent both professional and amateur scholars, both archaeologists and historians, and span many different approaches from archaeology to business history, covering a time-span from the Mesolithic to the twentieth century. What they demonstrate together is a vibrancy of research scholarship that was belied by its recent low profile. There has always been a great deal going on in Perth, and, as several of these papers testify, a strong civic spirit that has supported what Professor Whatley calls in his chapter 'one of the richest and most user-friendly local authority archives in Scotland in the AK Bell library'. The conference organisers, from Perth and Kinross Heritage Trust, Perth Archives, AK Bell library Local Studies and Perth Museum are to be congratulated in organising the conference and seeing this venture through to the printed page.

David Strachan sets us off to serious purpose by outlining the prehistory of the area around Perth, from the first scatters of prehistoric flint to the heavy masonry of the Romans and Picts. He emphasises how rich it was in important settlements, Moncreiffe, Abernethy, Forteviot and Scone, sometimes with millennia of strategic or ritual use and reuse spanning the Neolithic to the early Christian era, all long before the foundation of Perth. The Romans in this seem a mere interruption. 'The wooded island on the flood plain', which is what Perth's name implies, became the leading settlement eventually, because the river was shallow enough to provide a decent ford, yet navigable enough to bring ships up. So it is when trade and communication grew in significance that there was good reason for Perth, and it is trade and communication that have been its purpose ever since.

In the next chapter, Derek Hall revisits the fascinations of medieval Perth. The first settlement can be confidently dated from wooden and ceramic fragments, to the mid-eleventh century, showing that the medieval kings did not so much create as recognise a thriving settlement. Finds from its trade and manufactures throughout the middle ages - leather and silk materials, a jet chess piece, bone combs, even fourteenth-century ceramic stove tiles from Germany - indicate a certain level of luxury appropriate to a burgh that was also the site of a royal castle (albeit washed away in 1209, a year before the charter), no fewer than four religious houses and a number of nobles' lodgings. Richard Oram shows from environmental history that life for most people was often hard, in his grim demonstration of the effects of repeated visitations of famine, flood and epidemic from the late thirteenth century through to the sixteenth. No doubt he could have continued the tale throughout the seventeenth century as well. In the Little Ice Age, those who could afford to relieve their shivering by buying the latest German stoves were the lucky ones.

Alan MacDonald, in contrast, demonstrates from his study of Perth and parliament, 1300-1707, that the burgh authorities were obsessed with the prestige and display that the town could muster even in such difficult times. Before the assassination of James I in the toilet of the Dominican Friary in 1437, Perth was shaping up to become the capital of Scotland, hosting in the first half of the fifteenth century, fourteen of the twenty-one sessions of parliament when Edinburgh hosted only five. The murder put paid to that, but Perth always found it worth its while to have high profile in parliament, obtaining committee places to frame policy to its advantage, and canvassing support for its bridge. It wore out the patience of its fellow burghs in an endless dispute with Dundee over which should rank as the second burgh of Scotland in Parliamentary processions.

We are taken on a lively tour of the streets of sixteenth century Perth by Mary Verschuur, to show the life (and crime) of a town where craftsmen were unusually prominent in economic and civic activity. It was therefore thronged with booths selling consumer goods, and attractive to visitors and those who could afford lodgings in town, not least the heads of the religious houses round about. Perhaps for this reason, it turned into a hot-bed of religious dissent and provided its quota of Protestant martyrs, including the unfortunate Helen Stirk whose offence was not to pray to the Virgin when she was in childbirth. Perth produced determined and powerful women in other ways, including widows of craftsmen who carried on their former husbands' trades with aplomb and flair.

The post-union world is the subject of the second half of the book, beginning with Chris Whatley's fascinating and much-needed account of the Enlightenment in Perth, part of a larger study of the eighteenth-century culture of Scottish provincial towns. He emphasises its lively and distinct character, Perth's elite being determined not to be overshadowed by Edinburgh but to produce its own Enlightenment, focussed on the Scottish (rather than the cosmopolitan) and on the validity of the local (rather than an insistence on the general and universal). The town lacked the advantage of a university, but produced its own new institutions,

Perth Academy in 1760, and the Literary and Antiquarian Society and Perth Library in 1784: the great John Smeaton built a new bridge over the Tay: the council pulled down the old town cross in more than a symbolic effort to welcome a new pulse of industry, and encouraged the elegant rebuilding of the old town. Not so easy to regulate were the hearts and minds of a burgeoning population of handloom weavers. In 1794, a slogan painted on the bridge read, 'Britain must be a republic, liberty and equality', which was not the Enlightenment their social superiors wanted.

Taking a step back to look at the mapping of Perth, Chris Fleet shows how map makers reveal as much about their own preoccupations as about the city. Timothy Pont around 1600 provided an incomplete sketch with a focus on the country around: Adair nearly a century later focussed on routeways, with Perth as a hub: Petit's map, the first overhead plan, was concerned with a project for a new fort, and Roy's was a 'magnificent military sketch'. Stobie's map of Perthshire in 1783 emphasised the power and standing of the landed aristocracy, and each of the great nineteenth century maps had their own agenda of mapping the electoral boundaries, the route of railways or assisting the control of disease, culminating in the Ordnance Survey town plan of 1860 which showed individual trees and drying poles. Not least remarkable were the RAF aerial photographs of the Second World War. Last in the series is Google, which makes Perth look like anywhere else, revealing more about globalisation than about Perth.

Charles McKean traces the story of the architectural development of Perth after the Union and into the age of improvement, and asks why it is not more like that of an English county town of similar size. The favoured architect of Provost Marshall, Robert Reid, was rival to James Gillespie and Robert Smirke, preferred by the county, in an abortive joint town-and-county proposal for a civic centre. The magistrates eventually proved more interested in manufacture than in urban elegance, so the facades of Rose Terrace and Marshall Place served to conceal the smokestacks of industry. What mattered so often in Perth's history was the abiding tradition of the city as a place where you made things, not (as in English county towns) just a place where you sold them.

Rhoda Fothergill's account of nineteenth-century benefactors of Perth dwelt especially on Adam Anderson, the rector of the Academy from 1809 to 1837, and John Pullar and his sons, the famous 'Pullars of Perth', dyers and dry cleaners. Anderson was instrumental in many and diverse enterprises within the town, starting with the introduction of gas lighting, when he smoothed the fears of the population by a series of public lectures explaining the properties of coal gas. A similar lecture course followed on the introduction of modern weights and measures. He helped actively to bring about improvements to the river, the harbour and the inches, and especially the arrival of the magnificent water-works. Anderson was an intellectual, eventually becoming a professor at St Andrews: the Pullars by contrast were formidable entrepreneurs whose success in business was matched by their civic generosity. A nineteenth-century town depended on such examples of public spirit to operate, and businessmen were ready to spend their own money on the town even though they might complain about the rates.

The book ends with three chapters on business history which recapitulate some of these lessons. Alia Campbell tells the tale of Arthur Bell, who believed that the quality of his blended whisky should speak for itself, but whose sons saved the day by seeing that sales abroad needed advertising, especially in the Commonwealth countries. One of these was A.K. Bell, to whose library we owe so much. Dewars are likewise described by Jacqui Seargeant, in a remarkably similar story of a founder who introduced a high-quality brand of his own whisky, followed by sons who built the firm up to be one of the big three in Scottish whisky by the early twentieth century. In this case, one of the second generation brothers was an advertising wizard, who in 1898 brought America to a halt by projecting a new cinematograph film onto the side of a building in the centre of New York. Susan Payne tells the extraordinary story of General Accident, of how a company set up in 1885 to insure farmers, became Scotland's third largest company, a homely multi-national with its headquarters in Perth, largely because of its success in capturing world-wide motor insurance business at an early stage.

There is common thread that runs through these studies: the great businessmen were devoted to their enterprise and work, but often also to leaving a legacy: libraries, housing estates and sports grounds come out of their pockets. They often served as provosts and in other civic offices, just as their predecessors in the town crafts had done in earlier centuries. They were generously paternalistic employers, but often ruled with an iron rod and did not take kindly to unions, as though the graffiti on the bridge in 1794 had entered their souls as a warning. They had an immediate sense of the opportunities presented to a Victorian in the outside world, both in the British empire and America, yet their domestic horizons were immediate and local. They would have agreed with the eighteenth century mood that Perth was home and home was where the heart was.

Today, it is sad to consider how the ownership of these firms is now far away from Perth, and the uninformed might conclude that the city's hey-day was over. That, however, is entirely the wrong conclusion, and modern Perth has come top of the opinion polls for quality of life and as a desirable place to live. The conference ended with a presentation on the modern town plan by the city's then Head of Planning, Roland Bean, who has been responsible for overseeing the highly successful pedestrianisation of the principal streets, the fine new civic buildings of the centre and the revival of the river front. Perth is proving itself to be a better place to live in than it has ever been before. But this would not have been possible without a very real, and a very Perth-like, sense of place, combined with a determination recently to preserve its heritage and to present it beautifully. The spirit which inspired the conference and the completion of this book to publication will surely ensure that the city will continue to have a vast amount to be proud about.

Prof T C Smout
HM Historiographer Royal for Scotland

[1]A A M Duncan, 'Perth: the first century of the burgh,' Transactions of the Perthshire Society of Natural Science, Special Issue 1974, available on http://psns.tsohost.co.uk/archaeological/Full%20txt.pdf

Before the Burgh: 15,000 years of crossing the Tay

David Strachan

Introduction

As with my opening presentation to the Perth conference in September 2010, the purpose of this paper is by way of a prologue, setting the scene for the proceedings within. By exploring the evolution of the cultural landscape of Perth's environs from early prehistory, the aim is to assess how key human episodes, along with determining geographical factors, may have influenced the location of the pre-burgh settlement in the tenth century.

After the Ice – populating the landscape in the Mesolithic

The topography of the Perthshire landscape was created over the most recent glacial episodes of the last 30,000 years. While the earlier glaciers, some up to 2km in depth, eroded bedrock and transported huge quantities of debris, it was the retreat of the final ice sheets, around 12,000 years ago, and the actions of their melt-water rivers, that fashioned the moraines and outwash terraces visible in river valleys such as Strathtay and Strathearn today.[1]

Perth sits in a key geographical location, part of this grand geological story: just below the highland–lowland division, where glacial action created the river-systems that feed into the dominant geographical feature of the Tayside area: the estuary itself. Perth's wider environs encompass only part of the Tay's vast catchment area: from southern highlands to estuarine mud-banks. It is the backdrop to this prehistory of the area, and most importantly provides the region's powerful links between land and sea. In addition to the strong estuarine and riverine conduits that link the sea with the land, there are major terrestrial routes radiating from the Perth area itself: Strathtay, Strathmore and Strathearn. From earliest times these routes have connected highland and lowland, land and sea, and made the Perth area one of the key nodes in Scotland's east coast geography.

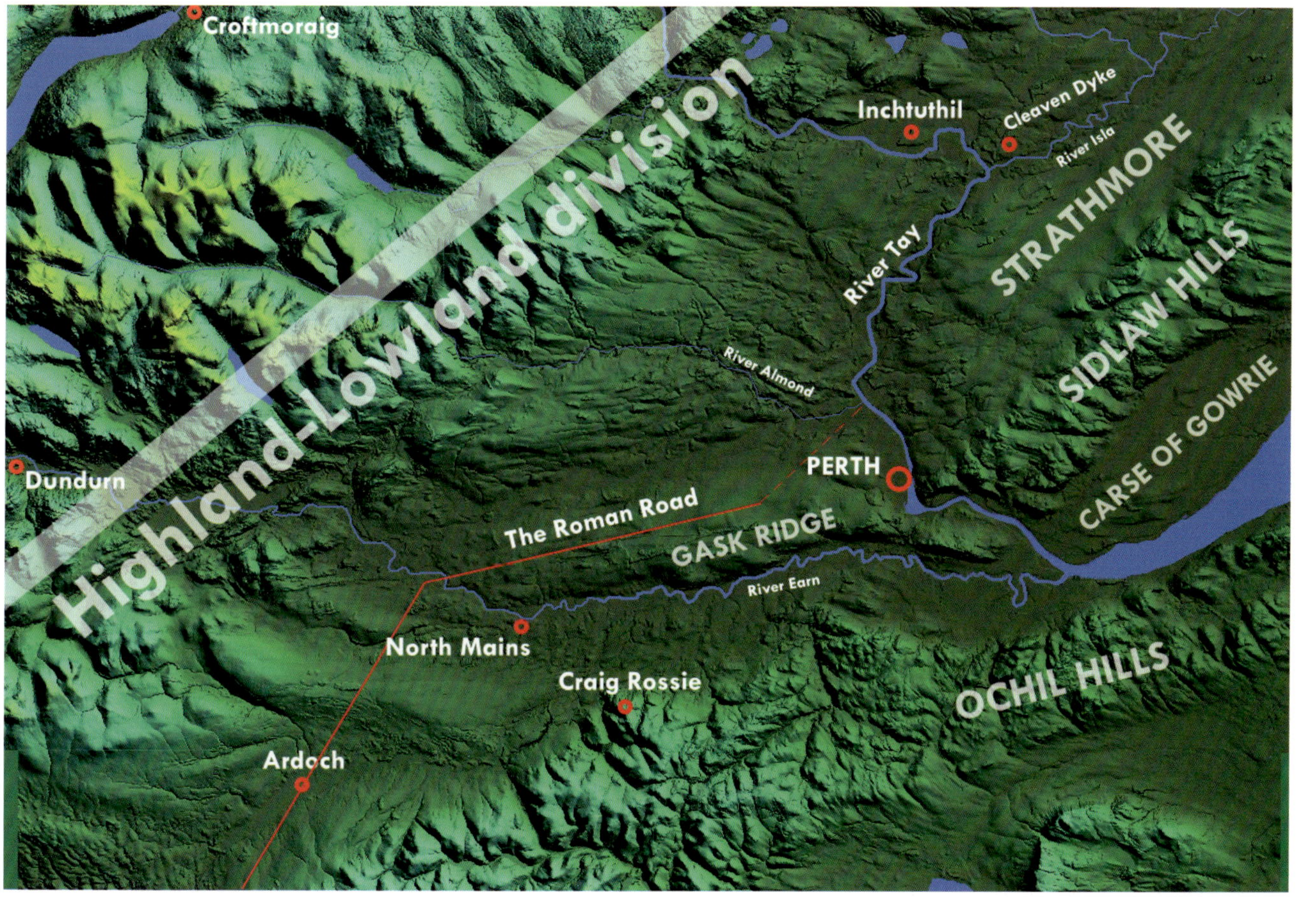

This relief map shows Perth and its environs: naming major rivers, landform features and key sites while dramatically illustrating the impact of the last glaciation (© Intermap Technologies Inc. All rights reserved. DPER100. 2011; annotation © PKHT).

Our earliest evidence of human activity in Tayside occurs remarkably soon after the all-obliterating effects of the last glaciers. The post-glacial landscape of rock, gravel and water gradually produced soils through water, frost and chemical action. With soil came plants, and early herb and shrub colonisers, such as sedges, birch and juniper, were followed by woodland of ash, hazel and oak.[2] Dense, tall oak-dominated wildwood was to cover Tayside, an environment which soon supported bears, wolves, wild cattle and pig, squirrels, otters, and of course fish and birds. The estuary itself is surrounded by a variety of converging landscape zones: riverine, lowland hills, carse and strath. It is from the rich and varied natural resources found in these different environments, that we have the evidence for the first humans around 10,000 years ago…

The Mesolithic (or Middle Stone Age) lasts some 4,000 years from around 8000 to 4000 BC. It is remarkable, however, that we have such little evidence of their activities given that the hunter-gather communities of this era inhabited the land for such a long period of time. The known Perth and Kinross material consists of only thirty or so artefacts that could be comfortably stored in a shoebox. These finds consist of small flint blades, most commonly 'scrapers', but also leaf-shaped arrowheads. We know from other sites in the UK, however, that these were nomadic groups who moved with the seasons visiting different environments and their resources, and their artefacts were mainly of wood, bone and other organic materials that generally perish over time. So both their lifestyle and small numbers explain why their remains are so difficult to find.[3]

Clusters of these stone finds, or lithic scatters, however, can indicate knapping sites, if not campsites. Field-walking by Reading University may have revealed a glimpse of such activity at Mains of Murthly, where a low density of worked quartz and flint was found on the southern side of Strath Tay.[4] It is significant, however, that the distribution shows a noticeable concentration on Kinnoull Hill, with its dramatic cliffs overlooking the Tay estuary, only 2km to the east of Perth. As it is today, it was clearly a favoured place 7,000 years ago, however to Mesolithic hunter-gatherers the panoramic views would have offered an ideal platform from which to view the landscape and plan routes and hunts. The possibility of a Mesolithic knapping and/or campsites on Kinnoull Hill must remain a possibility. Intriguingly, we also have the suggestion of a possible Mesolithic logboat from nearby Friarton, recovered in 1879 and recorded by the geologist James Geikie.[5] While the Friarton boat no longer survives, and cannot therefore be verified, both it, and the flint finds must be viewed in the context of the sea-level change: as around 5000 BC both the Carse of Gowrie and much of Strathearn was flooded as a result of the final melting of the North American and Scandinavian ice sheets.[6] This glimpse of activity in the very distant past is the first indicator of the Tay as a conduit to communication and transport, in addition to sustenance.

By way of a coda to our first study, it is significant that two projects at Loch Tay have recently produced surprising results from this time. A hill-top hunting camp was unearthed beneath a shieling high on Ben Lawers, where charcoal from a campfire produced a radiocarbon date of between 7200–6700 BC, and evidence for the knapping or retouching of stone tools on the site[7] while, from below the surface of the loch, preserved timbers have produced dates ranging from the Mesolithic to the Neolithic.[8] This sporadic distribution leaves us with an enigma: wherewith the Mesolithic between these clusters?

First Farmers and Magic Metal – the Neolithic and Bronze Age

The Neolithic (or New Stone Age) gradually saw the end of Mesolithic ways with the introduction of domesticated plants and animals, along with polished stone axes and pottery, by around 4000 BC. The construction of the first large-scale monuments in the landscape at this time reflects both a significant increase in population and a change in social order and aspiration. These early ritual and burial monuments begin the long-term process of creating the cultural landscape.

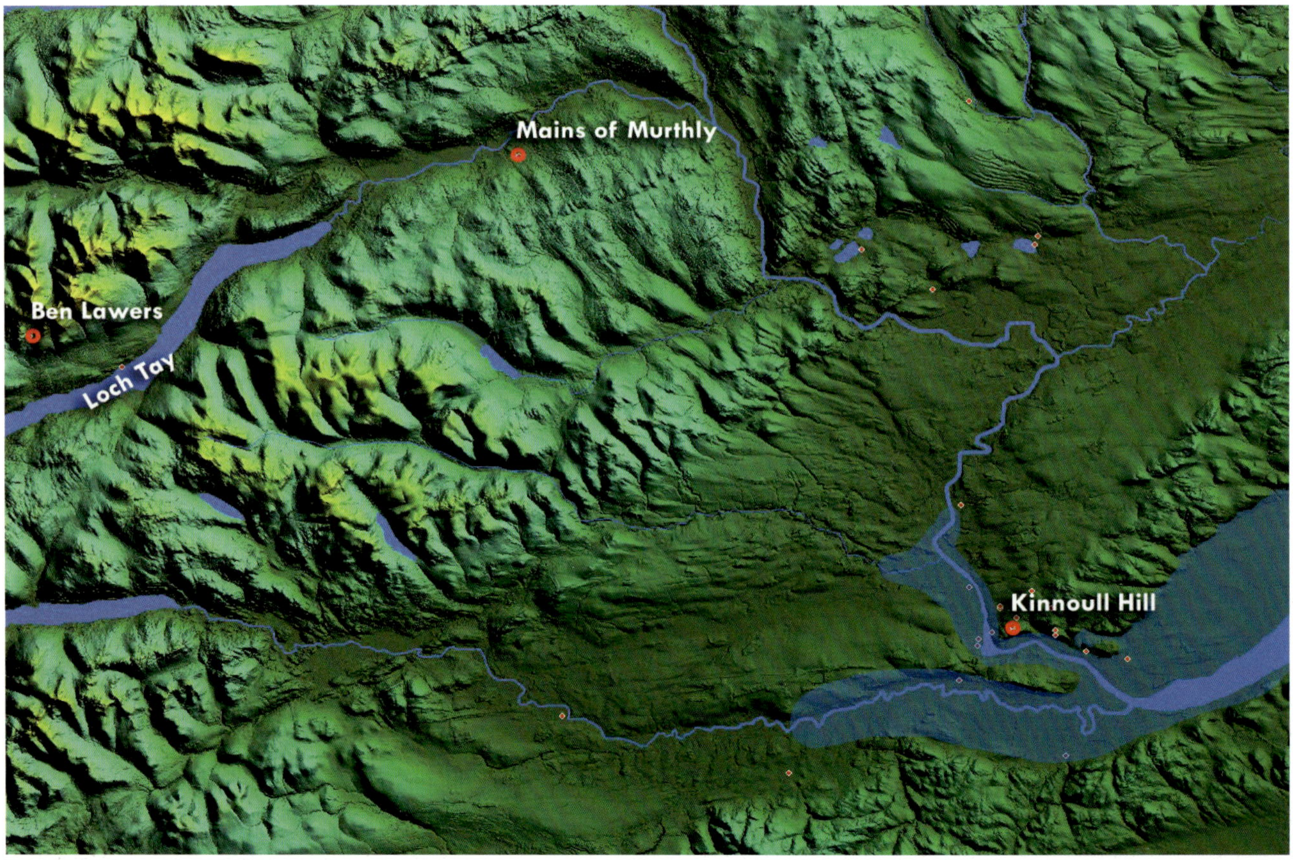

The distribution of known Mesolithic finds from the Perth and Kinross area, and the possible logboat from Friarton, Perth, with sea-level c5000 BC (© Intermap Technologies Inc. All rights reserved. DPER100. 2011; annotation © PKHT).

Among the earliest monuments are mounds and cairns which covered burial chambers. The current understanding is that excarnation was practised, with skeletal remains subsequently being deposited within the chambers. This 'ossuary' practice of de-fleshing before burial probably occurred at separate sites, on platforms within elongated mortuary enclosures such as the example excavated at Inchtuthil, on the banks of the Tay around 15km north of Perth. The site, which was around 50×10m and dating to c3900 BC, included a fence of oak posts constructed within the ditch of the enclosure. This had been set on fire and while it burned, gravel and soil were pushed into the ditch.[9] While there was no evidence of treatment of the dead, comparisons with similar sites elsewhere suggests that these timber mortuary structures were used repeatedly for interment of bones while they were free-standing structures. This form of burial practice appears to centre on worship of a *common ancestor* rather than the individual. The number of individuals collected within these tombs over long periods, however, must represent only a small percentage of the total population. So there was clearly a selection process at work. In the later Neolithic there is increased regional diversity to burial and the communal mounds go out of use around 2500 BC, with a subsequent trend to focusing on individuals.

The early Neolithic also saw the construction of large-scale arenas, possibly used for processional rituals, in the form of 'cursus' monuments: (usually) large elongated enclosures, often rectangular, defined by a ditch and bank. In national terms, there is a concentration of these in Perthshire, with twelve examples in the lowlands and straths; but all but one have been ploughed flat by subsequent agriculture and are no longer visible, although they do survive buried beneath the plough-soil. The exception is the Cleaven Dyke, which is arguably the best-preserved example in Britain. It was at least 2.1km in length, with two parallel ditches, set about 50m apart, and had a much-exaggerated version of long barrow, running between these ditches. This was built in about thirty-four segments within five main sections, and excavation has suggested this gradual process of extending the site began around 3500 BC.[10] It is suggested that the act of groups gathering, perhaps annually, to work on such communal projects may have been as important as the resulting monuments themselves. As we will discover, it is remarkable, given that these were amongst the first monuments built, that the example at Blairhall, near Scone, would appear to feature so prominently in events over four thousand years after it was constructed.

In the later Neolithic, a new ceremonial enclosure, the 'henge' was introduced, comprising a large circular ditch with external bank, usually with two opposing entrances. They often contained stone or timber circles and there are at least seventeen examples in the area. The massive ditch at North Mains, on the banks of the River Earn to the east of Muthill, enclosed an area 35m across and containing two rings of uprights. The outer was roughly circular and around 25m in diameter, with twenty-four pits, each up to 2m deep, while the inner ring was more oval and consisted of eighteen pits which showed little evidence of having held posts. The inner ring appears to have preceded the outer, which in turn was completed before the quarrying of the ditch. Dispersed in and around the enclosure were thirty-one cremations and inhumations in grave pits and stone cists.[11] While North Mains is large in terms of Perthshire examples, the henges do represent significant engineering projects, and it has been argued that the single-phase construction of henges indicates the appearance of a more hierarchical society, with chiefs, or a priest caste, who can arrange such large-scale operations.

Visitors span the 50m across the remarkable Cleaven Dyke, near Blairgowrie, that runs (into the distance) for around 2.3km and dates from around 3500 BC (author © PKHT).

The outline of probable Bronze Age round houses captured from the air in light snow in upland at Glen Fender, Blair Atholl (author © PKHT).

Both of the definitive Bronze Age monuments, stone circles and round barrows, have been shown to appear in the late Neolithic in Perthshire, and indeed current thinking plays down the transition as many other traits of the late Neolithic are shared with the early Bronze Age. The best-known stone circle in Perthshire, the well-preserved complex at Croftmoraig, near Kenmore, was first erected as a stone monument in the Neolithic and incorporated at least three phases of remodelling until around 1000 BC in the late Bronze Age.[12] It is uncharacteristic of the area, however, being an outlier of the recumbent stone circles found in Aberdeenshire, and of the seventy or so possible stone circles in Perth and Kinross, the majority are so-called 'four-posters'. These feature four prominent corner stones in an irregular quadrilateral, and while the sites would have included more than these four stones, often only they survive. Used again during communal ceremonies, and later for burial, their builders were clearly interested in astronomical events and some are aligned with movements of the sun and moon along the horizon. In addition to stone circles, standing stones survive, sometimes in aligned groups sometimes on their own; both simpler variations of the more complex stone circles. As with the henges, the burial mounds were in use over very long periods of time, during which modifications in burial tradition were incorporated. The artefacts frequently found in Bronze Age cist burials indicate contact with the wider world: the bronze and gold dagger recovered recently at Forteviot[13] or the necklaces of Whitby jet, gold personal ornaments and fine pottery found in cist burials in Strathmore, Strathtay and Strathearn. Like the cursus at Blairhall, the henges and burial mounds at Forteviot also clearly survived as impressive monuments into the Pictish period when they would take on a new lease of life.

Perhaps the most striking fact is that in contrast to earlier periods of prehistory, there is extensive evidence of Bronze Age settlement, and once again Perthshire boasts outstanding examples. The relic upland settlements in Glenshee, Strathardle, and above Pitlochry and Blair Atholl, were only possible because of much warmer and drier weather that allowed Bronze Age communities to cultivate higher ground. The sites are often accompanied by agricultural 'clearance cairns' and 'burnt mounds', the debris from the heating of large quantities of water for cooking and/or bathing. The late Bronze Age is seen as a period of great social change resulting directly from rapid and significant climatic decline, however, and while upland farms clearly go out of use, the very small sample of excavated examples makes it very difficult for us to say exactly when this occurred. A clearer signal of the process can be seen in the significant increase of bronze weaponry and the establishment of enclosed settlements, sometimes dramatically fortified, which suggest a pressure on available land.

The importance of the late Bronze Age as a period of social transition is also reflected in changes in burial and ritual practice. Cairns, burial mounds, cists and cremation burials all appear to cease, presumably replaced by open air cremation and/or deposition of remains in rivers, and there is a gradual decline in the construction of ceremonial monuments such as stone circles. At the same time, however, there is an increasing interest in water bodies, whether rivers, lochs or bogs, as sites for votive offerings of metal-work, and presumably worship. A good example is the hoard recovered from peat at Corrymuckloch, which dates from around 800 BC and consists of a broken sword, three socketed axe-heads, and an unusual ladle.[14] Another is the series of broadly contemporary bronze swords, deposited in the River Tay between

The distribution of forts, circular homesteads, souterrains and crannogs, indicating social organisation in the first centuries BC/AD (© Intermap Technologies Inc. All rights reserved. DPER100. 2011; annotation © PKHT).

Perth and Mugdrum Island while in excellent condition; hinting at the idea of a sacred river whereby such offerings were made to supernatural forces perceived as controlling or inhabiting the river. A far more prosaic, but equally informative, artefact from the same stretch of the Tay is the remarkable 9m long logboat from Carpow, near Abernethy, dating to around 1000 BC. Comprehensive study of the vessel has given insight both into existing boat-building technology, and the importance of river and estuarine transportation at that time, a local part of a much wider network of trade that stretched across much of northern Europe.[15]

Roman and native in Iron Age Perthshire

The introduction of iron-working, around 700BC, appears to have been partly a response to the breakdown in these trade networks, and the resulting lack of bronze. The appearance of fortified farmsteads and hill-forts, for example, is seen as indicating fledgling tribal chiefdoms in the early Iron Age. While debate continues as to the relative importance of symbolic power over working military architecture, clearly warfare, or the threat of it, becomes increasingly significant at this time. Many of the larger hill-forts along the Sidlaws and Ochils probably date from this time, and would have dominated the population residing on the fertile straths below. The distribution of souterrains, underground cellars associated with settlements, is a good indicator of grain production, while their relative absence in Strathearn may simply reflect a bias in data collection resulting from modern land-use. Ironically, large hill-forts are notably absent in the highland zone, being replaced here by smaller defended homesteads and the artificial island settlements called 'crannogs'. Once referred to as ring-forts, the homesteads appear to have been squat towers, with façades reminiscent of brochs, and the example at the Black Spout (c300 BC to c100 AD), near Pitlochry, has revealed many features usually associated with broch architecture.[16] Notably the distribution of the crannogs,[17] timber roundhouses built on artificial islands, is neatly complementary to the homesteads and may suggest a similar status. So clearly the distribution of these monument types, and their geographical setting, can give us some insight into social and economic patterns over quite a large area: with larger tribes protected by hill-forts in the fertile lowlands, and smaller and more fragmented communities occupying the highland glens.

The story continues with what we now call Scotland entering the historical record, with the much debated text of *The Agricola* by Tacitus, who describes the general Agricola's advance to the *Taus*, assumed to be Tay, in 79 or 80 AD. There is growing evidence that the area was subdued earlier, in the 70s, however, and continued with occasional military occupation, to varying degrees until 213. Initially, a network of military sites, in two roughly parallel lines, was established to protect the strategically important terrestrial route up the east coast route (avoiding the highlands): from Strathearn, through the Perth area, and up into Strathmore and hence Angus. The first line consisted of the so-called 'glen-blocker' forts, such as Fendoch and Dalginross, which protected this route by controlling access to the highland glens. One of these, the huge 53-acre legionary fortress at Inchtuthil, on the River Tay south-west of Blairgowrie, was the key site of the whole system, housing one of the four 5,500 strong legions in Britain. Behind this ran the military road with associated fortlets and watch-towers running from Dunblane to Bertha, to the north of Perth. Known as the

'Gask system' after the best preserved watch-towers which survive along the Gask Ridge, to the west of Perth, it is widely accepted as the Empire's earliest land frontier, a prototype for other linear frontiers such as Hadrian's Wall,[18] while it may also have provided logistical support for Inchtuthil, the largest Roman base in Scotland. Legionary fortresses were usually built as springboards for further invasion, however, Inchtuthil was never completed as troops were withdrawn to defend invasion of the Danube, resulting in Roman withdrawal to northern England. The strategic importance of the Tay in terms of wider Scottish geography is stressed by the intriguing thought that had the Roman Empire continued to secure all of mainland Britain, it would have been from this site on the Tay, just 16km to the north of Perth.

In the end, Rome had to create boundaries, although the construction of the Antonine Wall in 142 did see re-occupation of the forts at Ardoch, Strageath, Bertha and Dalginross, if only for around fifteen years. The remarkable survival of the ramparts and ditches of the fort at Ardoch, Braco, described as one of the best preserved earth and timber forts in the Empire, is a pertinent reminder that most other Roman sites in the area survived in similar condition until the improvements of the eighteenth century. As discussed below, this is especially relevant to the Roman fort at Bertha, at the Almond–Tay confluence about 4km to the north of Perth itself, but should also be considered in terms of the Roman road system from Strathallan, through Strathearn, to Bertha, which would have undoubtedly remained a major and unique thoroughfare in the region for centuries after Roman withdrawal. The Gask ridge itself affords a gradually raised approach, much like a natural ramp, bringing the road out of Strathearn towards Perth. At some point, to the north of Dupplin Loch, around 9km west-southwest of Perth, the road veered north-east towards the Roman fort at Bertha. Once Bertha has ceased to be a destination, for whatever reason, the traveller continuing the direction of the road, and completing their journey along the ridge, would arrive around the location of Perth. This influence of topography and existing terrestrial transport infrastructure has perhaps to date been underplayed by those who have looked solely at the dynamics of the river for a reason for Perth's location. Indeed, the location of the early medieval palace of *Rathinveramon* (the fort at the mouth of the Almond) at Bertha in the ninth century, if that is where it was, may equally have been as much influenced by the surviving road, and its links to the Tay, as to the survival of Roman earthworks which could be adapted for a new use. Mention of Bertha here also allows us to dispel the antiquarian assumption that the layout of Perth's medieval burgh had its origins in a Roman fort. This is simply not the case and results from confusion with the fort of Bertha; that name probably being an invention of the fourteenth century Scottish chronicler John of Fordun. Finally there is a pertinent coda to the Roman chapter in the form of the 30-acre fortress at Carpow, on the south bank of the Tay near Abernethy, which was the base for the final planned conquest in 208 led by the Emperor Septimius Severus. The campaign was doomed to failure as a result of his death in 211, effectively ending Roman interest in the area, but the significance of the key location at Carpow, both strategically and in terms of sea–land transport, is again dramatically stressed. Indeed, as depicted on coins of 208 and 209, it is the possible site of a bridge of Roman boats, or perhaps even a permanent timber bridge, from the fortress north across the Tay to a bridgehead camp on the north bank near St Madoes.[19]

The Roman fortress at Carpow on the Tay estuary, a base for the Severan campaigns of 208, it is the possible site of the bridge of Roman boats illustrated on contemporary coins (author © PKHT).

Picts and Scots: the creation of Alba and pre-burgh Perth

The centuries following the withdrawal of Rome used to be viewed as a Dark Age with the Picts considered 'a problem'; however, our understanding of Pictish culture has much improved in recent decades.[20] The name 'Pict' was first used by Roman writers to describe the tribes living north of Hadrian's Wall and while research has done much to illuminate our understanding of burial in particular, it is through their artwork, and especially the stone sculptures on early symbol stones and the later cross-slabs, that they are best known. There are many excellent examples of these and other types of site in the surrounding area that illustrate the importance of Perth's environs in the period following the withdrawal of Rome to around 1000 AD.

From the first few centuries AD a tradition of burial in single graves develops, usually marked by barrows (which are often square) and characteristically found in small cemeteries. It is possible that the early Pictish symbol stones, from the fifth to seventh centuries, marked such graves: with the motifs recording the deceased's name or family. There was also continuity from the earlier Iron Age, however, and some site-types that originate then also occur in Pictish times, such as the use of souterrains and re-occupation at some hill-forts. While still poorly dated, the morphology of the small, nucleated hill-forts such as Dunsinnan, Abernethy and Moncreiffe are reminiscent of the early medieval power centre at Dundurn. At this isolated rocky knoll, which controlled upper Strathearn directly east of Loch Earn, excavations have shown that the defended compounds and courtyards were developed at least three times from around 500–800, with evidence of metal-working and glass and other high status objects inferring royal control and trade. While the site may have originated in the Iron Age, this principal Pictish stronghold is presumed to be the place mentioned in the Annals of Ulster as being under siege in 683.[21]

The class I Pictish stone at the base of Abernethy round-tower is the earliest known from the area (author © PKHT).

At Abernethy we can clearly trace control of power from the Iron Age to Pictish and into the later medieval period. Abernethy Law hill-fort, excavated in the late nineteenth century, produced both Iron Age and later artefacts, suggesting occupation, whether continuous or sporadic, from perhaps 500 BC into the early medieval period.[22] The Pictish Chronicle records that King Nechtan reigned in the second half of the fifth century, and links him to the foundation of a church at Abernethy, and the early dedication to St Bridgid for the parish church in the centre of the village supports an early establishment. From the fifth or sixth century, the (Class I) symbol stone now erected by the round tower at the entrance to the churchyard, discovered while excavating foundations for a house in the village, is unlikely to have travelled far.[23] It bears some of the typical symbols: a 'tuning fork', a crescent and V-rod, and a hammer and anvil; however, these have been truncated by the re-cutting, probably for re-use as a building stone, presumably at some point in the medieval. Deeply incised into the pinkish granite slab, the surviving symbols, the earliest known from the village, are a dramatic reminder of a powerful earlier Pictish centre. With both a church and monastery already established in the Early Medieval, the later Class III stones recovered from the village, and the round tower itself (dating from the end of the eleventh century) chart a continued ecclesiastical presence until the monastery was reformed in the thirteenth century and re-founded as an Augustinian house in the 1270s. So the historical resonance at Abernethy is overwhelming: the early Pictish symbol stone and round tower at which King Malcolm III paid homage to William the Conqueror in 1072, both overlooked by the enigmatic hill-fort, a probable Pictish stronghold built on an Iron Age predecessor. We can glimpse here connections between Iron Age chiefs, through to Pictish kingship, to the origins of medieval society; however, only modern study, with scientific dating, will enhance our understanding of this and other similar sites.

Another key site in this narrative are the twin hill-forts on Moncreiffe Hill, which dominates Strathearn and the upper Tay estuary and controls the confluence of the river Earn and the Tay, with the Earn to the south and the Tay to the north. They are part of a wider network of regularly spaced hill-forts along the Ochils and the Sidlaw Hills, but are distinctive both as a multiple site and through this very strong geographical location. Moncreiffe is not unique, however, and is reminiscent of the cluster of hill-forts at another striking geographical feature: the distinctive peaks of Craig Rossie on the Ochil Hills above Auchterarder, visible throughout upper Strathallan and Strathearn. Here there are two hill top forts, Rossie Law and Ben Effrey, and also two on the lower slopes, Castle Craig and Ogle Hill. While it is possible that sites in such close proximity were occupied simultaneously, they may reflect a shift in geographical focus and importance over time. Hill-fort building appears to have declined in the early centuries AD, but was renewed in the third to fifth centuries, with occupation until at least the eighth century. This second phase of hill-fort use saw both refurbishment of earlier forts and the construction of new ones,[24] and the relationship between such forts can be questioned at Moncreiffe Hill, where the larger of the two, the nucleated Moredun Top, appears to have had at least two main phases of construction and use. It crowns the highest part of Moncreiffe Hill, commanding extensive views in all directions of the surrounding landscape, in particular views over the carse of Gowrie not shared by its much smaller companion (simply

Moredun Top, Moncrieffe Hill is a key site in the series of hill-forts found along the Sidlaw Hills and the Ochils (author © PKHT).

called Moncreiffe Hill) which perches on the south-facing western cliff of the hill. The complex morphology of Moredun Top, with a dun-like structure within a larger enclosure, itself with an annexe, or 'court', is reminiscent of Early Historic sites throughout Scotland. While the archaeology of the sites again remains enigmatic, there are records of a Pictish dynastic battle, a struggle for control of the Kingdom, at *Mónidchroibh* in 728. The name, which has become rendered as *Moncrief* by 1685, means the 'hill of the tree', and comes from the Scottish Gaelic *monadh*, meaning 'mountain' or 'hill' and *craobh* 'tree'; however, the eighth century use of the name shows it to be a Pictish name, also illustrating that *monadh* is a loan-word from Pictish (or British) into Scottish Gaelic and Pictish probably had a close cognate of Scottish Gaelic *craobh*.[25]

The ninth century was a period of major social and political change, with the Perth environs, perhaps partly as a result of Moncreiffe's importance, becoming increasingly significant in the story of the unification of the kingships of the Picts and the Scots into the new kingdom of *Alba*. The major lowland royal centre of Forteviot was to play a crucial role in this complex process, which produced the early medieval nation, and is the focus of ongoing research by Glasgow University.[26] Probably written in the eleventh century, the Scottish manuscript the *Chronicles of the Kings of Alba* records that King Kenneth MacAlpin, the 'first king of Scotland', died at a palace at Forteviot in 858. This was one of only two palaces mentioned, and a high-status church is attested by the iconic early-ninth century sandstone arch recovered from the bed of the Water of May beside the traditional site; the Haly Hill, to the west of the village. The location appears to have been dictated by the existing cultural landscape, as to the south of the modern village is one of the most extensive Neolithic and Bronze Age ceremonial landscapes in Scotland, including henges and burial monuments and an immense pit-defined enclosure. Significantly, one of the largest Pictish cemeteries in the area was constructed beside the earthwork remains of these monuments, already ancient by this time. This link between a prehistoric complex and early medieval royal centre has drawn comparisons with Tara, the inauguration site of the High Kings of Ireland, and it is suggested that the adoption and ceremonial re-use of these much earlier monuments may have inferred ancestor linkage in order to legitimise the new kingship. Indeed, it is possible that an inauguration mound existed at Forteviot, the centre of a royal landscape that would be demarcated by the Dupplin and Invermay high crosses on either side of the strath.

The spread of Gaelic culture through intermarriage with the Pictish aristocracy, along with the Viking incursions from ninth century, saw considerable pressures on Pictish kingship. Ultimately it was the descendents of MacAlpin who appropriated the southern Pictish Kingdoms, and it was probably under Constantine II, Kenneth's grandson, that the kingship inauguration site moved to Scone, around 900. The first clear record of the inauguration mound, or 'moothill', and royal monastery at Scone is in 906, and this has recently been verified by excavation that has produced radiocarbon dates from the moothill ditch from around this date.[27] Scone now put the area at the symbolic heart of the Kingdom, and as at Forteviot, its location appears to have been inspired by the existing cultural landscape, as in landscape archaeology terms, there are striking parallels between Scone and Forteviot: both overlooking prehistoric ritual landscapes subsequently adopted and adapted by the Picts.

In the low-lying land to the north of Old Scone aerial photography has once again revealed a concentration of prehistoric monuments long levelled by the plough, but which survive buried beneath the plough-soil to produce remarkable 'crop marks'. The major prehistoric ritual complex at Blairhall comprises an early Neolithic cursus, orientated east-northeast/west-southwest, which has a later prehistoric cemetery of at least ten round burial mounds built about and across it. Notably, five of these form a line running parallel to, and about 60m to the north of, the cursus, while another two are built over each ditch of the cursus. Clearly the cursus and its orientation were important to the barrow builders, but moreover to the north of these are two enigmatic rectangular ditched enclosures that also respect this alignment of monuments. The function of these enclosures, with sub-divisions and annexes is not at all clear, as there are few, if any, parallels in the area. The relationship between these monuments is telling. Both the barrows and enclosures respect the orientation of the cursus, so the earlier monuments were still extant when the later ones were constructed; indeed together they would have formed a coherent layout *incorporating the old and the new.* The site has never been excavated, and so the exact relationship between the monuments remains an enigma. While it is not uncommon for cursus monuments of the Neolithic period to become the focus of Bronze Age burial mounds, it is possible that some of the barrows may be Pictish in date, as indeed, may the rectangular enclosures.

Notably, this process of incorporation and adaptation is not restricted to the Blairhall complex: it is just one part of a larger picture. Around 660m west-southwest of the line of barrows at Blairhall is the Sheriffton Cottage crop mark complex, a cemetery comprising two rows of conjoined square barrows and two round barrows. While the latter are arguably more likely to date to the Bronze Age, the square barrows, which have shown central burial pits, can be more confidently dated to the early centuries AD. It is important to recognise that this line of square barrows was constructed to align with the Blairhall complex linear barrows. More remarkable then, that these both align with a third possible Pictish site, existing c650m west-southwest of the Sheriffton Cottage square barrows. Here, encompassed within the southern half of the 120 acre Roman temporary camp of Grassy Walls (thought to have accommodated the entire Severan army in the campaigns of 208–11) are two unenclosed settlements of ring-ditch houses and associated souterrains. The western of these is built on the convergence of a possible track-way and the route of the Roman road running north-northeast/south-southwest from the Tay at Bertha.

The close proximity of Roman monuments, and the Tay crossing, is significant here. The Roman fort of Bertha has, since the nineteenth century, reasonably been suggested as *Rathinveramon*, the other early medieval palace referenced as the place of death of MacAlpin's brother in 862, and featuring in tenth century references. The site controls the Almond–Tay confluence, and was the northern terminus of the Roman road, which may well have survived as a major terrestrial route, and both a Roman bridge and quay have been suggested at the site. All of which begs the question – why did a pre-burgh settlement not develop at Bertha? Had the Roman road survived in use, could Bertha have offered a more convenient route to Scone from the west?

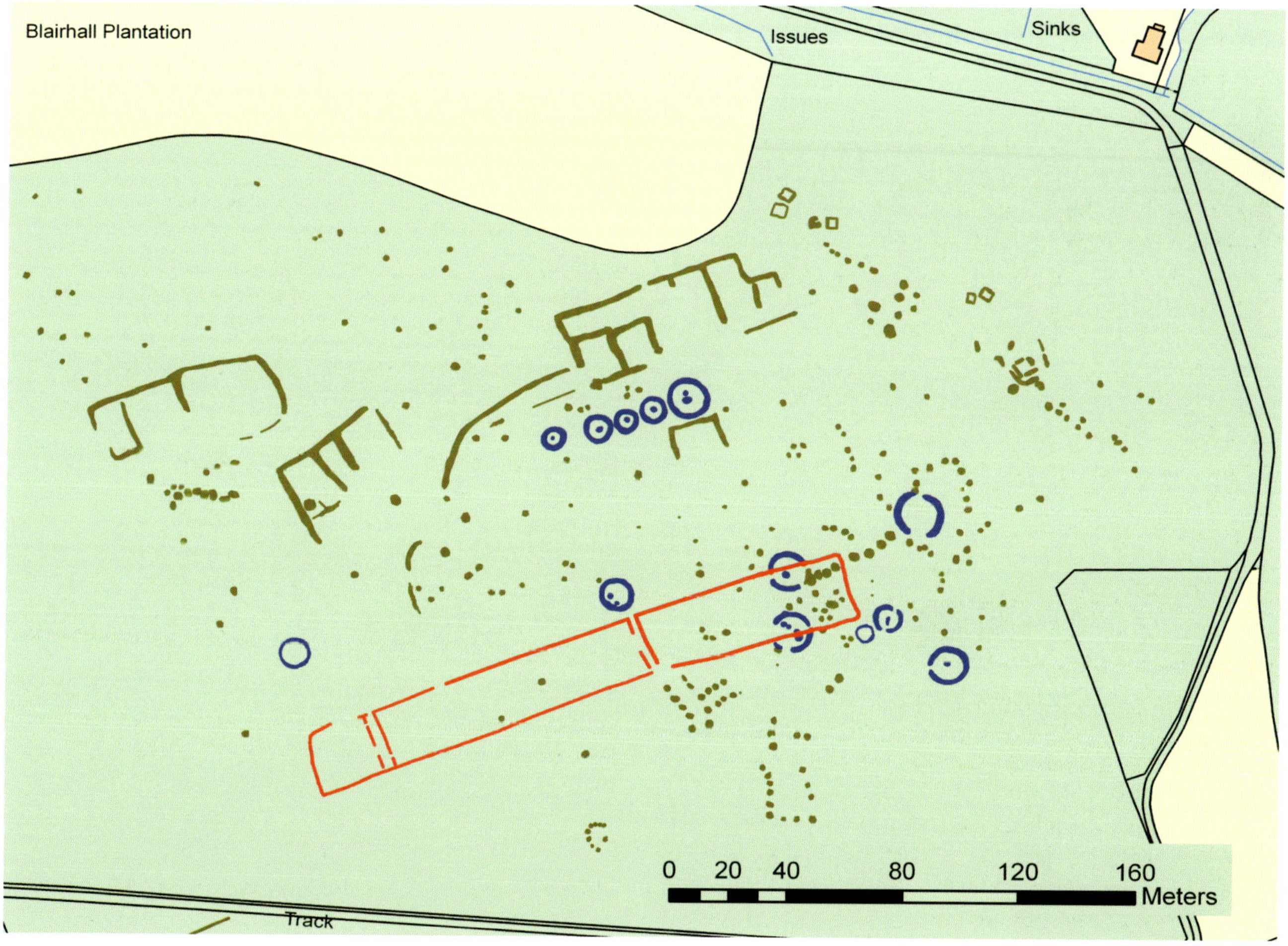

The Blairhall crop mark complex showing the Neolithic cursus (red); the ditches and burial pits of circular burial mounds (blue); and the later rectilinear features that respect the orientation of the cursus (© Crown copyright and database right 2011. All rights reserved. 100016971; crop mark transcription © PKHT).

There are a number of possibilities. The Roman bridge, if it existed, would have been of wood and unlikely to be in use after six hundred years. Perhaps re-bridging was not an option and crossing by ford was too difficult (although interestingly the 'Derder's ford' marked on Roy's eighteenth century map is annotated as 'disused' by the first edition Ordnance Survey map in the late nineteenth). The Tay is narrow, but deeper at Bertha, and so perhaps it was the ease of fording the wider section at Perth that was the attraction. It is also possible that the answer lies with the remaining importance of other local sites, old and new, at Moncreiffe, Abernethy and Forteviot, in addition to Scone. Perhaps maritime transport was as much a consideration, and Perth was the furthest point upstream accessible by larger boats, which also offered the lowest crossing point for a ford or bridge.

Other topographical considerations may also have been at play. The disadvantage of the site is of course the hazard of the flooding, which was increasingly played out through the medieval period as the burgh expanded. However, the benefits of the relatively sheltered position of Perth, protected from prevailing westerly winds by the slightly higher ground to the west Gask Ridge, perhaps outweighed this. In addition, the threat of flooding would have initially been much less: the historic core sat on a slightly raised platform of land, surrounded by lower ground to the north and south, and during extreme flood may have appeared as an island.[28] The origin of Perth's name itself supports both of these facts. *Perth* is a P-Celtic British or Pictish survival, comparable to the Old Welsh *Pert* is likely to mean 'wood' (and indicates that the name existed prior to the increasing dominance of Gaelic in the new Alba of the tenth century).[29] In addition, the only place that trees could have grown along this marshy flood plain would have been on a raised platform of land, which, well-defined and bounded by marsh and river would have appeared distinctive. Perhaps this additional protection was also considered advantageous. Excavations in Perth High Street[30] have revealed a ditch of around 1000 AD, suggested as part of the precinct enclosure around the earliest phase of St John's Kirk, and it is likely that the eastern end of High Street and the Watergate was probably already well established by this date, so we can begin to envisage a river crossing with a small settlement and church on a raised platform surrounded by wetland: the origins of medieval Perth.

Conclusion

So in conclusion, Perth clearly had an important role in early Scottish history, developing at the centre of a nationally important political landscape albeit influenced by the political geography of its environs. By the development of the pre-burgh settlement there had already been almost 5,000 years of monument building in the surrounding area, and during the politically uncertain ninth and tenth centuries their influence in locating new royal and religious sites appears to have taken precedence at the expense of geographical concerns. In contrast, the pre-burgh settlement seems to have evolved in response to pragmatic logistics: where best to cross, bridge and ship. As we will discover in the following papers, Perth, as a key east coast inland port, would secure prosperity and assure its royal burgh status. The processes leading to the selection of site were complex, however, with a long-established history, and prehistory.

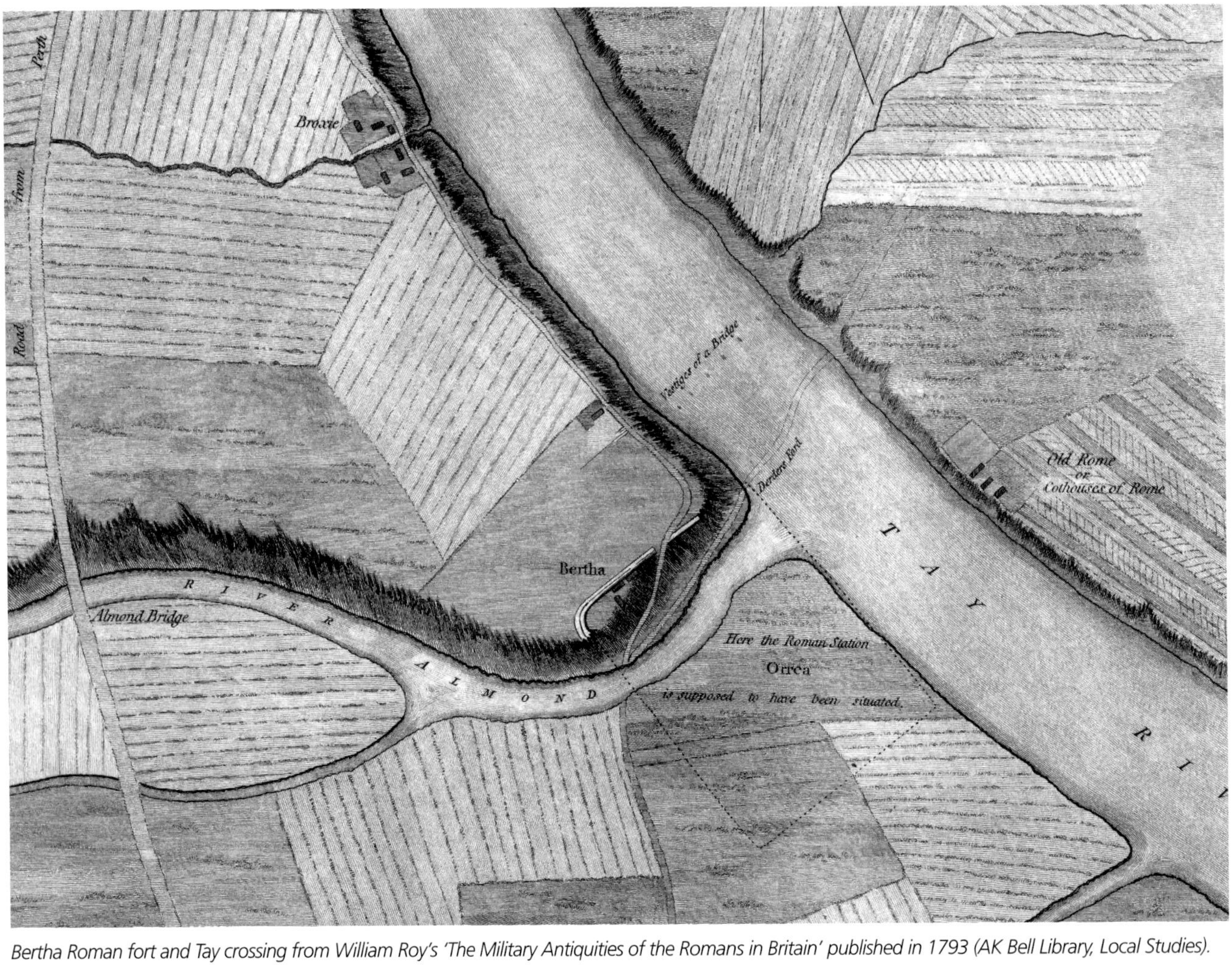

Bertha Roman fort and Tay crossing from William Roy's 'The Military Antiquities of the Romans in Britain' published in 1793 (AK Bell Library, Local Studies).

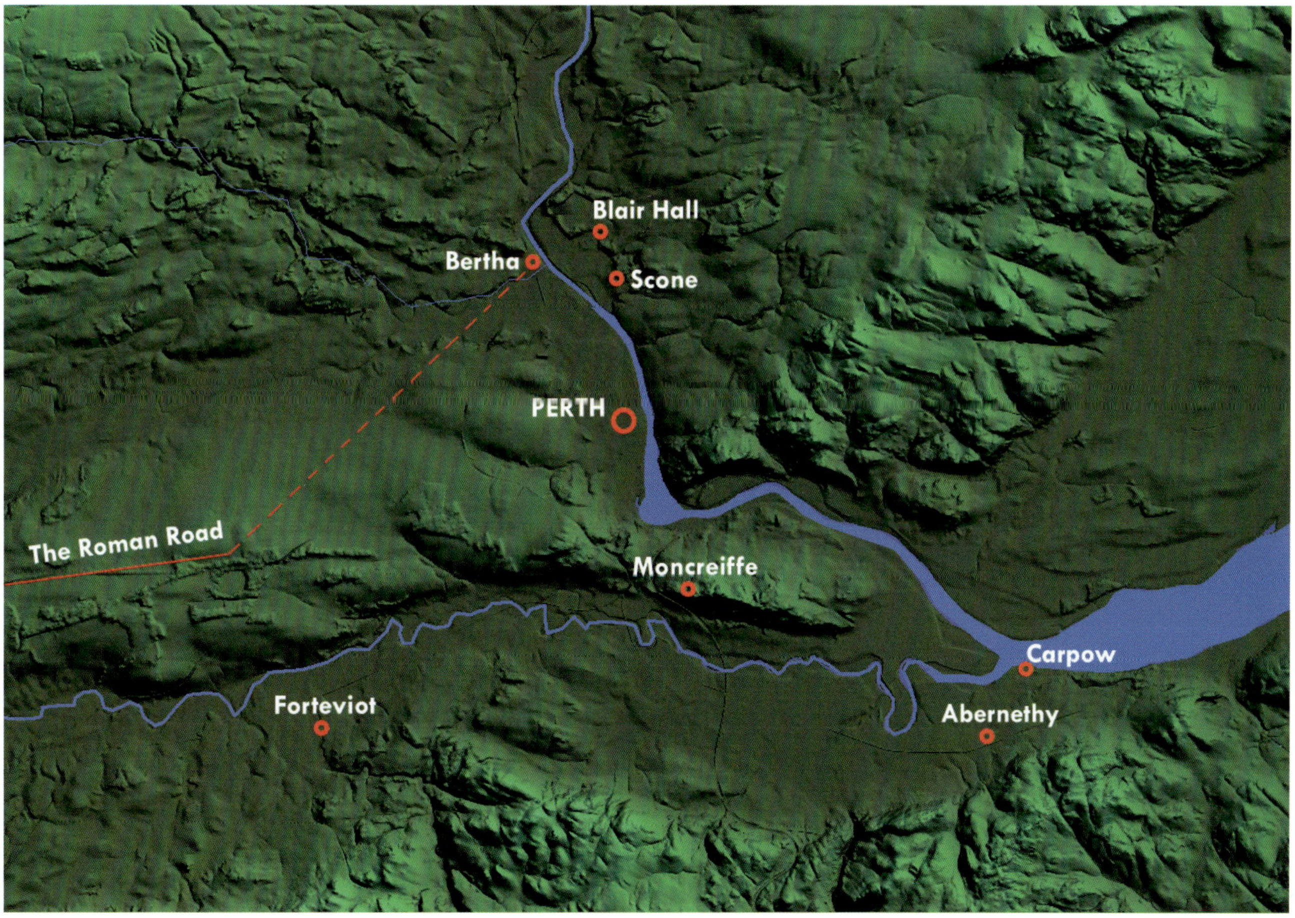

The environs of Perth showing key power centres around 900–1000 AD (© Intermap Technologies Inc. All rights reserved. DPER100. 2011; annotation © PKHT).

Twenty years into developer funded archaeology, we can clearly see benefits to our understanding in the medieval burgh, but this is less so for the surrounding rural areas, where far fewer sites have been investigated in advance of modern development. While this has been recently addressed through research at Forteviot and Scone, there is still much to learn about pre-burgh Perth, and its environs, through modern archaeological investigation. The majority of sites are the levelled crop mark sites, however, with truncated remains surviving beneath plough-soils. Often recorded by aerial photography decades ago, legislation in the form of scheduling can protect them from development, but we are unsure of the full impact of continued ploughing with modern equipment – and there is increasing evidence to suggest many have already been lost forever.

End Notes

1 Armstrong, M et al 1985 *Geology of the Perth District*. British Geological Survey.
2 Finlayson, B 1998 *Wild Harvesters: The First People in Scotland*. Canongate.
3 Saville, A 2004 *Mesolithic Scotland and Its Neighbours: The Early Holocene Prehistory of Scotland, Its British and Irish Context, and Some Northern European Perspectives* Society of Antiquaries of Scotland monograph.
4 Bradley, R personal communication (pers comm)
5 Mowat, R 1996 *The Logboats of Scotland, with notes on related artefact types*. Oxbow Monograph 68.
6 McKirdy, A et al 2007 *Land of Mountain and Flood: The Geology and Landforms of Scotland*. Edinburgh.
7 Atkinson, J pers comm
8 Dixon, N pers comm
9 Barclay, GJ and Maxwell, GS 1991 'Excavation of a Neolithic long mortuary enclosure within the Roman legionary fortress at Inchtuthil, Perthshire.' *Proc Soc Antiq Scot*, 121.
10 Barclay, GJ and Maxwell, GS 1998 *The Cleaven Dyke and Littleour: Monuments in the Neolithic of Tayside*. Society of Antiquaries of Scotland monograph.
11 Barclay, GJ 1980 'North Mains, Strathallan, Tayside Region, NN 928 162, barrow, class II henge and two ring-ditches' *Proceedings of the Prehist Society*, 46.
12 Piggott, S and Simpson, DDA 1971 'Excavation of a stone circle at Croft Moraig, Perthshire, Scotland' *Proceedings of the Prehist Society*, 37 1; Bradley, R and Sheridan, A 2005 'Croft Moraig and the Chronology of Stone Circles' *Proc Soc Antiq Scot*, 71.
13 Brophy, K et al 2010 *Strathearn Environs & Royal Forteviot Project Report 2006–2009*. Perth.
14 Cowie, T et al 1996 'The Late Bronze age hoard from Corrymuckloch, near Amulree, Perthshire: an interim report' *Tayside and Fife Archaeological Journal* 2.
15 Strachan, D 2010 *Carpow in Context: a Late Bronze Age Logboat from the Tay*. Society of Antiquaries of Scotland monograph.
16 Strachan, D forthcoming *The Black Spout, Pitlochry*.
17 Dixon, N 2004 *The Crannogs of Scotland: an underwater archaeology*. The History Press.
18 Woolliscroft, D and Hoffmann, B 2006 *Rome's First Frontier*. Tempus.
19 Reed, N 1976 'The Scottish campaigns of Septimius Severus' *Proc Soc Antiq Scot*, 107.
20 Driscoll, S, Geddes, J and Hall, M (eds) 2011 *Pictish Progress: new studies on North Britain in the Early Middle Ages*. Leiden: Brill.
21 Alcock, L, Alcock, EA and Driscoll, ST 1989 'Reconnaissance excavations on Early Historic fortifications and other royal sites in Scotland, 1974–84: 3, Excavations at Dundurn, Strathearn, Perthshire, 1976–77' *Proc Soc Antiq Scot*, 119.
22 Christison D, and Anderson, J 1898-9 'On the recently excavated fort on Castle Law, Abernethy, Perthshire, with notes on finds' *Proc Soc Antiq Scot*, 33.
23 Proudfoot, E 1997 'Abernethy and Mugdrum: towards reassessment' in Henry, D (ed) *The Worm, the Germ, the Thorn*. The Pinkfoot Press.
24 Alcock, L 2003 *Kings & Warriors, Craftsmen & Priests: In Northern Britain AD 550–850*. Society of Antiquaries of Scotland monograph.
25 Watson, WJ 1926 *The History of the Celtic Place-names of Scotland*. Reprinted 1993, Edinburgh; Peter McNiven pers comm.
26 Driscoll, ST 2010 'Pictish Archaeology: Persistent Problems and Structural Solutions' in ST Driscoll, J Geddes and MA Hall (eds) *Pictish Progress: New Studies on Northern Britain in the Early Middle Ages*. Brill: Leiden.
27 O'Grady, O pers comm.
28 Bowler, D 2004 *Perth, the Archaeology and Development of a Scottish Burgh*. Perth.
29 Watson, WJ 1926 ibid.
30 Moloney, C and Colman, RJ 1997 'The development of a medieval street frontage: evidence from excavations at 80–86 High Street, Perth', *Proc Soc Antiq Scot* 127, 707-782.

Excavations at 80–86 High Street, Perth (© Scottish Urban Archaeological Trust Ltd).

800 years under your feet – the archaeology of medieval Perth

Derek Hall

Introduction

This paper considers the information that has been gained from more than thirty-five years of rescue archaeological excavation in the medieval burgh. New evidence for early settlement in Perth is discussed and the reader is taken on a short walk around the modern town in an attempt to compare it with its medieval predecessor. Finally consideration is given to what can be done next and the importance of publication and communication.

Pre-burghal settlement

The place name Perth may mean 'brake, brush or copse' and has been taken to refer to the former topography of the site on which Perth grew up. It is interesting therefore to note that the very earliest levels of the excavations at 75 High Street, Perth (Marks and Spencer) encountered several tree stumps that were left after clearance of the site prior to its occupation. The question of how old early settlement might be is one that only in recent years have we started to answer. Excavations across the street from Marks and Spencer at 80–86 High Street encountered a narrow wattle lined ditch that ran on a different alignment to the medieval property boundaries that overlay it[1]. Carbon dating of the wattle lining produced a date of the mid eleventh century; it is possible that this feature represents a boundary around an earlier church on the site of St John's Kirk. It seems fair to assume that early settlement on the site of Perth may have been represented by an early ecclesiastical site where St John's Kirk now stands with an associated secular settlement across the other side of the major routeway leading to a fording point across the River Tay. Other evidence for an early ecclesiastical site includes a cross slab recovered from a garden in Scone but said to have originally been found close to St John's Kirk. Further evidence has been provided in recent years by the carbon dating of carbonised sherds of Shelly Sandy Ware pottery from the 75 High Street excavations. This pottery has been identified as originating in the Thames Valley in south eastern England and the suggested chronology for its use and manufacture is based on excavations on the Thames waterfront at Billingsgate Fish Market.[2] The results of those excavations led to the suggestion that that particular pottery type dated no earlier than 1150. Those associated with the post excavation analysis of the 75 High Street excavations were not happy with this date and suggested that as this pottery was coming from the earliest phases of the site it ought to date before the granting of Perth's foundation charter in the 1120s. In an attempt to break the impasse, samples of sherds from carbonised cooking vessels were submitted for C14 dating initially from Perth and the Billingsgate site in London. Dates of the mid eleventh century were received from both sites, at least hundred years earlier than the London chronology. Further C14 samples were then selected and submitted from excavations at the Bryggen Wharf in Bergen, Norway where this pottery fabric has also been recovered and similar dates were received. In summary we now have thirty-eight carbon dates from three different towns suggesting the use of this pottery in the mid eleventh century. What is probably of most interest is who is using these imported cooking vessels in early Perth? That is a question that requires further excavation and research.

The foundation of the burgh of Perth

The original foundation charter for Perth is missing but it is generally accepted to have taken place in the 1120s; discussion of early settlement above indicates that, as has been suggested in the past, King David the First was not founding his new burghs on greenfield sites but in places where thriving settlements already existed. Previous work on the development of the layout and ground plan of medieval Perth has suggested that Watergate was probably the original focus and that on the foundation of the burgh this then changed to an east/west alignment focused on the High Street (the former routeway to the ford across the Tay).[3]

If you say to somebody that Perth is a medieval town it can be difficult to convince them of this when they walk around the modern town due to the lack of surviving early buildings. The earliest such building in the town is probably the Fair Maid's House in North Port although parts of it are probably no earlier than the seventeenth century. The only true medieval building is St John's Kirk and since its refurbishment in the nineteenth century it is probably only the tower that still contains surviving medieval fabric. We do have pictorial evidence for medieval buildings surviving in the town in the eighteenth and nineteenth centuries and in fact the Kinnoull Lodging, which stood in the Watergate until the mid 1960s, was also of medieval date.

This leaves us with a combination of archaeology and historical research as our best way of reconstructing life in the medieval burgh. So far there have been sixty-five excavations and over 150 watching briefs (monitoring of building work) in Perth and they have provided us with good cover of the medieval town. The largest of these were the 1975–77 excavations at 75 High Street, Perth (Marks and Spencer) which confirmed what Lis Thoms had discovered at St Ann's Lane in the early 1970s: that Perth's archaeological deposits were deep and anaerobic (no oxygen so no decay)[4]. This means that just about anything can survive, from upstanding wooden buildings and wattle trackways right through to leather and silk. Besides surviving organic material Perth's medieval middens can also produce more personal objects such as a jet chess piece and bone combs.[5]

In the early core of the medieval town up to 3m or 4m of archaeology can survive and it appears that in the past it was common to build

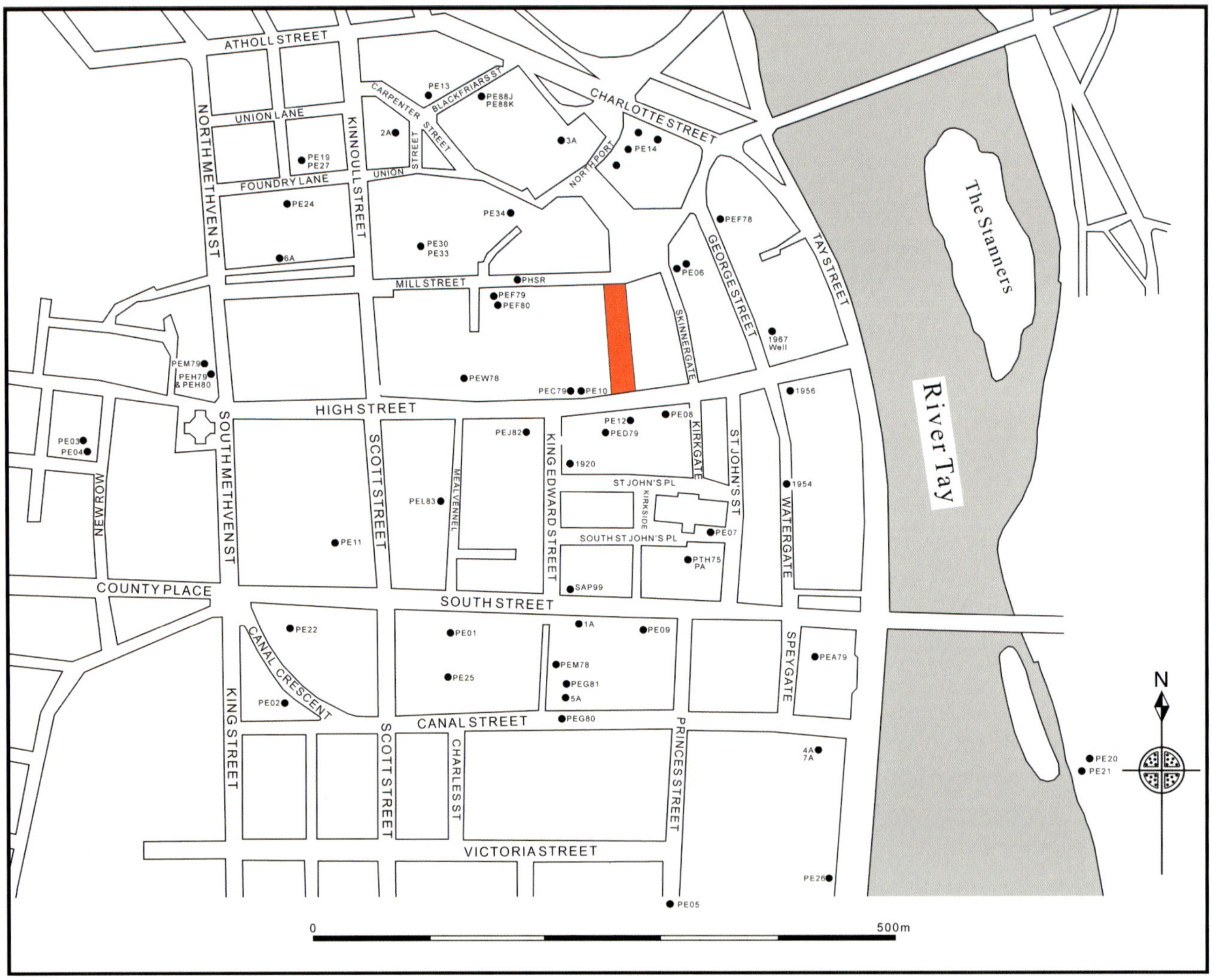

Location plan of excavations in Perth, 75–95 High Street (Marks and Spencer) in red (after Bowler, DP 2004 Perth, the Archaeology and Development of a Scottish Burgh).

Excavations at 75–95 High Street, Perth (© Scottish Urban Archaeological Trust Ltd).

on top of existing demolished building remains rather than dig deep foundations. This depth of archaeology means that deposits can still survive even in those parts of the town where deep cellars have been dug and there will often be up to 1m of archaeology surviving under cellar floors. Perth retains its medieval layout until the late eighteenth century when expansion begins to take place with the construction of the likes of Marshall Place to the south and Atholl Crescent to the north. Let's have a look at some elements of the modern town and how they reflect their medieval predecessors.

High Street

With the High Street pedestrianised since at least the 1990s it feels much wider and open than in the days when traffic ran up and down it. From excavations on either side of the High Street it appears that in the medieval period is was even wider than today, maybe as much as up to 2m on either side. This is because it was also used as the burgh's market place, the market cross formerly stood in the High Street at its junction with Skinnergate and Kirkgate; it is still marked with a cross in the street surface. From several excavations in Scotland's medieval burghs there doesn't seem to have been a separate market place like you will find in England, wider High Streets may therefore have been the norm. Where the surface of the medieval High Street has been exposed it has tended to be laid and packed gravel; whether it was like this all the way across is currently not known. From excavations in advance of the construction of the 'Next' shop at 103 High Street we have evidence for a booth that used to extend out into the street from the shop front.[6] From excavations behind Boots the Chemist on Mill Street we have a well-laid road surface heading north towards Curfew Row and the Castle, this is a street that no longer exists in the modern town plan.[7] Before the new House of Fraser store was built in the early 1980s, excavations located a line of buildings on the original medieval High Street frontage some 2m back from the modern street frontage. As a sign of pressure

Jet chess piece (bishop) from Meal Vennel excavations, Perth (© courtesy of Perth Museum and Art Gallery).

Detail of wattle fence line at Kirk Close excavations, Perth (© Scottish Urban Archaeological Trust Ltd).

for space on the medieval High Street a vennel running south from the High Street had been turned into a very narrow building with a hearth and animal pen, possible evidence for a medieval fast food outlet![8] Put simply the medieval High Street must have been a very busy, bustling thoroughfare with lots going on.

Good preservation of archaeological deposits can present its own problems as objects and artefacts will be found for which it is difficult, if not impossible, to find parallels from anywhere else. This is especially true of a couple of wooden objects from Perth High Street that have been identified as a wooden cog wheel and a port hole cover!

From a site on the south side of the High Street at Kirk Close we have evidence for a toilet attached to one of the buildings, indicating provision for health and hygiene in the medieval burgh.[9] Enough textile and leather has been found to have a good idea of the sort of clothing and footwear that was being worn in everyday life. More personal objects such as a jet chess piece and a merchant's seal were found at the Meal Vennel excavations which took place in advance of the construction of the new St John's Shopping Centre in the mid 1980s.[10] Evidence for foreign contact and travel is provided by pilgrim badges from Canterbury in England, Amiens in France and Santiago de Compostela in Spain. Similar evidence is also provided by the vast range of imported medieval pottery that has been found in Perth: there are 52,000 sherds from the 75 High Street excavations alone. There are even occasional sherds from later medieval maiolicas from Portugal or Spain. Most of the burgh's later archaeology no longer survives due to the digging of cellars. There is also evidence for climate change since the medieval period with the discovery of several ice skates manufactured from modified horse leg bones; presumably these were used to cross the frozen River Tay at a time when there was no bridge.

Burgh backlands and Industry

The distinctive nature of the long narrow burgage plots in the medieval town can still be seen even today. Excavations in advance of the construction of the multi-storey car park in Canal Street picked up evidence for the various industries that were taking place in these backland plots in the medieval town.[11] These activities include malt barns, kilns and cobles that were connected with the brewing process; a coble is a clay-lined tank for steeping the grain. This is a good example of the archaeology matching the historical evidence as the King James VI Rental Books have references to such structures in this part of the burgh.[12] Evidence for a similar process was also recovered from excavations on the former Pullar's site, now the Council offices at Pullar House. There is evidence for ironworking at Meal Vennel, which was formerly on the limit of the early burgh. There was a substantial manufacture of knives and barrel padlocks at this site and evidence for a blacksmiths forge represented by an anvil base and associated forge. Precious metal working, probably of silver, was taking place on the High Street at the House of Fraser site.

Sherd of Malagan lustreware pottery from Horsecross excavations, Perth (© D Hall).

Skinnergate and Kirkgate

Skinnergate was called that because of the focus of leather working in that part of the town. There has been limited opportunity to do any excavation in this area but deep deposits were located during the hand excavation of the new lift shaft at Gillie's furniture store. From that site part of a ceramic stove tile was also recovered; in the fourteenth century ceramic stoves from Northern Germany became popular and must have been quite expensive. All other such Scottish tiles have been found at monasteries and abbeys, the Skinnergate example must have been from an important high status building somewhere on that street.[13]

The Kirkgate runs from the Market Cross to St John's Kirk and there has been limited work along it but Scottish Water mains replacement a few years ago located deep midden and various street levels and produced a fine decorated buckle; there is documentary evidence for metal working on that street as well.

Town Defences

Unusually in Scotland, Perth was defended with a ditch and town wall. Evidence for the town ditch has been located in the excavations behind Boots the Chemist on Mill Street. Here a revetted stone face to the ditch, with a flight of steps leading down into it, was found, along with a dump of stone 'cannon' balls that were probably ammunition for a catapult (arbalest). Finding evidence for the wall has been a lot harder, largely because most of it has probably gone when the stone was taken away and used in buildings elsewhere in the town or in Cromwell's citadel on the South Inch. A rubble-filled trench was found on the right line at 75 High Street (Marks and Spencer) and excavations in Albert Close discovered a stone foundation at some depth, again on the right line. Monitoring of sewer replacement along George Street in the 1990s located a substantial fragment of buried upstanding stone wall on the same line as the wall in Albert Close which has a plaque on it claiming that it is a fragment of the town wall, it is not but it is on the right line.

Castle

Perth's Royal castle was washed away in 1209 and never rebuilt. It has always been assumed to be on the site of the museum but excavations at the Horse Cross in advance of the building of the Concert Hall revealed a massive linear feature running across the site from north to south, which must be the ditch for the castle. This would put the castle roughly where the multi-storey car park behind the Council offices now stands. A later re-cut of this ditch had a well built stone bridge which formed part of a routeway that probably led to the Blackfriars monastery. The Horse Cross excavation also discovered a human body rammed into a pit, this could be evidence for robbery and murder or execution. Intriguingly the body still had two fourteenth century coins buried with it.[14]

The harbours

One reason that Perth was founded in its present location is the access afforded to boats so far up the river Tay. Perth can be regarded as an 'entrepôt'; a distribution centre for traded goods out into the hinterland. The medieval harbour lay at the foot of the High Street and then moved down to the end of Canal Street, then to the Lime Shore and Merchants Quay at the South Inch and finally to Friarton where it stands today. Again there has been limited archaeological work on the site of the early harbour but the underpinning of the old City Chambers at the end of the High Street in the 1970s revealed massive jointed timbers at least 3–4m down below modern street level. The burgh tollbooth stood at this point across the High Street controlling access from the harbour into the town. Excavations at the former site of the Baptist Church on Tay Street in 1984 located evidence for the later medieval harbour being represented by a series of harbour walls that predated the culverting of the town lade.[15]

The friaries

Perth in its medieval heyday was a bustling place and there was presumably a lot of money around. For this reason four medieval religious houses were drawn to it, the Dominican (Blackfriars) founded in 1231, the Carmelite (Whitefriars) founded in 1262, the Franciscan (Greyfriars) founded in 1460 and the Carthusian monastery founded between 1426 and 1429.

The location of the Carthusian monastery is still not known although topographically it does seem more likely to have been in the vicinity of the bus station. After the Reformation of 1559 its gateway was transplanted onto St John's Kirk and a contemporary engraving is the only evidence we currently have for what it might have looked like. Excavations prior to the construction of sheltered housing at Carpenter Court, on the north side of the town, located fragments of the southern and eastern ranges of the Blackfriars monastery and part of its associated graveyard.[16] The Greyfriars lay somewhere in the vicinity of the graveyard of the same name and prior to the recent refurbishment of the cemetery, deep clay bonded wall foundations were located under its boundary wall, which could be part of the medieval precinct line.

Whitefriars is the friary that lay furthest out from the burgh. It was first excavated in 1982 in advance of the construction of the Jeanfield Road industrial estate and produced a high level of local interest.[17] Probably the most important find from that excavation was the official seal matrix of the friary, which would have been used to sign letters and other documents. When a planning application came forward for further development in the vicinity in 2006–7 it was clear that the rest of the friary would be affected and a planning condition for further archaeological works was attached. Following some trial excavation to assess the level of survival across the site the first phase of excavation started at the Jeanfield Road end of the site. As in 1982 the first archaeological evidence on the site was for post Reformation burials dug into the demolished remains of the friary. There is no documentary evidence for burial in this area at this date; Wellshill Cemetery, which lies across the road, is of nineteenth century date. A coin with one of the burials was of a date just after the Reformation of 1559 suggesting that these may have been Recusant Catholics who wished to be buried on the former site of the Carmelite friary. What was clear during the excavation was that we were dealing with family groups and not just isolated burials.

When the friary demolition levels were encountered there was good evidence for the friary's roof covering in the form of roof slates, supported by a documentary reference to the reroofing of the Carmelite church with 14,000 Caithness slates. The friary buildings only survived at foundation level due to the amount of stone robbing that had taken place but good evidence for the layout of the church and the northern part of the cloister was recovered. There was also a marked change visible in the buildings with a lot of new construction work taking place; this resulted in a complete rebuild of the church and must relate to the period when the Bishop of Dunkeld moved down to Perth to escape Highland raids and took over the friary complex. The Bishop's rebuild was not on the existing footprint of the Carmelite church but parallel to it, possibly reflecting the poor state of the Carmelite's buildings when the Bishop arrived. His arrival also promoted an increase in burial on the site with up to three or four times more inhumations compared with the Carmelite phase.

While the excavations at Whitefriars in 2007 were not completed, and the site was carefully backfilled, more than 100 human burials were excavated, recorded and lifted from the site. A similar number still remain in that part of the site that was not completed. Limited evidence was beginning to appear for an earlier church, which the documents suggest belonged to Dunfermline Abbey in the twelfth century. It is possible that this is why Whitefriars lies so far out of town and that the Carmelites were given an existing church for the foundation of their friary in 1262.

St John's Town

If we now return to the burgh where as already stated St John's is the earliest building. For many years Perth was known as St Johnstown, and it is still the name of the local football team. Recent environmental improvements around the Kirk revealed skeletons under the minister's car-parking space on the south side, and the foundations of a former side porch to the church. There was also surviving evidence for the medieval fabric of St John's lying directly under the nineteenth century refurbishment of the building.[18]

Seal matrix from Carmelite friary excavations of 1982 (© courtesy of Perth Museum and Art Gallery).

The future of the past

In winding up I would like to offer some personal thoughts on Perth's archaeology. I have always wondered if there could be earlier building remains surviving in many of the standing structures in the town. At some point a controlled building survey might be useful which could back up the work that already takes place as a result of planning conditions on new development. Chemical sourcing of greyware pottery from Perth is suggesting that it is from Jutland and could be hinting at an early connection with the Baltic; it would be nice to find more evidence of this.[19] I have argued that it might be possible to suggest the origin of some of the inhabitants of the early burgh by looking at what pottery they were using. The Scottish pottery industry seems to start quite late (thirteenth century) and it seems likely that when David the First is founding the new burghs in the twelfth century some of the people that he is bringing to populate them might be bringing their own pottery with them. So far the only evidence that this might be the case is provided from the excavations at Horsecross where sherds of Ely-type ware were found, one of the plots on the site was owned by Thomas de Lynn in the fifteenth century and Ely and Kings Lynn are only twenty-eight miles apart. One of the most important relationships is between Perth and Scone and Oliver O'Grady's recent work there is a good start at trying to understand how this relationship worked in the past.

In the tail end of a recession where does this leave us? I feel that continued communication with the public is important, they are paying for this after all, popular archaeological publications are important and in 2011 the first publications of the Perth High Street Excavations will begin to appear, finally reinforcing Perth's position in the study of European urban medieval archaeology.[20]

In summing up I would say they are deep, they are dark, they are smelly but we should cherish our archaeological deposits.

Staved wooden bowl under excavation at Kirk Close, Perth (© Scottish Urban Archaeological Trust Ltd).

End Notes

1 Moloney, C and Colman, RJ 1997 'The development of a medieval street frontage: evidence from excavations at 80–86 High Street, Perth', *Proc Soc Antiq Scot* 127, 707-782.
2 Blackmore, L and Pearce, J 2010 'Shelly-sandy ware and the greyware industries; a dated type series of London medieval pottery: Part 5', 81-82.
3 Bowler, DP 2004 *Perth, The Archaeology and Development of a Scottish Burgh*, Tayside and Fife Archaeological Committee Monograph; Lynch, M, Spearman, M and Stell, G (eds) 1988 *The Scottish Medieval Town*. Edinburgh.
4 Perry, D et al 2011 *Perth High Street Archaeological Excavation 1975–77. The excavations at 75–95 High Street and 5–10 Mill Street, Perth*, Fascicule 1.
5 Hall, DW 2002 *Burgess Merchant and Priest; Burgh life in the Scottish medieval town*, Birlinn Books.
6 Roy, M and Falconer, C 2000 'Excavations at the Abbey National Building, 103 High Street, Perth' *Tayside and Fife Archaeological Journal* Vol 6, 95-98.
7 Brann, ML and McGavin, N 1995 'Mill Street' in Bowler, DP et al 'Four excavations in Perth, 1979–1984', *Proc Soc Antiq Scot* 125, 918-930.
8 Clark, P and Blanchard, L 1995 'King Edward Street' in Bowler, D P et al 'Four excavations in Perth, 1979–1984', *Proc Soc Antiq Scot* 125, 931-938.
9 Blanchard, LM 1987 'Kirk Close' in Holdsworth, P Excavations in the Medieval Burgh of Perth 1979–1981, *Soc Ants Scot Mono Ser* Number 5, 18-47.
10 Cox, A 1996 'Backland activities in medieval Perth: excavations at Meal Vennel and Scott Street', *Proc Soc Antiq Scot* 126, 733-821; Hall, MA 2002 'Cultural interaction in the medieval burgh of Perth, Scotland 1200–1600', in G Helmig, B Scholkmann and M Untermann (eds) *Centre, Region, Periphery – Medieval Europe Basel 2002* Volume 1 (Hertingen), 290-301.
11 Coleman, RJ 1996 'Burgage plots of medieval Perth: the evidence from excavations at Canal Street', *Proc Soc Antiq Scot* 126, 689-732.
12 Milne, R (ed.) 1891 *Rental Books of King James VI Hospital, Perth... with a short history of the institution and notes*. Perth.
13 Haggarty, G and Hall, DW (2010) 'Throw some more fuel on the fire'– the stove tiles of medieval Scotland' (eds) De Groote, K, Tys, D, & Pieters, M *Exchanging Medieval Material Culture: studies on archaeology and history presented to Frans Verhaeghe*. (=Archeologie Monuments- & Landschapsonderzoek in Vlaanderen, Relicta Monografieen 4, 67-74.)
14 Cox, A 2007 'Excavations at the Horse Cross, Perth', *Tayside and Fife Archaeological Journal* Vol 13, 112-206.
15 Bowler, DP and Cachart, R 1994 'Tay Street, Perth: the excavation of an early harbour site', *Proc Soc Antiq Scot* 124, 467-489.
16 Bowler, DP and Hall, DW 1995 'Kinnoull Street' in Bowler, DP et al 'Four excavations in Perth, 1979–1984', *Proc Soc Antiq Scot* 125, 939-947.
17 Hall, DW 1982 'Perth the excavations' in Stones, J Three Scottish Carmelite Friaries, *Soc Ants Scot Mon Ser* No 6, 99-110.
18 Fyles, C, Hall, DW and Edwards, J 2005 'Watching brief on environmental improvements around St John's Kirk, Perth', *Tayside and Fife Archaeological Journal* Vol 11 18-45.
19 Hall, DW and Chenery, S 2005 'New evidence for early connections between Scotland and Denmark? The chemical analysis of medieval greyware pottery from Scotland' *Tayside and Fife Archaeological Journal* Vol 11, 54-69.
20 Perry, D et al 2011 *Perth High Street Archaeological Excavation 1975–77. The excavations at 75–95 High Street and 5–10 Mill Street, Perth*, Fascicule 1.

Perth in the Middle Ages: An Environmental History

Richard Oram

Introduction

Traditionally the history of medieval Scotland has been written in conventional terms of political and religious development, of conflicts for power between crown and magnates, and increasingly in the second half of the twentieth century, in the language of identity, independence and the 'making of the kingdom'. More recently, however, Scotland's past has begun to be explored from the perspective of environmental history, an approach that focuses on the interplay between humans and the world around them. Such a focus departs from traditional interpretations of the past that view humans as the only significant actors moving across a largely passive natural stage. It originated in the 1960s with recognition of the impact of contemporary human actions on the environment and the resulting environmental impacts on human society. Use of environmental history methods in the study of the medieval period has allowed us to see that humans are and were neither the only nor the most significant agents of change. It also permits us to see that major episodes of historic social and political transition could be caused as much by episodes of environmental disturbance as by moments of technological advance, or that economic trends were driven as often by the impact of pathogens and climatic variation as by human social behaviour.

Environmental history has begun to transform our understanding of Scotland's historical development. It has, for example, revealed the degree to which conflict could be driven by crises of supply which themselves arose from sometimes subtle, sometimes dramatic shifts in the climate. It likewise exposes the link between subsistence crises and often radical social reconfigurations. For exploration of the history of a burgh, a community whose success or failure depended on control and trade of resources produced in its hinterland, and on the demand for its raw materials and finished products from a growing consumer market, environmental history permits us to see how that community dealt with non-human factors which threatened its prosperity; it could reconfigure itself to accommodate changed circumstances and roll with the blows, or fail to learn and adapt and suffer decline, contraction and collapse.

Perth is an ideal case study for an environmental history of a medieval burgh in Scotland. Blessed with relatively abundant medieval and early post-medieval records, the location of extensive archaeological excavations and palaeoenvironmental studies, and the beneficiary of modern hydrological studies of the Tay, Perth possesses a range of data which enable us to reconstruct the complex interaction between the human community and environmental agents which together shaped its historical development.[1] Through studying these different forms of evidence, we can see areas of pressure from early in the burgh's history, notably in terms of unsustainable levels of exploitation of resources like fuel and building materials.[2] When we link this local evidence with climate data drawn from elsewhere around Scotland and throughout the North Atlantic region, we gain a subtly textured picture of long-term processes of environmental change, particularly of shifts in weather patterns. In that picture we can see the impact on primary food production and on availability of raw materials for crafts, industry and domestic needs, and the consequent stresses on social organisation when those needs could not easily be met.[3] In sum, we can see how the environment directly influenced the lives of ordinary people for better or for worse. This short essay, however, cannot examine all aspects of Perth's environmental history across a five hundred-year period. Instead it will focus on evidence for the impact of weather events, famines and epidemics on the people of Perth between *c*1100 and *c*1600 as a first outline of an environmental history of the medieval burgh.

Weather events

It is essential to first establish the broad context in terms of trends in climate and weather. In the early twelfth century when Perth first emerges into historical record as an urban community, Scotland and the wider North Atlantic region was entering the closing stages of what is often referred to as the 'medieval warm period'.[4] This episode, where average annual temperatures were generally several degrees above the mean, had commenced in the tenth century and had created the conditions which, for example, allowed Norse colonisation of Iceland and Greenland, and saw in Scotland a rise in the altitudinal range at which crops could be grown, ripened and harvested in even marginal districts. It should not, however, be thought of as an era of unbroken 'barbeque summers' and mild winters; chronicle accounts for the 1190s, for example, report violent, unseasonal summer hail storms across northern Europe which destroyed crops and triggered famine, while in 1196 Scotland also experienced widespread famine with high mortality.[5] One particularly significant deviation from a milder norm was the winter of 1204–5 in Scotland, which was reported as intensely cold with severe frosts from December to March, which killed many sheep, cattle and wild animals.[6] For an arable economy a poor summer season, delayed and below average harvest and bad late winter conditions impeding the start of the new year's agricultural cycle could be bad, but for a stock-based economy the consequences of high-level mortality amongst the over-wintered flocks and herds could be devastating. In arable cultivation, below-average yields in one year could be followed by bumper crops in the next; where livestock numbers were culled by extreme events, it could take years to restore populations to pre-event levels. In the 'medieval warm period' such events, however, were short-term deviations from an average and what matters for agricultural cycles are long-term trends; down to about 1250, the general trend was good but from then on conditions began to deteriorate.

Winter livestock deaths in distant parts perhaps made little immediate impression on the consciousnesses of most Perth folk, but the geographical location that underpinned the burgh's regional dominance soon exposed them to a direct and very traumatic experience of climate change. In late September 1209 extreme rainfall over the Perthshire hills triggered floods on the rivers Almond and Tay which, combined with high tides possibly worsened by easterly winds, caused the rivers to spill over into the broad flood plain on which Perth was built. The floodwaters overwhelmed the town with such rapidity that even the king and his magnates who had gathered there for a council were caught unawares and forced to escape in boats or take refuge in the upper storeys of buildings. The flood's greatest casualty, however, was Perth bridge which was completely swept away by the force of the river and the debris it was carrying.[7] The bridge was swiftly replaced, but charter evidence reveals that over a decade after the flood burgage plots that had been overwhelmed by the waters were still standing vacant.[8] Perth had been served notice of the potentially crippling economic consequences of a major environmental event.

Although there was no further similar incident affecting Perth and the lower reaches of the Tay directly until the 1260s, chronicle accounts detail a succession of events through the second half of the thirteenth century that would have had significant repercussions for the community. Contrary to popular traditions of the later thirteenth century as a 'Golden Age' of abundant harvests, economic prosperity, and peaceful growth, climate data and historical accounts reveal it to have been a time of great environmental change. The beginning of a downward trend in annual mean temperatures heralded the start of a period of climatic disturbance and greater frequency of extreme conditions. Far from being the time of 'wyne and wax, gamyn and gle' recalled by chroniclers looking back from the war- and disease-ravaged later fourteenth century, it was a stuttering pause of incipient crisis before a plunge into the abyss.

Food shortage and famine

For 1259–60 we have records of food shortages and price-inflation stemming from harvest failures; violent storms throughout a dry summer; a wet harvest season (threatening food-shortages to come); and destructive gales in late autumn and early winter.[9] The result in 1261–2 was that 'all parts of Scotland suffered from a great famine caused by the harvest being ruined.'[10] Similar weather continued through 1263, including the gales that battered the Norwegian fleet off Largs.[11] Further misery came in 1267 when a mild, dry summer brought hopes of an abundant harvest but dashed them first by plant-eating insect infestations and then by violent easterlies in late October which pounded the coast between the Tweed and Tay causing tidal surges to flood low-lying estuarine agricultural land in areas like the Carse of Gowrie.[12] Winter 1267–8 saw severe weather which continued into a cold, wet and windy spring and summer for 1268, when 'there was a high death-rate amongst animals, that is amongst red deer, fallow deer, forest ponies, but most of all sheep,' and which ended with a winter so harsh that the ground could not be ploughed between the end of November 1268 and the beginning of February 1269 to prepare for sowing.[13] The new decade brought continuing misery, with general famine in 1270 and, in 1272, 'a great lack of productivity of the land and unfruitfulness of the sea, as well as turbulence of the air, as a result of which many people fell ill and many animals died.' It was not just Scotland that experienced these disasters, for it was reported that 'great famine hit France, England, Scotland and many areas, for the cattle mostly died, the crops died and the poor died of their poverty.'[14] English records show a continuation of such conditions into the 1280s, with harsh winters and late springs producing livestock deaths, delayed harvests and the resulting risks of reduced yields in wet and windy autumns.

It may seem like a fine semantic line to draw a distinction between 'dearth' and 'famine', especially when even seasonal and localised food shortages resulted in deaths amongst those on the economic margins, but the shortages recorded in the thirteenth century appear inconsequential alongside the disasters of the early fourteenth century. Severe and widespread famine hit northern Europe between 1315 and 1322 as a consequence of a succession of weather-related harvest failures, resulting in a mortality rate of around ten per cent across the continent.[15] We have no record for how Scotland fared during this event; our few surviving accounts for the period are rather preoccupied with the later stages of the wars with England and the Scottish invasion of Ireland of 1315–18. Evidence from the north of England and Ireland, however, suggests that Scotland was no less severely affected during the famine years than other parts of Europe and, indeed, there is good reason to believe that the pastoral economy of Scotland suffered at least as badly as the arable economies of other regions; livestock need grass and other fodder, but grass- and hay-growth was affected in just the same way as cereal crops.[16]

Shortage of food for the human population and fodder for livestock was not the only consequence of the human and environmental crisis of the late thirteenth and early fourteenth centuries. Supply of foodstuffs and the raw materials for crafts and trade had also been severely dislocated by warfare after 1296. The deliberate ravaging of important estates in the vicinity of Perth, most notably that of Scone Abbey, disrupted local patterns of supply and demand, made worse by the garrisoning of Perth by the English and the long war of attrition fought locally with supporters of Robert Bruce until the Scots recaptured the burgh in January 1313. Again, however, we lack detailed accounts of the wider impact of that conflict, but we can see that later episodes of famine in Scotland did stem from a combination of weather events and localised impacts of warfare. One of the most extreme cases is recorded by Walter Bower, who introduces the great cultural-religious taboo of cannibalism as a symbol of how desperate conditions had become:

> *At that time [1339] the whole of the adjacent land was to such a degree laid waste that there was almost no inhabited house left, but wild beasts and deer coming down from the mountains were often hunted around the town. So great was the dearth and lack of provisions that the common folk were starving everywhere; and eating grass like sheep, they were found dead in pits. Nearby there lurked in a ruined building a certain peasant called Christy Cleke with his fierce woman; they lay in wait for women, children and young people, and after strangling them like a wolf, lived on their flesh.*[17]

There is no independent corroboration of this tale and it may simply have been invention to impress on Bower's readership the full horror of the war, but it captures powerfully the sense of social dislocation and utter desperation which successive years of devastating warfare engendered.

Did climate change drive these events? Studies of a range of what are known as proxy climate data, that is sources of indirect evidence derived from the growth patterns of trees reflected in their annual tree-rings, from ice cores taken from the Greenland ice-sheet, and from oceanic sediments, reveal that a significant shift in the northern hemisphere climate system was gathering pace at this time. One key factor in this shift was reflected in changes in ocean surface temperature. Movement in these temperatures altered the pattern of weather systems coming in from the Atlantic and affecting the British Isles. In particular, ocean-surface warming raised atmospheric moisture and triggered increases in storminess with some extreme summer wind and rain events, and periods of great heat or coldness often seen in records of hot, wet summers and prolonged snow and ice in late winter. Conversely, extension of the southward range of sea ice increased the incidence of winter storms as cold surface temperatures cause high surface air pressures associated with anticyclonic circulation which draws cold air further south and into collision with warmer moist air moving east across the Atlantic. The result is winter storm systems tracking east across the North Atlantic followed by late springs, adverse summer growing conditions, and wet and delayed harvests.

From around 1300 there had been a marked shift towards colder annual temperatures in the northern hemisphere, signifying the 'end' of the 'medieval warm period'.[18] Anticyclonic circulation established a seasonal pattern of harsh and bitterly cold winters, delayed and relatively cool springs, hot and dry summers and warm, wet autumns from around 1308. Then in 1315 a dramatic change occurred with summers turning cold and delivering almost continual frontal systems which, as English and Irish chroniclers of the time attested, deposited rains across Britain and Ireland, delayed harvests and brought shortages of grain and fodder; the result was the Great Famine. The Greenland ice cores reveal that this episode stemmed from a rapid rise in ocean surface temperatures in the North Atlantic in the summer months, an overheating which continued through the winter to trigger an upward spiral in temperatures and a dramatic increase in atmospheric moisture. These conditions peaked around 1318–9 but it was not until 1325 that a further change was manifest in a return to summer droughts. That episode was short-lived, however, with some indication of renewed wet conditions by the early 1330s, but this was swiftly followed by a plunge to the lowest temperatures experienced in the North Atlantic region since well before 1000. While this plunge in temperatures has been described as 'a period of polar cooling that is minor by glacial standards'[19] it was the catalyst for dramatic changes in social organisation and economic structures along the North Atlantic periphery of Europe.

While there remains debate over the chronological range to which the term should be applied, the climatic cooling evident through the fourteenth century can be seen as the first stage of the so-called 'Little Ice Age' which lasted until the middle of the nineteenth century. Again, as with the generic, 'medieval warm period' label, the 'Little Ice Age' was not a period of unmitigated climatic deterioration and relentless cold weather. The 1350s had seen unprecedented low temperatures but that had been followed by a period of milder summer and winter conditions; it was a very cold episode which commenced soon after 1400 which may have seen the effects of the cooling becoming entrenched. Winter storms in the North Atlantic were more regular, more violent and more prolonged, and the south-west to north-east circulation of warmer water which helped to give the British Isles their generally milder climate moved south as colder, polar circulation systems extended. The direct result was that the North Atlantic winter storm track which passed over Iceland and the Faroe Islands became fixed instead over Britain; storm systems fed in from the west off the Atlantic to collide with cold air drawn by anticyclonic circulation from Russia, resulting in snow. The sea ice retreated northward slightly in the middle of the fifteenth century but it would be wrong to call this a period of warmer mean temperatures; it was less cold than what had preceded it.

While we have few detailed narrative accounts from Scotland for the central decades of the fifteenth century to illustrate what this fluctuating weather pattern meant for harvests, parliamentary legislation of the period hints at poor harvests through the 1450s and resultant high food prices. Parliamentary acts in January 1450 over supplies of food, hoarding and price inflation points to underlying problems with the harvest.[20] This was followed in the August 1452 parliament by similar legislation intended to force hoarded grain to be released into the market,[21] and orders for the similar release of all stored food beyond what was needed for the sustenance of the owners and their dependents, with particular reference to 'searchers' for such stores being established in Edinburgh and Leith, point to particular problems in the Lothians,[22] but all the major trading burghs faced similar issues. Favourable treatment of merchants who were bringing cargos of food to Scotland was ordained in legislation of the July 1454 parliament, which perhaps indicates that the harvests had been poor or had failed again.[23] Efforts to increase the levels of grain, peas and beans produced in Scotland – both to secure domestic supplies and reduce the drain on money through the need to import basic foodstuffs – can be seen in legislation of the March 1458 parliament, which instructed the sowing of minimum amounts of wheat and beans on any property where an eight-oxen plough was used.[24] A supply crisis was again the subject of legislation in June 1478, probably arising from a series of harsh winters and wet autumns in the mid-1470s, and 1482 legislation again giving favourable treatment to foreign merchants who brought merchandise and victuals to Scotland indicates that there was an extended period of shortages.[25] It is probable that this protracted supply crisis added to the general atmosphere of political insecurity which permeated the kingdom at this time and worsened the already tense relationship between the king and landholders who were facing declining incomes as the climatic cycle dropped to a new nadir.

The period c1490 to c1520 saw some recovery in annual temperatures, but there are indications of poor harvests in 1524–5, the summer of 1525 being recorded in Perth as 'the deir symmer' on account of the high price of meal produced by grain shortages.[26] More detailed local documentary records become available from the middle of the sixteenth century, including two chronicles with strongly regional foci – the Chronicle of Fortingall and Chronicle of Perth – surviving for the period c1550 to c1670.[27] These records confirm climate data that point to a return

Ben Lawers from the south – the extreme winters of the sixteenth century killed wild and domestic livestock, damaging Perth's trade in wool and skins, and worsening food shortages for the human population (author).

to cooler circumstances in the middle of the sixteenth century; the winter of 1554–5 is recorded as especially severe throughout the southern Highlands. Severe frosts had begun in November, but the main episode started with frosts from 13 December through to 25 December, when snow began to fall lasting through to 17 January – 'it was the grettast snaw and storm that was sein in memorie of man lewand that tyme' – when, after a brief thaw, snow began to fall again and the coldest weather was experienced between 22 and 26 February.[28] Late winter 1561 saw similar extreme weather, with 'mekill snaw…frost and stormis' lasting through March and 'evill frost snaw gret vindis' in early April.[29] A period of extreme instability followed in the 1560s and 1570s. Summer 1567 was 'rycht dry and het that brynt … kill corne and gyrs [grass] in mony partis of Scotland' followed by an 'evyl haryst' in September and October.[30] High grain prices resulted, extending through into the summer of 1569, which was followed by a good harvest and mild winter in 1569-70 and a second good harvest in 1570.[31] The winter of 1570–1, however, was very poor with widespread deaths amongst sheep and goats; harsh frosts lasted from mid-January until late March, so severe that rivers froze over and the ground was too hard to plough until the beginning of April.[32] After a respite of three years, the mid-1570s saw a run of poor conditions starting in the summer of 1574, which was wet and windy resulting in a poor harvest and high grain prices. The following winter saw severe snows, harsh frosts and hailstorms lasting through from December until March 1575. It seemed at first that 1576 was going to be a better year, but rains started in June and the wet weather extended through to September and brought a very poor harvest. As the chronicler put it 'ewil haryst ewil vintyr ewil Merche' with the sowing of the oats delayed that year until the start of the fourth week of March, and in 1577 wet weather continued right through the summer;[33] all this time, whilst Perthshire was alternately saturated or frozen, Edinburgh and the Lothians were parched to near drought conditions. Winter 1578 was also exceptionally wet, resulting in spates which caused the collapse of two arches of the bridge over the Tay at Perth and severe flood damage to the town on 20 December; a second major spate of the Tay in January 1582 carried away a further five arches of the bridge.[34] More recent experience of the impact of extreme weather on the national economy makes the cumulative effect of the successive blows delivered to Perth by these events easier to comprehend, but we can never truly understand the trauma which such episodes brought in an era where there was no insurance cover to offer any financial relief and aid was dependent entirely on charitable provision from your equally hard-pressed fellows.

Such direct experience of the effects of climate change were, for many of Perth's craft- and trade-dependent inhabitants, matched across this period by indirect consequences. For most of the period down to the late 1200s, the people of Perth were probably beneficiaries of the generally more benign climatic regime. With Europe experiencing an economic boom and rapid population growth, which triggered an explosion in demand for basic commodities like wool and hides, there were opportunities for relatively undeveloped regions like Scotland to secure niche roles as suppliers. As a community whose prosperity was founded on a combination of their own agricultural production, the channelling of the raw or semi-finished produce of the burgh's

Perth from Friarton – nowadays richly wooded, the landscape around the medieval burgh had been effectively stripped of significant growing timber by around 1200 as the burgesses cleared woodland to provide building materials and fuel (author).

hinterland through its market, and craft and trade activities based on control of that supply of materials, the milder conditions encouraged Perth's expansion to meet growing domestic and European demand.[35] Before 1200, Perth had already established itself as a centre for the trade in wool and dyed cloth, but, as King William's confirmation of the burgh's privileges also reveals, there was a significant involvement in the trade in hides.[36] As excavated evidence from the High Street suggests, this trade included goatskins and probably fleeces as well as cattle hides, many of the goatskins and kidskins perhaps supplying the prominent glovers' craft.[37] The numbers of animals represented by the bone and horn-core evidence represents more than would have been kept by the burgesses for their own domestic needs and points instead to a funnelling of the output of the pastoral uplands in Perth's hinterland through the burgh market. Such specialism was profitable during times of stable climate and high consumer demand, but as the account mentioned above of the impact of the severe winter of 1204–5 indicates, and as the sixteenth-century references to livestock deaths during the extreme winter weather of that period underscore, the supply of livestock or skins of slaughtered animals to the burgh could be disrupted severely by the weather.

Disease

In tandem with the catalogue of weather-related crises affecting Perth throughout the Middle Ages, recurring outbreaks of widespread disease from the late 1310s amongst animals (epizootics) and human populations (epidemics) introduced biological agency as a causal factor in major environmental, socio-economic and cultural change. The first clear surviving evidence for widespread livestock disease relates to sheep scab outbreaks that affected Lothian in 1268 and north-east Scotland in 1328. Although rarely fatal, such an outbreak was a critical concern for a society heavily dependent upon sheep-derived income, for the festering pustules which erupted on the animals' skins and which burst to contaminate the fleeces, which were themselves being shed by the infected sheep, rendered the wool foul and unsellable.[38] Royal mandates issued in the early 1320s aimed at preventing the spread of sheep diseases referred to variously as scab, 'pilsoucht' or 'pluk' illustrate the level of concern.[39] Juries were set up and given responsibility to identify infected flocks locally; infected sheep had to be slaughtered within eight days, with a fine of £10 – a substantial figure – for failure to comply; and all movement of livestock was prohibited. Comparison with the modern Foot-and-Mouth epidemics in cattle is unavoidable and perhaps provides us with some insight into how such similar events affected our ancestors.

While sheep scab was a recurring problem, something new occurred in a devastating plague amongst oxen and cattle across Europe between c1315 and 1325.[40] Herds in south-eastern England were first affected in 1318–9,[41] with the outbreak reaching the border by August 1319 probably in infected livestock brought to supply Edward II's army besieging Berwick.[42] Again, the loss of contemporary Scottish records renders it impossible to calculate its impact or the extent of its northern spread, but references to 'the great cattle slaughter' in Irish annals,[43] and English manorial accounts which indicate that in some areas over seventy-five per cent of cattle and draught oxen perished,[44] give a stark image of the likely effect in Scotland. Where oxen provided the vast majority of traction power for ploughs and wagons, the loss of teams crippled the seasonal agricultural round, hindering ploughing operations or overland transportation of bulky goods. Even more extreme than the winter deaths recorded in 1204–5, the scale of loss amongst herds would have taken years if not decades to recover from, severely damaging levels of output and consequently pushing up costs in everything from dairy production to crafts which involved the processing of leather and horn. References to further outbreaks of cattle disease continue throughout the remainder of our period, one of the last occurring in 1590 when local accounts record 'a plague among the bestiall' in the burgh's hinterland.[45]

Any economic crisis triggered by livestock disease in the early 1320s paled into insignificance behind the human pandemic which spread from the east after 1347 and reached Scotland in 1349, which we have come to know as the Black Death. In contrast to the abundant records from contemporary European, English and Irish writers, only one fourteenth-century account survives of the first episode of plague in Scotland. It states simply that 'there was in the kingdom of Scotland so great a pestilence and plague amongst men… as… had never been heard of by man', that 'fully a third of the human race was killed', and that its main victims were amongst 'the meaner sort and common people' rather than the magnates.[46] A second plague epidemic reached Scotland in 1362–3, which, according to Walter Bower, killed one third of those who had survived the first pestilence.[47] It was followed in 1380 by a third occurrence, which Bower again claimed killed one third of the remaining people.[48] A fourth outbreak struck in 1392 but with an apparently reduced death-rate. The understated reference to these incidents in fourteenth- and fifteenth-century accounts has resulted in plague almost disappearing from the reckoning in most modern academic histories of later medieval Scotland.[49] Only Alexander Grant has offered the sober but unsubstantiated opinion that 'plague still appears to have been the worst disaster suffered by the people of Scotland in recorded history'.[50]

As with accounts of weather events and recurring food shortages in the fifteenth century, the relative absence of accounts of epidemics from historical narratives, certainly when compared with the extensive plague literature from elsewhere in Europe, may be more a problem of survival of sources than evidence for initially limited and then declining impact. In common with the fifteenth-century issue of food supply, it is in parliamentary and burgh administration records that references to outbreaks continuing to affect the country down to the mid-seventeenth century occur and where the first measures to control epidemics were set out. Parliamentary legislation in October 1456, in response to an epidemic which began in 1455, set in place measures intended to contain the spread of the disease and to protect the property of victims and their neighbours; it was the earliest such legislation in Britain.[51] Burgh authorities followed this parliamentary lead; Edinburgh had measures in place by 1499, which provided a model for other communities, including Perth to follow.[52]

Although the disease that we have come to label as the Black Death is commonly identified as bubonic plague (the result of the bacillus *Yersinia pestis* being transmitted by flea-bites) descriptions of the medieval outbreaks and modern medical understanding of how bubonic plague spreads have raised doubt over that identification.[53] Further question marks have been raised against identification of documented fifteenth-century 'pestilences' as outbreaks of the same disease that had struck in 1349. In 1402, for example, there was a major epidemic of dysentery affecting the eastern part of the kingdom, with deaths reported as far north as Dundee.[54] Walter Bower's description of the epidemic in 1420 which caused great mortality amongst 'not only magnates but also numberless men of the people', which the common people named 'le qwhew', has led to its identification as some form of influenza.[55] Influenza might also have been the 'swiftly-spreading pestilence' which broke out in Edinburgh in February 1431 and in Haddington in 1432, and which led to arrangements for the possible relocation from Perth to St Andrews of a meeting of the Exchequer due to be held in February 1432.[56] The high mortalities of the famine of 1439 were accompanied by an epidemic labelled 'the wame ill' which, according to the chronicle accounts, killed as many people as in any previous pestilence, with a second epidemic spreading from England later in the year which caused the death of those infected within twenty-four hours.[57] The description of this epidemic has led to identification of the pathogen at work as *Vibrio cholerae* – cholera. In the majority of instances, however, we simply have the contemporary label of 'pestilence' used to describe outbreaks where different pathogens, or combinations of different pathogens, may have been at work.

Successive 'pestilence' epidemics struck Perth through the sixteenth century. In 1512, during a general epidemic throughout the kingdom, King James IV's councillors wrote to the burgh council with instructions for implementation of plague-control measures there in line with the terms of the 1456 act.[58] An epidemic of what was referred to as the 'Mallochis pest' struck Perth in September 1537.[59] This may have been the start of the epidemic that in 1542–3 led to a claim by leading burgess Oliver Maxton that the burgh had been 'in point of uter distructioun thre yere sine or tharby be the pest, and the maist part of the hale commontie fled for deid, and left the said burgh dissolait, without ordour or officiar'.[60] Although Maxton was probably overstating the impact of the disease on the daily functioning of the burgh and the lives of its inhabitants to make his actions during the course of the epidemic appear more significant, it is unlikely that his claims were so outrageous as to provoke dismissive ridicule. The picture, then, is of a community paralysed by the outbreak, effectively leaderless, and with significant numbers of townsfolk fleeing in fear of contagion and thereby compounding the burgh's difficulties in coping with and containing the epidemic.

Fear of pestilence remained strong throughout the 1500s, especially the threat of its entry to Scotland from abroad through trade with an infected area of mainland Europe. As a seaport and trading burgh that had regular contact with places where plague outbreaks were recurrent this was very much a live issue for Perth. In November 1580, for example, it was reported to the Privy Council in Edinburgh that a ship containing 'guidis and geir' of some Perth burgesses had entered the Tay estuary and been found to be carrying plague, some of its crew and passengers having already died. Although the ship-master had been ordered to sail to the Isle of May at the outer limit of the Firth of Forth and remain there in quarantine under pain of death, the ship had passed upstream and begun to discharge its cargo. The Privy Council therefore commanded the captain to take his ship to the May, ordering no-one on land to have unlicensed communication with them under penalty of death. Anyone who had come ashore already was to be apprehended and executed, houses where they had lodged to be closed, and the ship, boats, and all goods within it to be burnt.[61] The burgh authorities were rigorous in their prosecution of their responsibilities, for they understood full well the consequences of failure to round up those who had broken quarantine and any goods that had already been dispersed. Their diligence on this occasion ensured that no outbreak occurred.

Prompt action by the government in Edinburgh and the local administration in Perth and the district around the Firth of Tay appears to have contained any threat in 1580, but four years later the burgh was not spared. One of the most severe recorded visitations of plague to affect Perth started in autumn 1584 and lasted a full year before burning itself out in autumn 1585, reportedly killing 1427 townsfolk of all ages, which would have represented around one third of the population.[62] The king had been in the burgh when the epidemic struck and, despite the instructions issued by his Privy Council to restrict movement of people from infected into uninfected areas, he personally fled to Stirling and ordered the closing of all ferry routes and bridges across the Forth to prevent the southward spread of plague. Four of his household were not as fortunate as James in escaping from Perth, being amongst the first victims of the outbreak.[63] By early November the epidemic had spread widely through the district around Perth and down into Fife, apparently moving along the main lines of communication, which led to James and his Privy Council placing fresh restrictions on movement through the infected areas.[64] By March 1585 it was clear that hopes that the winter months would see an end to the outbreak had been misplaced and more drastic measures were authorised to staunch any further spread.

For a community which lived by its trading, the most severe of these measures was the suspension of all public gatherings and markets in Perth until the epidemic was clearly over and their temporary relocation to some nearby, uninfected place. All Perth burgesses, except for a handful licensed to move and certified as being 'clene' of any infection, were prohibited to go to the relocated market, their few certified fellows being charged with buying food, clothing and other necessary items sufficient to support the town.[65] The ban was repeated in April, pointing to a major dislocation of Perth's trading activity, and as late as 19 to 21 August it was still being reported that the plague was 'spreding in diverse pairtis of Louthean, Fyffe, and about Perth'.[66] Indeed, the instruction issued on 21 August – three days before local records noted the official ending of the epidemic – for a public proclamation citing the Earl of Atholl in a court action to be made at the market cross in Coupar Angus 'becaus of the infectioun of the pest within oure burgh of Perth', suggests that the prohibition of public assemblies in the burgh had continued right through the summer months.[67] Along with the loss of what was probably around twenty to thirty per cent of its population, this six-month suspension of its market and trading rights was a body-blow to a community which had already been experiencing a marked decline in its economic prosperity.

The costs of a major epidemic such as that of 1584–5 should not be under-estimated. The disruption of its trade through its harbour and market was not simply a question of inconvenience to local traders and consumers; producers in the burgh's commercial hinterland had been permitted to dispose of their goods through the markets in unaffected burghs in the wider region and external merchants had gone to those rival markets to buy and sell trade items. Dundee in particular, which apparently remained plague-free until October 1585, had benefited from its old rival's misfortunes. Indeed, when the epidemic had broken out in Edinburgh in summer 1585 the king had instructed the removal of the 'cunzie house' (mint) to Dundee instead of the traditional northern centre of government functions, although the arrival of plague at Dundee four months later saw a second relocation of the mint to the newly plague-free Perth.[68] Perth needed to recover as much of its lost revenues as possible, particularly in the form of customs and tolls from goods that should have been accounted for through the burgh's market, not only to meet its fiscal obligations at the Exchequer but also to pay off public debts incurred by the burgh council in its efforts to contain the epidemic and support both the infected and those whose ability to earn any income had been utterly disrupted by the bans on trade and free movement and assembly of people. In September 1586, the council launched an action in the Convention of the Royal Burghs against Dundee for the recovery of tolls and other revenue lost to that burgh during the epidemic, citing as the main reason for its action financial losses occasioned 'throw the lang continwance of the pest within the said burgh.'[69] Although some help was forthcoming on this occasion, the relief set in place made little impact to offset the full cost of the anti-plague measures that the town had borne.

Most of the succession of calamities outlined above affected medieval Scotland generally and stimulated wide-ranging socio-economic and cultural changes. For Perth, and for many other Scottish burghs, the more local impact of these events wrought equally profound socially transformative developments. Rapid population expansion in the burgh put pressure on local resources, driving the conversion of woodland and scrub areas into agricultural land. The possibilities for profit that Perth's market presented brought further pressures to bear as communities in the burgh's hinterland began to adjust their production efforts to supply the demand for specific raw materials from the craftsmen and merchants in the burgh, and from the foreign customers whom they were supplying. Clearance of woodland around Perth was already far advanced by the later twelfth century, with landlords encouraging their tenants to create 'assarts' – new intakes from previously uncultivated ground – for arable cultivation or for expanded, better-quality pasture.[70] Records suggest that by the mid-fifteenth century the closest source of large timbers was over 20km from Perth around Birnam, while by the early 1500s large oaks and pine could only be obtained in areas like Glen Lyon and western Rannoch some 60 to 100km away, or imported from the eastern Baltic.[71] The shortage of wood for fuel and building purposes may have been already so severe in the early 1200s that specific provision was made by King William in his c1209 confirmation of Perth's burgh privileges for the extension of his peace to those bringing fuel-wood or building-timber there, the only commodity provided for in this way in his charter.[72] The deforestation of the lower parts of the river-valley systems around Perth which such evidence suggests may have been a contributory factor in the devastating spate of 1209, for the loss of woodland which could have absorbed much of the rainfall probably saw increased run-off of rain-water causing rapid rises in river levels. It also had a second consequence: silting-up of the Tay estuary. As woodland cover declined and agriculture expanded, the increased run-off of water into the river carried progressively higher volumes of silt. By the fourteenth century, sandbanks in the tidal reach of the river below Perth made navigation upstream to the port more difficult, and by the sixteenth century its burgesses were referring to it as a 'dry town' and 'far from the sea'.[73] The impact of deforestation remained a problem for the remainder of the Middle Ages, as regional concentration on livestock rearing prevented regeneration of woodland in upland Perthshire through grazing pressures. As a consequence, shortages of fuel and building materials became a constraint on expansion and economic development which could only be offset partly by the import of coal and timber through Perth's port, which was itself in decline through the deforestation-related silting of the Tay. While some merchants benefited from the import of these in-demand commodities, in the longer term, the unsustainable exploitation of the natural resources of Perth's hinterland inflicted greater harm on the burgh's prosperity.

In balance to the negative dimension of intensification of grazing pressures, the suitability of much of Perth's hinterland for a concentration on livestock management brought great prosperity to important segments of the burgh's community for most of the twelfth and thirteenth centuries. Wool production was central to wealth-generation during this period and Perth secured a position as the main outlet for the clip from the flocks of some of the largest corporate sheep-farmers in medieval Scotland, the great monasteries. Coupar Angus Abbey, it has been suggested, acted as the agent for the Cistercian monasteries north of the Forth, collecting their produce and channelling it through the Perth wool-market.[74] Perth's merchants and cloth-producers benefited hugely from this trade, but disruption to supply or questions over quality caused by winter losses or outbreaks of scab threatened that prosperity. Wool exports from Perth declined sharply from the earlier fourteenth century and especially in the 1400s,[75] possibly partly due to declining flock sizes as a consequence of deteriorating climatic conditions and partly due to changes in market demand. There was a particular loss of regional market dominance as a wool-export centre to Dundee, but as Edinburgh came to control most of Scotland's trade in that commodity both towns began to turn to the export of coarse woollen cloth. Here too, however, by the early sixteenth century Dundee had completely overshadowed its old up-river rival.[76] Wool and woollen cloth production, however, was only one dimension of the regional emphasis on livestock farming; for Perth much of the money lay in skins and hides.

Conclusion

In the early sixteenth century Perth was regarded as a 'craftis toun' (crafts town) in that its commercial activity was dominated by the crafts rather than by its merchant community to a scale far greater than in any similar-sized burgh.[77] Of those crafts, the third most important of the nine leading activities in terms of wealth was the skinners, who included amongst their ranks the specialist skin-dealers including the glovers. In total, the crafts paid more than half the taxes raised in Perth, a position without parallel in any other Scottish burgh. Any event which had a negative impact on livestock numbers in Perth's hinterland, therefore, would have had a disproportionately significant impact on the burgh's wealth-generating and revenue-paying abilities. Epizootics and weather-related livestock deaths, therefore, threatened the livelihoods of significant numbers of Perth's inhabitants to a greater degree than in any other Scottish burgh. The succession of environmental checks delivered to the livestock-related crafts and trades in the burgh were not simply par for the course turns in the economic cycle. Such major episodes as the epizootic of the early 1320s probably inflicted prolonged economic damage on not only the skinner craft community but also on the wider interdependent network of crafts and trades, while the livestock deaths in the extreme winters of the sixteenth century and the cattle-plague of the 1590s added to a catalogue of woes afflicting a burgh in long-term decline.

In conclusion, however, it should be stressed that it was people ultimately who experienced the prospering or decline of their burgh and who responded to the environmental changes that affected them. Local shortages of specific materials could be offset in part by the ability to secure them from further afield, provided there was a vibrant trade in other commodities generating the prosperity to pay for the imports. That vibrant trade, however, depended on people both to create demand and service the supply; epidemic disease helped to depress both sides in that equation with awful regularity for the remainder of the Middle Ages. Our records of high mortality in the burgh in the aftermath of harvest failures may reflect more the drawing power of an urban centre on the rural poor who lacked the communal resources of a burgh to cushion the impact of such recurrent crises rather than deaths amongst the normally resident population, but it also possibly highlights the shocking death-toll brought by exposure of migrant labour who lacked immunity to the festering mass of common urban pathogens. Perth may have been little different from other Scottish burghs which suffered successive demographic shocks from plague or subsistence crises from the fourteenth century onwards, in its apparent ability to replace its losses with fresh blood from its rural hinterland, but that ability was dependent utterly on its wider economic health. As its economic base continued to contract in the sixteenth century, however, that attractive power declined and economic migrants gravitated towards more prosperous alternatives, Edinburgh above all others. A legacy of the interplay of environmental mismanagement, climate change and epidemic disease, at the close of the sixteenth century a burgh which had been in the top four of Scotland's international trading centres three hundred years earlier had sunk to the status of a purely regional market.

End Notes

1 For an overview of this material, see D. Bowler and others, *Perth: The Archaeology and Development of a Scottish Burgh* (Perth, 2004).
2 A. Crone and F. Watson, 'Sufficiency to scarcity: medieval Scotland, 500–1600', in T.C. Smout (ed), *People and Woods in Scotland* (Edinburgh, 2003), 60-81, especially 66-7.
3 See, for example, R.D. Oram and W.P. Adderley, 'Lordship and environmental change in central Highland Scotland c.1300 to c.1450', *Journal of the North Atlantic*, 1 (2008), 74-84; R.D. Oram and W.P. Adderley, 'Lordship, land and environmental change in West Highland and Hebridean Scotland c.1300–c.1450' in S Cavaciocchi (ed), *Economic and Biological Interactions in Pre-Industrial Europe from the 13th to the 18th Centuries* (Florence, 2010), 257-268; R.D. Oram and W.P. Adderley, 'Re Innse Gall: A Norse Colony in the Irish Sea and Hebrides?', in S Imsen (ed), *The Norwegian Domination and the Norse World c.1100–c.1400* (Trondheim, 2010), 125-148.
4 For general discussion, see A. Dawson, *So Foul and Fair a Day: A History of Scotland's Weather and Climate* (Edinburgh, 2009), chapter 4.
5 Walter Bower, *Scotichronicon*, D.E.R. Watt (ed) and others, iv (Edinburgh, 1994), 411, 417, 419.
6 Bower, *Scotichronicon*, iv, 437.
7 Bower, *Scotichronicon*, iv, 457
8 *Liber Ecclesie de Scon* (Bannatyne Club, 1843), nos 82, 96.
9 Bower, *Scotichronicon*, v (Edinburgh, 1990), 325.
10 Bower, *Scotichronicon*, v, 335.
11 John of Fordun, *Chronicle of the Scottish Nation*, W.F. Skene (ed) (Edinburgh, 1872), 295; Bower, *Scotichronicon*, v, 341.
12 Bower, *Scotichronicon*, v, 359, 361.
13 Bower, *Scotichronicon*, v, 369, 373
14 Bower, *Scotichronicon*, v, 381, 385, 387.
15 W.C. Jordan, *The Great Famine: Northern Europe in the Early Fourteenth Century* (Princeton, 1996).
16 Oram and Adderley, 'Lordship and environmental change'; Oram and Adderley, 'Lordship, land and environmental change', 260-63; Oram and Adderley, 'Re Innse Gall', 139-42.
17 Bower, *Scotichronicon*, vii, 143, 145.
18 Oram and Adderley, 'Lordship and environmental change', 77 and Figure 2.
19 P.A. Mayeski and others, ' Holocene Climate Variability,' *Quaternary Research* 62 (2004), 252.
20 Records of the Parliaments of Scotland (RPS) 1450/1/23; RPS 1450/1/24.
21 RPS 1452/3.
22 RPS 1452/4; RPS 1452/5.
23 RPS 1454/3.
24 RPS 1458/3/29.
25 RPS 1478/6/83; RPS 1482/3/8; RPS 1482/12/84.
26 *The Chronicle of Perth*, J. Eagles (ed) (Llanerch, 1996), 21.
27 *The Black Book of Taymouth* (Edinburgh, 1855), 107-48, *Chronicle of Perth*.
28 *Black Book of Taymouth*, 124-5.
29 *Black Book of Taymouth*, 129.
30 *Black Book of Taymouth*, 135.
31 *Black Book of Taymouth*, 136.
32 *Black Book of Taymouth*, 137-8.
33 *Black Book of Taymouth*, 141-2.
34 *Chronicle of Perth*, 39.
35 R.D. Oram, *Domination and Lordship: Scotland 1070–1230* (Edinburgh, 2011), 271.
36 D. Ditchburn, *Scotland and Europe: The Medieval Kingdom and its Contacts with Christendom, 1214–1560* (East Linton, 2000), 166, 168; Oram, *Domination and Lordship*, 292-3; G.W.S. Barrow (ed), *Regesta Regum Scotorum, ii, The Acts of William I* (Edinburgh, 1971), no.467.
37 R.M. Spearman, 'Workshops, Materials and Debris – Evidence of Early Industries', in M. Lynch, M. Spearman and G. Stell (eds), *The Scottish Medieval Town* (Edinburgh, 1988), 134-47 at 140.
38 Ditchburn, *Scotland and Europe*, 142.
39 Edinburgh University Ms. Borland 207 fol. 136; T.M. Cooper (ed), *Register of Brieves 1286-1386*, Stair Society, x (1946), 59, no.74.
40 T.P. Newfield, 'A cattle panzootic in early fourteenth-century Europe', *Agricultural History Review*, 57.2 (2009), 155-90; B.M.S. Campbell, 'Four famines and a pestilence: harvest, price and wage variations in England, 13th to 19th centuries', in B. Liljewall, I.A. Flygare, U. Lange, L. Ljunggren and J. Söderberg (eds), *Agrarhistoria på många sätt, 28 studies on manniskan och jorden. Festskrift till Janken Myrdal på hans 60-årsdag* (Stockholm, 2009), 23-56.
41 John de Trokelowe, *Annales*, H. Riley (ed) (London, 1866), 104-5; *Flores Historiarum*, H. Luard (ed) (London, 1890), 186-7.
42 *Chronicon de Lanercost* (Bannatyne Club, 1839), 240; Thomas Gray, Scalacronica (Maitland Club, 1836), 148; V.H. Galbraith, 'Extracts from the Historia aurea and a French "Brut" (1317–47)', *English Historical Review*, 43 (1928), 205, 210.
43 Newfield, 'Fourteenth-century cattle panzootic', 169-70.
44 B.M.S. Campbell, 'Physical shocks, biological hazards, and human impacts: the crisis of the fourteenth century revisited', in S Cavaciocchi (ed), *Economic and Biological Interactions in Pre-Industrial Europe from the 13th to the 18th Centuries* (Florence, 2010), 13-32.
45 *Chronicle of Perth*, 30.
46 *Chron. Fordun*, 359.
47 *Chron. Fordun*, 369; Bower, *Scotichronicon*, vii, 319.
48 Bower, *Scotichronicon*, vii, 381.
49 R. Oram, '"It cannot be decernit quha are clean and quha are foulle": Responses to epidemic disease in sixteenth and seventeenth-century Scotland', *Renaissance and Reformation*, 30 (2007), 13-39 at13-14.
50 A. Grant, *Independence and Nationhood: Scotland 1306–1469* (London, 1984), 75.
51 RPS 1456/7.
52 Oram, 'Responses to epidemic disease', 22, 24-7.
53 S.K. Cohn jnr, *The Black Death Transformed: Disease and Culture in Early Renaissance Europe* (London, 2002).
54 Bower, Scotichronicon, viii, 45; J.F.D. Shrewsbury, *History of the Bubonic Plague in the British Isles* (Cambridge, 1971), 149.
55 Bower, Scotichronicon, viii, 117; Shrewsbury, *History of the Bubonic Plague*, 150.
56 Bower, Scotichronicon, viii, 265, 277; Shrewsbury, *History of the Bubonic Plague*, 150; RPS 1431/10/2.
57 *Auchinleck Chronicle*, 160 (printed in C.A. McGladdery, *James II* (Edinburgh, 1990)).
58 Peacock, *Perth: Its Annals and Archives*, 476-7.
59 *Chronicle of Perth*, 21.
60 *Acts of the Lords of Council in Public Affairs 1501–1554*, R.K. Hannay (ed) (Edinburgh, 1932), 522-3.
61 *Register of the Privy Council of Scotland*, D. Masson (ed), iii (Edinburgh, 1880), 330 (hereafter RPC).
62 *Chronicle of Perth*, 23. That is not an impossibly high death-rate. Similar mortality levels were suffered in Brechin and Leith in the 1640s.
63 *Calendar of Letters and Papers Relating to the Affairs of the Borders of England and Scotland, J Bain* (ed), i (Edinburgh, 1894), no.258.
64 *RPC*, iii, 696-7.
65 *RPC*, iii, 727-8.
66 *RPC*, iii, 737, RPC, iv, 6-7.
67 *RPC*, 2nd series, viii,. P Hume Brown (ed) (Edinburgh, 1908), 219.
68 *RPC*, iii, 751; *RPC*, iv, 26.
69 *RPC*, iv, 105.
70 D.E. Easson and A. MacDonald (eds), *Charters of the Abbey of Inchcolm* (Scottish History Society, 1938), no. XXXVII.
71 G. Burnett (ed), *The Exchequer Rolls of Scotland, vi, 1455–1460* (Edinburgh, 1883), 35; R.K. Hannay (ed), *Rentale Dunkeldense* (Scottish History Society, 1915), 91, 122, 271.
72 G.W.S. Barrow (ed), *Regesta Regum Scotorum*, ii, *The Acts of William I* (Edinburgh, 1971), no.467.
73 M. Lynch, 'The Social and Economic Structure of the Larger Towns, 1450–1600', in M. Lynch, M. Spearman and G. Stell (eds), *The Scottish Medieval Town* (Edinburgh, 1988), 261-86 at 271.
74 A.A.M. Duncan, *Scotland: The Making of the Kingdom* (Edinburgh, 1975), 513.
75 Ditchburn, *Scotland and Europe*, 168; Lynch, 'Social and Economic Structure', 271.
76 Ditchburn, *Scotland and Europe*, 177; Lynch, 'Social and Economic Structure', 270.
77 M. Verschuur, 'Merchants and Craftsmen in Sixteenth-Century Perth', in M. Lynch (ed), *The Early Modern Town in Scotland* (London, 1987), 36-54 at 38.

Deforestation and more intensive cultivation of the catchment area of the Tay increased the flow of silt into the river, leading to the silting up of the estuary and ultimately to a decline in sea-borne trade involving the burgh (© PKHT).

Perth and Parliament, *c*1300–1707

Alan MacDonald

Perth is distinguished among the burghs as one of the very first to appear on a parliamentary list. In 1357, John Mercer, Robert Gatmilk and John Gill sat as one of the first ever urban representatives to be listed as attending a Scottish parliament.[1] Perth was represented right from the start and it would have been an exceptional parliament that did not have any representatives from Perth in attendance. Indeed, Perth was involved even before the start. In 1296, when the first Franco Scottish treaty was ratified in Scotland the seals of six burghs were appended, along with those of the leading churchmen and nobles. One of those burghs was Perth.[2] At some point between that date and 1357, it became normal for towns to be represented at parliaments and Perth took its place alongside the other leading burghs of the kingdom in that process.[3] Only Edinburgh, Aberdeen and Dundee have more names in the lists of those who represented the burghs in parliament. Being one of the foremost burghs, Perth often had two or even three representatives until 1621 when the privilege of having more than one was restricted to Edinburgh alone.

It was also virtually unheard of for one of Perth's commissioners not to be appointed to the key parliamentary drafting committee, the Lords of the Articles. Every piece of business went through this committee, which had to include the most powerful nobles and churchmen, and the commissioners from the most important burghs. In that forum, the burgh's commissioner played a significant part in ensuring that the interests of the burghs in general, as well as those of Perth itself, were promoted.

There was much more to the job of a parliamentary commissioner than the donkeywork of the legislative process. For a burgh as prominent as Perth, it was especially important to ensure that you made a good public impression. This can be illustrated by how much Perth spent on those that it sent to parliament. Commissioners received a daily allowance while at parliament and it varied from one burgh to another. In the early seventeenth century, Dunfermline paid £1 6s 8d, Ayr £1 10s, while Glasgow, Haddington and Perth paid the highest rate of £2. By the middle of that century, this had risen to £5 per day.[4] It mattered to a burgh like Perth that its commissioners lived more expensively than their counterparts from more lowly towns; they had a reputation to sustain.

The size of the commissioner's entourage was equally important in that respect. Commissioners took servants to care for their horses, run messages and look after their luggage. If a burgh sent three commissioners to parliament that could easily mean that a delegation of six or more people might be sent, for whom the burgh would provide clothing and living expenses. In 1661, the two 'lackeys' who accompanied the provost (Sir Patrick Threipland of Fingask) to parliament were furnished with 'clothes, showes, stockins and hatts' at the considerable cost of £56 12s.[5] One of the most important things that the servants carried was the 'pockmantie' (ie the portmanteau, literally, mantle-carrier), containing the town's footmantle, the ankle-length black velvet robe worn by the burgh's commissioner in the opening ceremony, the riding of parliament.

Perth treated the matter of sending its commissioners to parliament so seriously, it even made an occasion of their departure and return. This was quite unusual among the burghs in general and serves to demonstrate just how important the burgh considered the role to be. In the 1640s, the burgh records show that Perth's commissioners received a 'bonnarlla' (ie *a bon aller,* a send-off) at what was called their 'way going' in the form of mulled wine; and further drinks were provided for them at their 'home coming', when they might receive a pint of 'sack' (a sweet white wine).[6] Gestures like this emphasised the significance of the occasion and the gratitude of the burgh for services done, cementing, through formal ceremonies, the relationship between the burgh and its commissioners.

What was in it for Perth?

All of this expense and pomp demonstrates the significance attached to parliament by a burgh like Perth, and there were good reasons for this. Parliament was *the* place to secure and uphold your rights. Nothing could trump an act of parliament in a court of law, so obtaining one was important. Between 1550 and 1650, Scotland's towns obtained 245 acts of parliament in their favour. Over 100 of those were accounted for by just five burghs (Edinburgh, Aberdeen, Glasgow, Dundee and Perth), with Edinburgh alone securing nearly fifty. The wealth and status of those five burghs gave them influence, enabled them to buy favours, got them onto committees, and eased the passage of their acts.

Perth obtained sixteen acts in its favour in that 100-year period, the third highest number, behind only Aberdeen and Edinburgh. These acts, many of which simply ratified the burgh's existing privileges, might look rather mundane to modern eyes, but we should not be too quick to dismiss their significance. Anyone who knows anything about the history of Perth knows that its bridge has always been a headache. In 1578, 1609 and 1641, acts of parliament were secured to help the burgh to either repair or rebuild their bridge.[7] Exceptionally, tens of thousands of pounds of central government funding were granted to the project. Perth's position at the lowest bridgeable point of the Tay meant that its bridge was nationally important for economic and strategic reasons, so the crown was willing to help out. When the burgh's commissioners returned home with news like that, they would have earned their pint of sack.

Then, as now, it was important to garner support in parliament, especially among prominent individuals. In 1606, the burgh's council minutes record how Perth sought to smooth the passage of the ratification of its new royal charter by giving half a tun of wine each to the earl of Montrose (the king's commissioner to parliament) and the earl of Dunbar (the king's treasurer) and a further puncheon of wine to the king's commissioner.[8] The size of this gift is best understood by conversion into bottles: tuns and puncheons were barrels, the former containing roughly 1,140 litres, equivalent to over 1,500 bottles, the latter containing about 450 litres, or 600 bottles!

Alongside such extravagances, smaller favours were also granted to ensure the goodwill of officials. Since Perth's leather-working industry was so important to the local economy, it was common for Perth's commissioners to carry new pairs of gloves as a gift for the clerks of parliament, the sort of promotional activity that we don't perhaps associate with the pre-industrial age.[9]

Perth as parliamentary venue

For most burghs, their parliamentary stories would end here but Perth was a member of that select band of towns where parliaments actually met. Until around the middle of the fifteenth century, the Scottish parliament met in religious houses, usually the abbeys of Scone, Cambuskenneth and Holyrood until around 1400, with the Dominican convent at Perth favoured in the early fifteenth century.[10] All of these had close associations with the monarchy. The first recorded parliament at Scone met there in 1265, and Scone became one of the principal venues for parliaments during the fourteenth century (it was host to twenty-one parliaments out of a total of thirty seven in the fourteenth century). As the nearest town, it is almost certain that such gatherings would have had an impact on Perth, even before parliaments began to meet in the burgh itself.

The Dominican convent at Perth was established by Alexander II in the thirteenth century, and its royal lodgings were a favoured royal residence until the assassination of James I there in 1437. The parliaments that met at Perth between 1321 and the death of James I all appear to have met in that setting. However, after the murder of the king, parliaments ceased to meet in religious houses, and they rarely met in Perth. Indeed it was probably the assassination of James I that thwarted a process by which Perth was emerging as the capital of Scotland. All over Europe, royal governments were becoming more bureaucratised and thus the itinerant nature of government was declining. The same process was happening in Scotland during the fifteenth century and, before 1437, Perth looked like the most likely location for the government to put down its roots, situated as it was in a central position, a safe distance from England and close to the traditional coronation place.

In the first half of the fifteenth century, Perth was the favoured location for parliament. In that period there were twenty-one sessions of parliament, fourteen of which met at Perth, while Edinburgh hosted only five. In the 1420s, James I even famously proposed to move the recently-created University of St Andrews to Perth, a further indication of his desire to enhance its status as his main centre of power. However, royal favour switched decisively to Edinburgh as the century wore on. Between 1450 and 1500, there were forty-four parliaments, all but three of which met at Edinburgh, with Perth hosting parliament only once.

The focus of power had begun to move decisively away from the ancient heart of the kingdom, with the coronation of James II at Holyrood in 1437 marking a deliberate rejection of Scone as Scotland's symbolic focus. Yet the history of Perth as a parliamentary venue did not end in the fifteenth century, for parliament returned to the burgh in times of crisis during the seventeenth century. In 1604 and 1606, parliament met at Perth because of outbreaks of disease in Edinburgh, usually referred to as the plague, but likely to have been a more locally-contained, water-borne disease such as typhoid. In 1604, 'the town mustart fourteen hundred men in armes and gude ecupadge'. Its three sergeants, the armed officers who accompanied the magistrates on their duties and carried out judicial summonses and arrests, were given new sets of clothes and one Alexander Peebles was given the burgh's 'handzanyie' (that is its ensign, or flag) 'to be borne be him this tyme of parliament'.[11] This was the first time that parliament had met in Perth since 1459 and the council were obviously determined to ensure that they put on a good show. Appearances were important when the most powerful men in the land were coming to town.

Two years later, when parliament once more had to meet in Perth because of disease in the capital, a 'wapinschaw' was held 'to sie quhat preparatione may be had anent the parliament'.[12] This suggests that even more preparation was being made to ensure that, as in 1604, the able-bodied freemen of the burgh would come out in 'good ecupage' for the visiting parliamentarians and their retinues. The council also ordered the 'taking away of the red [rubbish], middingis and stane aff the calsay [the paved streets]' in preparation for parliament.[13] Early modern towns tended to accumulate ordure in their streets but it was not fitting to have piles of it lying around when parliament came to town. Also, because of the number of people likely to descend upon the burgh, the council gave ten burgesses the daunting responsibility of being 'governouris and gydaris of the multitude' during parliament.[14] Given the size of the retinues of noblemen, it is quite possible that a parliament with a membership of around 150 would have involved the influx of well over 1,000 people to the burgh, providing a considerable economic boost.

By the seventeenth century, the house of the Dominican friars was no longer available, so where exactly did parliament meet at this time? A laconic entry in the council minutes records a command to the master of works in 1604 to see to 'the reparatioun of the new kirk' for the parliament, but the parliamentary record itself is clear that it met 'within the tolbuth of the said burgh of Perth' in both 1604 and 1606.[15] This presents something of a puzzle. Perth's new tolbooth lay at the eastern end of the High Street, at some distance from the church, on a different street.

However, recent research has shown that parliament was a more advanced institution than was previously appreciated, requiring a more complex venue for its deliberations.[16] As well as gathering in a single chamber at the beginning and end of the parliamentary session, the membership split up into its constituent estates of bishops, nobles, lairds and burgesses, each of which needed a separate room in which to discuss the business of the parliament. The Presbyterian historian, David Calderwood, records a petition being submitted to 'everie estat, as they satt severallie' (ie separately) during the 1606 parliament at Perth. So it is likely that rooms in St John's church were used to house at least some

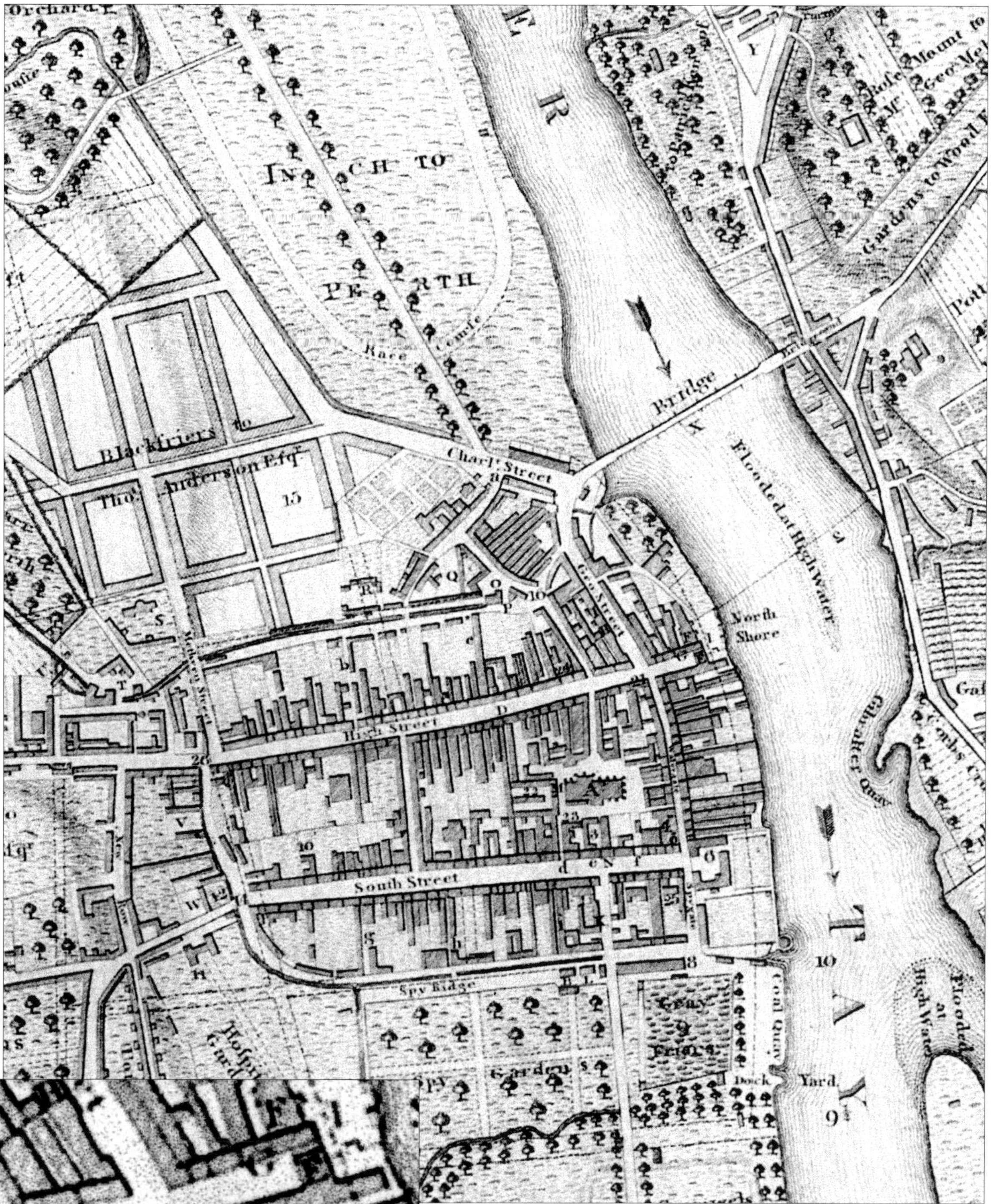

Perth in 1792: the street layout is virtually unchanged from the early seventeenth century (AK Bell Library, Local Studies).

Detail of the above showing the relationship between the tolbooth (top right, marked 'E', blocking the end of High Street) and St John's church (bottom left, marked 'A') (AK Bell Library, Local Studies).

of these meetings. Although the fact that the burgh council met in the 'revestry' (ie the vestry), might even suggest that it was possible to describe part of St John's church as the 'tolbooth' of Perth, just as in Edinburgh, where a significant portion of the west end of St Giles' church was partitioned off in the 1560s for municipal and parliamentary use.[17]

After 1606, it would be another forty-four years before parliament returned to Perth for what proved to be the last time. In the winter of 1650–51, the Scots were retreating in the face of Cromwell's invading English army and were forced to abandon Edinburgh. Sadly, however, the burgh accounts and council minutes from that time are lost, perhaps as a result of the disruptions caused by the Anglo-Scottish war, so we know nothing of how the town accommodated the estates on that occasion.

Perth's tolbooth, possibly a seventeenth-century parliamentary venue (AK Bell Library, Local Studies).

Riding and Rivalry

The parliament at Perth in 1606 has gone down in history as the 'Red Parliament'. The Chronicle of Perth records why: 'This parliament was riddin be the nobilitie, all in robbis of reid scarlet, and facit with quhyte furris'.[18] James VI decided that the finery worn by the nobles was not fine enough, so he commanded them to wear scarlet robes for all future parliaments, which was done for the first time at this parliament.[19]

Even before this innovation, the 'riding of parliament' already involved a lot of pomp and was taken very seriously by participants. On the first day of parliament, the entire membership gathered in the forecourt of Holyrood Palace and processed up the hill to the parliament house where they would dismount, enter the chamber and be placed in their seats. The riding projected the majesty of parliament. At the same time, it emphasised hierarchy: your place in the procession was directly related to your importance. It might come as a surprise to discover that the more important you were the closer to the rear of the procession you would be. The reason for this was that the procession created a visual crescendo, culminating with the honours of Scotland (the crown, sword and sceptre) and the monarch. Thus, when the members arrived at parliament, the lowliest had to wait longest for the king who had to wait for nobody. When it came to voting, however, the order was reversed, so that the people of highest status had the opportunity to lead their social inferiors by example.

Places were hotly contested and disputes led to heated confrontations, protests and even physical violence. One dispute in 1593 delayed the start of parliament for almost five hours. Another nearly led to a duel. In 1587,

> thaire arrose ane heiche contentioun betuix the erles of Crafurde and Bothuell, the lordis Fleming, Settoun, Home and Innermeithe. The counsell sat thairupone, and fand that the lord Flemyng sould have the prioretie afoir the rest of the lordis. Quhairupone the lord Home challendgit the lord Fleming with the singular combat, quho wer not suffered to fecht, albeet they wer baith weill willing.[20]

The nobles were very hung up on family status, but some burghs were equally concerned about their place in the pecking order. The longest-running dispute was between Dundee and Perth.

In December 1567 a 'tumult happynnit upoun the gait of Edinburgh betuix the nychtbouris [of Dundee] and the inhabitantis of Sanctjohnnestoun in the tyme of the... parliament', in other words, the servants of the burghs' commissioners had a fist-fight.[21] This marks the beginning of what would be described in the early seventeenth century as 'that long lasting debait betuix the tounes of Perth and Dundie anent the 2d place of precidencey amongest the burrowes', which, according to one Victorian historian of Perth, 'raged with ludicrous *vehemence on the part of the Dundonians*'![22] By the sixteenth century, Dundee had overtaken Perth in terms of the volume of its trade, making it the second wealthiest burgh in Scotland, behind Edinburgh. But Perth was in no mind to let its upstart neighbour lord it over them. In 1579, with the dispute still unresolved, the convention of burghs was ordered by an act of parliament to decide the issue 'according to the auncientie [i.e. the age] of the ... burrowis' and to rank all burghs, 'swa that perpetuall ordour may be establischit'.[23] When the convention met in the following year, commissioners from Dundee and Perth agreed that their dispute should be submitted to arbitrators chosen by the convention. Before anyone could take a breath,

Stirling's commissioner intervened, declaring that 'quhatsumever thing beis done or decernit betuix ... Dondie and Perth tuiching the second place ... prejudge nocht Striveling and the privilege it hes to the second place'.[24]

In spite of this unhelpful intervention, it was decided that Dundee and Perth should each choose three merchants to meet at the parish church of Rait in the Carse of Gowrie, and that those six should choose an 'overisman' with a casting vote. To ensure that this crucial individual was chosen fairly, a complicated process was devised: each group of three should name five neutral men from burghs other than Dundee and Perth, both lists would then be put into a hat (literally) on a single piece of paper, along with another piece of paper which was blank. If Perth's representative chose the paper with the names on it, Dundee would choose from Perth's nominees and vice versa.[25]

It is not hard to imagine the groans of exasperation that must have been heard at the next convention of burghs when it transpired that nobody had turned up at Rait, let alone carried out the convoluted process of choosing the 'oversman'. So, the convention ruled that Dundee and Perth should bring their evidence in writing to a convention at Edinburgh in April 1581.[26] At that meeting, there was 'lang debaitt and controversie' between Perth and Dundee, while Stirling again registered its claim to second place. Written arguments were 'hard, red and at lenth avysitlie considerit'. However, they decided that because the dispute was 'swa debaitabill and intricate', they'd ask the privy council to decide. Perth's commissioner protested, while Stirling's again asserted his burgh's right to second place. To add to the confusion, those from Aberdeen and Linlithgow weighed in with assertions of *their* right to 'thrid place': whatever the outcome of the contest between Perth and Dundee, others were forming a queue to square up to the loser.[27] But the privy council would have none of it, threatening the burghs with being put to the horn (ie outlawed), if they did not make a decision. So Perth was given 'priority... before... Dundie' but only until the next parliament, or until a judgement could be made by the king and privy council. The commissioners of Dundee 'alluterly dissentit'.[28]

When parliament met in November 1581, Dundee alleged, among other things, that Perth's claim to second place was of recent vintage. Parliament handed the decision back to the burghs once again, insisting on a final resolution at their next convention in the summer of 1582.[29] The guildry book of Perth gives a full account of the lengths to which Perth's dean of guild, Henry Adamson, went in 1582 to achieve a positive result. He rode to Edinburgh to raise a letter at the court of session ordering the convention of burghs to resolve the dispute. He secured the signatures of the treasurer, William Ruthven, earl of Gowrie (a good friend to Perth), and the abbot of Dunfermline. He then rode to Stirling for the king's signature, returning to Edinburgh to have the letter sealed with the royal signet.[30] It seemed to work: the royal letter (clearly drafted by the council of Perth, given its entirely one-sided stance) had been crucial: it ordered the burghs to 'considder onlye the maist auld and ancient burgh', while noting 'the ancie[n]tie and antiquitie of our said burgh of Perth'. So, the convention of burghs (incidentally meeting at Perth), 'declarit the burgh of Perth to haif the first place afoir Dondy... in all tym to cum'.[31] But Dundee refused to take this lying down and complained to the next parliament, arguing that a convention at Perth could hardly be neutral. Parliament sent the case straight back to the burghs, ordering them to make a final decision 'without delay'. In 1582, the earl of Gowrie's support had been valuable. By 1584, the political tables had turned. Gowrie had headed a coup in August 1582 (the Ruthven Raid) but the resulting regime was overthrown in the following July. Gowrie himself was arrested, ironically at Dundee, while trying to flee Scotland and was executed for treason. Dundee's reward came quickly: at parliament in May 1584, the king granted it 'second place... nixt [to] Edinburgh' and Perth's protests were brushed aside.[32]

Perth continued to insist on the validity of the judgements already made in its favour. In exasperation, the convention of burghs tried to get Edinburgh to decide the dispute, on the logical basis that its position as the premier burgh was undisputed, but the capital flatly refused. Dundee tried to get the next parliament to make a final decision but parliament passed the matter to the court of session.[33] Nobody wanted to be the one to make the decision.

By 1594, Perth was back in royal favour and the king ordered the earl Marischal, whose responsibility it was to order the members for the riding of parliament, to place it second after Edinburgh in that year 'and in tyme coming'.[34] This also sounds like a final judgement, but Dundee refused to back down and seven years later, the dispute seemed no closer to resolution: if anything, relations between the two burghs were getting worse, as Perth's new royal charter of November 1600 appeared to remove most of Dundee's rights on the Tay.

On 1 July 1601, Perth's commissioners at the convention of burghs at St Andrews wrote to their council, telling them that the convention wanted to reach a final resolution and that Dundee was agreeable. Perth's representatives at the court of session were told 'to haist... heir and desist fra all forder proces'. With similar urgency, the council was asked to send someone to St Andrews 'on the secund of this moneth, althocht he suld ryd the haill nycht'. On 3 July, the case before the court of session was suspended because the convention of burghs was to 'submit the matter... to the amicabill decisioun of certane uther burrowis'. On the same day, commissioners from both burghs agreed 'to submit all their grudgeis and controvereis' to a special convention of burghs at Edinburgh five days later.[35]

It duly met, but, when it was decided that the most important task was 'to tak away all grudge of the prioritie', Perth 'refuissit to submit' unless that particular issue was 'left furth', insisting that the original judgement of 1582 should stand. As far as they were concerned, it was only the navigation rights on the Tay that were at issue. The case returned to the court of session. Perth authorised its representatives to borrow whatever sums were necessary for the case, while Dundee borrowed over £3,000 'in the defense of certane wrangous actionis and persuittis intendit aganes thame' by Perth.[36] The case was so important that when the court of session sat on 30 December 1602 to give its final judgement, the king himself was present. Although Perth's arguments didn't mention precedence, its submission began with its strongest suit:

> the gryt antiquitie, gud and pleasant cituatioun of the said burgh, of auld the residence of your hienes progenitouris with thair princeis, bairnes, and fameleis, and quhair parliamentis, publict conventiounes, generall counsellis and assembleis of the esteattis of the realme wer hauldin.

It went on to say that its new charter had exempted its merchants from any exactions that might harm their trade, protesting that the rights obtained by Dundee over parts of the Firth of Tay were invalid because those places had been granted to Perth.

Dundee's response cited various grants from the thirteenth century onwards which gave it jurisdiction on the north side of the Firth and granted it the right to insist that all ships entering the Tay had to 'break bulk' at Dundee. It also provided a detailed account of why it should have 'the first place [after Edinburgh] in all parliamentis, assembleis, counsallis and counventioumes'. The first was that Dundee 'is mair ancient', having existed before Perth's claim to foundation by William the Lion (1165–1214). William had indeed granted Perth its oldest extant charter (in 1210), but other sources demonstrate foundation by David I (1124–1153) in the 1120s. It also stated that, Dundee 'beiris the double of the chairgis of Perth in the subsideis of the realme' (that is, it paid more tax). But wealth is difficult grounds for precedence, for it is a very fickle thing. If this argument had been accepted, every parliament would have had to be preceded by a long and fraught process of assessing each burgh's wealth. Another assertion was that 'Dundie is more civilie governit than Perth'. This referred to the fact that Dundee had only two craftsmen on its council compared to Perth's even division of merchants and craftsmen. The only problem was that this made Edinburgh (with six craft councillors) less 'civillie governit' than Dundee. For obvious reasons, this argument could not be admitted. There were some much smaller burghs that had no craft councillors at all, and Dundee would not have accepted that those burghs were superior. Finally, Dundee claimed to have had priority before 1582 when judgement in favour of Perth had been obtained with the help of 'mony sinister means usit be William erle of Gowrie'.[37] This was clearly aimed at the king who would not easily have forgotten his captivity at Huntingtower in 1582–3, and would still have the Gowrie Conspiracy, a supposed attempt on his life in Perth in August 1600, fresh in his mind. Yet the generous charter granted to Perth only three months after the Gowrie conspiracy shows that, for James, there was nothing to forgive.

So, the judgement favoured Perth:

> As to the first place and rank acclamit be ather of the saidis burrowis of Dundie and Perth in parliamentis, generall conventioumes, counsellis of the esteattis of this realme and assembleis of burrowis, Our... soverane lord findis and decernis that the said burght of Perth and thair commissioneris sall have the plaice befoir the said burght of Dundie and thair commissioneris in all the foirsaidis publict meittingis, And the said burgessis of Dundie thair saidis successouris and commissioneris sall mak na impedimentis to thame thairin in na tyme cuming.

And that was an end to it – the highest civil court in the land had given its judgement and Dundee was forced to relent.

Conclusion

Looking at Perth's relationship with parliament tells us things about Perth and things about parliament as well. Perth's efforts to obtain legislation in its favour (and its success in doing so), the money it spent to kit out its commissioners and their entourages, to provide a fitting venue for parliaments, and to pursue its dispute over precedence with Dundee, tell us two important things. First, they tell us that parliament was the most important institution in Scotland, the sovereign body of the realm, with power above even that of the king (why else would Perth, in 1606, have bothered to get parliamentary ratification of its royal charter of 1600?). Secondly, they tell us something important about Perth: it was one of the five wealthiest and most influential towns in Scotland; it had a prominent voice in the councils of the realm; and, even though by the sixteenth century it was no longer as wealthy as its great rival Dundee, it was recognised as second only to Edinburgh in terms of the esteem accorded to Scotland's towns in public ceremonial occasions. And in celebrating 800 years since William the Lion granted a charter to Perth, that is something of which the burgh and its people can rightly be proud.

End Notes

1 *The Records of the Parliaments of Scotland to 1707* [RPS], K. M. Brown et al. (eds) (St Andrews, 2007–2011), A1357/9/3. Date accessed: 24 February 2011; M. D. Young (ed), *The Parliaments of Scotland: Burgh and Shire Commissioners,* 2 vols (Edinburgh, 1992-3), vol. ii, p.784.

2 A. A. M. Duncan, 'The early parliaments of Scotland', in *Scottish Historical Review,* vol. 45 (1966), pp.36-58, at p.51.

3 A. R. MacDonald, 'The Third Estate: Parliament and the Burghs', in K. M. Brown and A. R. MacDonald (eds), *The History of the Scottish Parliament Volume 3: Parliament in Context, 1235–1707* (Edinburgh, 2010), pp. 95-121, at pp. 96-7.

4 A. R. MacDonald, *The Burghs and Parliament in Scotland c.1550–1651* (Aldershot, 2007), pp. 84-7.

5 Perth and Kinross Council Archive [PKCA], B59/25/4/2.

6 PKCA, B59/25/4/1/4A, account for 1645–6.

7 *RPS,* 1578/7/24, 1609/4/55, 1641/8/347-8.

8 PKCA, B59/16/1, fo.123r.

9 PKCA, B59/25/4/1/4A, account for 1645–6.

10 For details on the medieval parliamentary venue, see R. Oram, 'Community of the Realm: the Middle Ages', in M. Glendinning (ed), *The Architecture of Scottish Government: From Kingship to Parliamentary Democracy* (Dundee, 2004), pp. 15-81.

11 PKCA, B59/16/1, fos. 84-5; J. Maidment (ed), *The Chronicle of Perth* (Edinburgh, 1831), p. 10.

12 PKCA, B59/16/1, fo. 122v.

13 PKCA, B59/16/1, fo. 122r.

14 PKCA, B59/16/1, fo. 123r.

15 PKCA, B59/16/1, fo. 84r; RPS, 1604/4/17.

16 A. R. MacDonald, 'Deliberative Processes in Parliament, c.1567–1639: Multicameralism and the Lords of the Articles', in SHR, vol. 81 (2002), pp. 23-51.

17 See MacDonald, *The Burghs and Parliament,* ch. 6, esp. 140-44.

18 *The Chronicle of Perth,* p. 11.

19 J. H. Burton, et al (eds), *Register of the Privy Council of Scotland [RPC],* first series, 14 vols (Edinburgh, 1877–98), vol. vii, 160-61.

20 J. Dennistoun (ed), *Memoirs of the Affairs of Scotland by David Moysie,* 1577–1603 (Edinburgh, 1830), p. 65.

21 RPC, vol. i, pp. 604-5.

22 J. Haig (ed), *The Historical Works of Sir James Balfour,* 4 vols (Edinburgh, 1824), vol. i, p. 242; R. S. Fittis, *The Perthshire Antiquarian Miscellany* (Perth, 1875), p. 358.

23 RPS, 1579/10/75.

24 J. D. Marwick (ed), *Records of the Convention of the Royal Burghs of Scotland* [RCRBS], 7 vols (1866-1918), vol. i, p. 84.

25 *RCRBS,* vol. i, pp. 84-5.

26 *RCRBS,* vol. i, pp. 107-8.

27 *RCRBS,* vol. i, p. 114.

28 *RCRBS,* vol. i, pp. 118-9.

29 *RPS,* 1581/10/66.

30 L. Stavert (ed), *The Perth Guildry Book, 1452–1601* (Edinburgh, 1993), pp. 327-8.

31 PKCA, B59/26/1/9/2; B59/26/1/9/7/1.

32 *RCRBS,* vol. i, pp. 175, 186-7, 195-6.

33 *RCRBS,* vol. i, pp. 232-3.

34 PKCA, B59/26/1/9/1.

35 PKCA, B59/16/1, fos 4-5; National Archives of Scotland [NAS], Court of Session Register of Acts and Decreets, CS7/195, fos 89v-92v; *RCRBS,* vol. ii, pp. 111, 116.

36 PKCA, B59/16/1, fo. 42r; Dundee City Archives, Town Council Minute Book, vol. 2, p. 118.

37 NAS, Court of Session, Register of Acts and Decreets, CS7/201, fos 387r-393r.

Town Life and the Life of the Town in the Sixteenth Century

Mary Verschuur

Welcome to Sixteenth Century Perth! This paper will take the form of a walking tour (a mental one at least) of Perth in the sixteenth century and will introduce you to some of the principal buildings and some of the people who went about their daily lives around the middle of the century, between 1540–70 or thereabouts. The sources that I have used to re-construct these descriptions of town life and the life of the town are documentary as opposed to archaeological. They comprise, amongst other things, notaries' protocols, burgh court and other court records, writs and miscellaneous documents, wills and testaments and the records of the merchants' gild and craft incorporations. The Blackfriars rentals, collected to fund a hospital in the post-Reformation decades, also proved to be very useful in identifying the locations and owners of many of the properties. The map below provides an outline of the burgh and the street pattern as it appeared in mid-sixteenth century. It will serve as a point of reference for the paper that follows.

Market Cross

Let us imagine that we are standing at the Market Cross. It is situated at the junction of Northgate with Castlegavel (now Skinnergate) and Kirkgate. I have not come across any contemporary descriptions of the Cross, but besides serving as a symbol of the burgh's right to trade, its location marked the focal point of town life and was a place of public punishment and of public proclamations. Were it sometime in mid-July 1549 we might witness John Small on his knees at the cross asking forgiveness of his victims, Thomas Tuly and his wife, whom he had attacked and wounded with his knife. Were it July 1551, we would see Christine Frew 'locked in irons at the market cross' where she had been sentenced to remain for twenty-four hours for having slandered or otherwise offended John Berne's wife.[1]

The Cross was also a place of public proclamation where one might hear a statute passed by the council and bailies being read aloud 'that no person allege ignorance thereof'. The one read in December 1551 regarding the laying of muck on the sides of the streets, at the ports and on the North and South Inches suggests that waste disposal was both a problem and a hazard whereby the streets were covered, passage through them 'stopped' and the Inches 'rotten'. The statute forbade any further deposit of horse droppings in the places mentioned under pain of forfeiture of one's horse and a fine of £10, which was earmarked for upkeep of the Tay Bridge.[2]

If you looked east from the Cross towards the river or south along Kirkgate you might see markets taking place in both streets on certain days. The fish/salmon market was held on Northgate 'below the cross' throughout most of the sixteenth century but was moved to the South Gate Port by an act of council in 1598.[3] Salmon was an important commodity in Perth's overseas commerce barrels of which might be traded for French wine or bought by merchants from other towns for sale or export elsewhere.[4]

It is hard to imagine stalls and barrows crowding the narrow passageway that is now Kirkgate, but one afternoon in June 1556 Patrick Robertson, a saddler living in Perth, was standing on his forestair in Kirkgate overlooking the activity of a street market. As he watched, an altercation broke out between two of the stall holders causing the onlooker to step down into the street to aid one of the people involved. Robertson was subsequently called as a witness when the protagonists continued their argument before the Court of Session.[5]

St John's church

Passing along Kirkgate towards the parish church of St John (probably the only building that Perth's sixteenth century residents would recognise today) we would come to a barrier separating the street from the churchyard. This wall had been erected by William Ross, a baxter burgess whose property was located on the west side of the street next to the church. Ross obtained permission from the burgh council to erect a low wall between his property and the churchyard on condition that he construct a stile or a gateway to allow access to the church. He was further required to mark the obstruction with a lamp to be kept alight until the conclusion of evening services.[6] Once across the stile we would come face to face with the parish church, focal point of religious practice within the burgh. The church was surrounded on the north and west sides by the town's official burial ground, which served the community until 1580 at which date it was moved by order of the Kirk Session to the Greyfriars yard.[7] Within the church itself, the spark that set fire to the Scottish reformation was ignited in May 1559. John Knox's sermon 'vehement against idolatry' provoked an outburst of iconoclasm from which there was no turning back. As told by Knox the iconoclasm that followed his sermon was precipitated by a youth who threw a stone at the tabernacle on the altar as a priest prepared to say mass. It is my contention that the town was well prepared to follow up on Knox's call, but it took me a whole book to tell that story so I will invite you to read it there while we continue our walk.[8]

May 1559 was not the first time that violence had erupted in St John's church. On All Saints Day in 1543, Robert Lamb interrupted a friar who was preaching on the efficacy of praying to the saints as a means of salvation. Lamb challenged the preacher to desist and instead 'to utter the truth' which caused some unrest amongst the congregation but little sympathy for Lamb's sentiments. He had to exit hurriedly to escape the wrath of the congregation.[9] Lamb's point of view may have been unpopular but Protestant thought was infiltrating the burgh in 1543. Two months later, he and four others were condemned to death for 'breaking

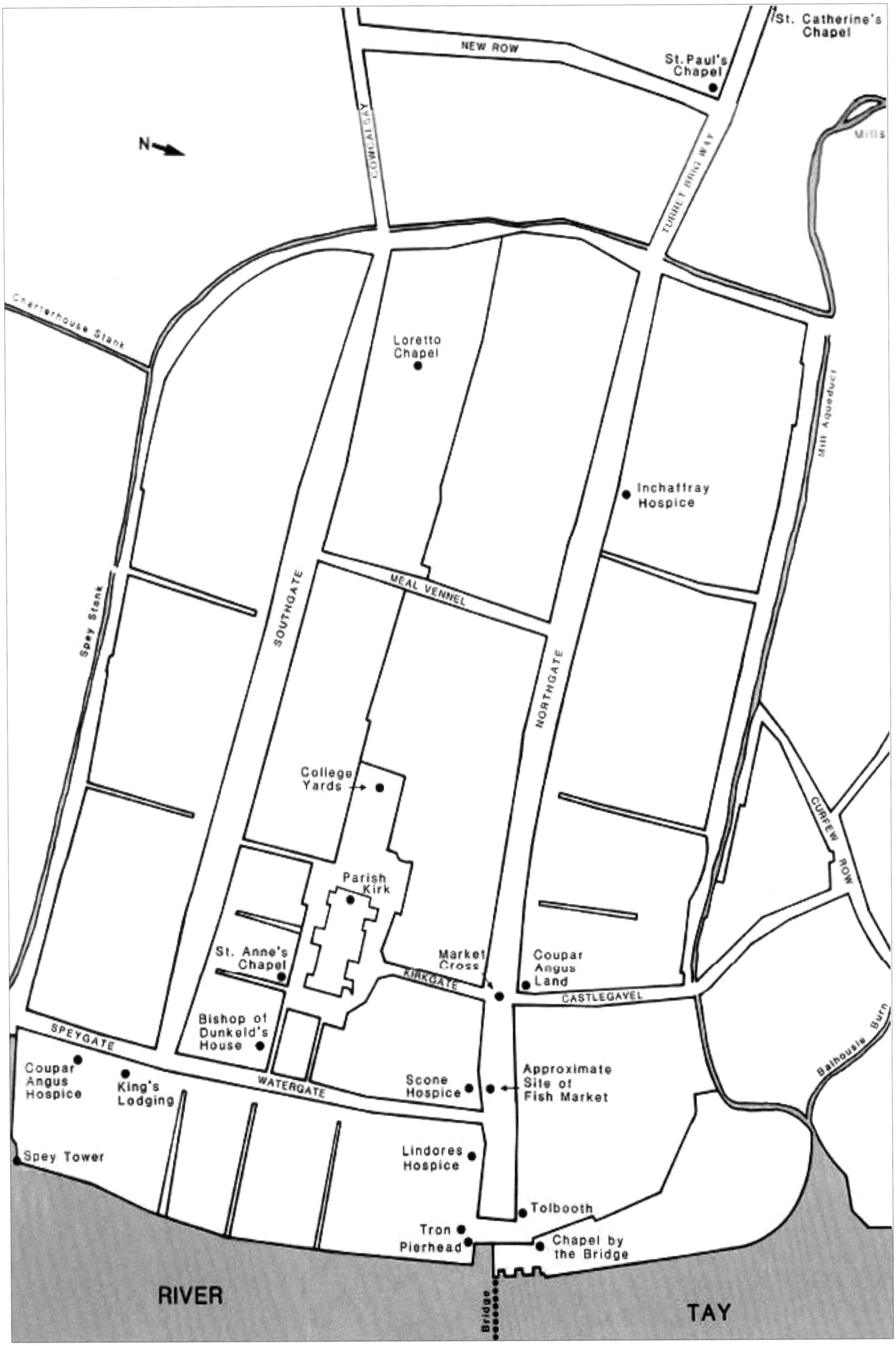

Plan of Perth, showing major landmarks, c1550.

the acts of Parliament' by disputing upon the scriptures and for such minor offences as breaking the Lenten fast, lampooning the pope and Cardinal Beaton and refusing to pray to the Virgin Mary in childbirth, in the case of Helen Stirk.[10]

There were other more mundane disturbances during church services than those of the religious reform minded. In 1551 Oliver Craigie, a wright, was fined by the deacon of his craft for 'molesting' the kirk and disrupting the evening service. Craigie well may have been drunk and disorderly as opposed to expressing any reforming zeal. Certainly, an argument over some secular affair was more than likely the case when David Donaldson was alleged to have cuffed Patrick Balmane in the church in 1549. Their fight continued at the vestry door when the two men drew knives on one another.[11] The burgh court records certainly confirm that knives, along with stones, were the weapons most often used to inflict bodily injury when arguments turned to physical violence.

Since the church offered the largest enclosed space in town, it was sometimes given over to secular uses ranging from meetings of the burgh council to serving as a dry place in which carpenters could store their wood. The churchyard walls provided a convenient place for weavers and dyers to dry their cloths and, as with the Inches, the yard was a place to dump waste. All these activities were, of course, frowned upon![12] But let us leave the churchyard and head towards St Anne's Vennel through which we will gain access to Southgate. As we do so we will pass St Anne's chapel, located on the edge of the churchyard and said to have had a place for the entertainment of poor people attached. It was considered for, but not selected as a site for the post-reformation poor hospital.[13]

Southgate

Southgate stretched in an east–westerly direction from the Tay to the South Gate Port. It was not as densely occupied as was Northgate but there were booths and workplaces all along both sides of the street except at the extreme west end where there was some vacant land. Southgate was home to a number of families and crafts who played a prominent part in the political and religious events of the sixteenth century. This was where Robert Lamb lived as did James Hunter, William Anderson and several of the others implicated in activities that raised the ire of the Governor Arran and Cardinal Beaton who came to town in January 1544, causing some to flee in anticipation of their arrival and others to await summary trial and sentencing and to go to their deaths as the 'Perth Martyrs'. John Kinloch and Walter Piper, sr. and jr., craftsmen who were in the forefront of political and religious activism in the 1540s and 1550s, also lived and worked on Southgate.

On the east side of Schoolhouse Vennel, on or adjacent to Thomas Wilson's land, stood 'the house of the grammar school'. The master of the grammar school during the 1550s and early 1560s, Mr Andrew Simson, leased a house a few doors east of the Schoolhouse Vennel. This property probably served later as the home for Mr John Row, Perth's first minister who in addition to his duties to his parish, taught Greek and Latin to his pupils in Perth and served the General Assembly of the new Scottish kirk in innumerable capacities.[14] There were few other important buildings or landmarks on Southgate other than the Loretto Chapel that occupied a site on the north side of the street towards the west end. This chapel was described as being wasted and ruinous in 1566, but whether this resulted from the enthusiasm of the reforming mob or merely from neglect is a matter of conjecture.[15]

Taking a quick peek down Speygate you might catch a glimpse of the Greyfriars friary or the Spey Tower, which housed the town's arsenal. You'd probably notice a somewhat larger residence on the east side of the street which was the King's (Queen's) Lodging. The records indicate that the house had a gallery overlooking a garden that stretched down to the river's edge.[16] Two merchant burgesses of Perth undertook some 'furnishing' of the lodging in 1540 but it is unclear whether this was in the form of household goods or simply maintenance work. Following the surprise attack on the burgh in 1544 the building suffered some damage when a doorway had to be re-built amongst other minor repairs.[17] The Lords Ruthven (later Earls of Gowrie) were appointed keepers of the lodging in 1546 and thereafter it remained in their charge until the fateful events of the Gowrie Conspiracy were played out in the house in August 1600. Perth was certainly unlike most other burghs for having been the location of the assassination of one Stewart monarch and the attempted assassination of another![18]

Northgate

Let us proceed now along the Watergate towards Northgate. I think that historians and archaeologists alike would like to find some proof of wharves or boat landings between the river and the street but I have found no documentary evidence to indicate such features in the sixteenth century. However, in 1558 Adam Foreman, prior of the Charterhouse, let a lodging to Thomas Scott on the south side of the 'peyr heid', the lease clearly defined the property as being located south of the bridge and therefore adjoining property that ran towards the river off the east side of Watergate. The rent, incidentally, was one half tun of wine and a monk's habit of white 'stemmyng' ie worsted woollen cloth.[19]

Two vennels ran from the east side of the street down towards the river's edge and two from the west side led into the churchyard. The documentary evidence suggests a good deal of building and improvement of properties on Watergate where commercial activity, booths and workshops were most concentrated at the Northgate end of the street. Several local lairds and the Bishop of Dunkeld had town houses on Watergate. The street was also home to merchants, tailors and shoemakers. Patrick Adamson, a well-known figure in the post-Reformation kirk, grew up living on the west side of the street (next to the North Vennel to the Kirk) with his sister Violet who became the wife of schoolmaster, and later minister, Mr Andrew Simson. A James Lawson inhabited a house two doors north of the Adamsons but to date I have failed to find any connection between this family of Lawsons and the minister of the Reformed kirk of the same name (James Lawson) who is said to have come from Perth. The James Lawson to whom I refer was murdered on his doorstep by Thomas Lyn in 1542. Was it this catastrophe that caused his wife Elena Wryt to leave Scotland with her daughter and seek refuge in 'Elsonrod', presumably Elsinore in Denmark? Lawson's son Robert appears to have remained in Perth under the guardianship of his curator Alexander Ray and he and Ray were called into burgh court in October 1547 to prove that Elena Wryt had indeed died. One witness, Alexander Bunche, a Perth burgess, testified that he had been in Elsonrod in October 1546. He told the court that he had attended Elena's death from the plague and her burial there, and that he had escorted Elena's daughter back to Perth. Another witness, John Christy, stated that although he had not been present when Wryt died he had bought the dead woman's clothing and personal effects.[20] Possibly the younger woman's return to Perth raised the question of proving her mother's death. (Incidentally Robert Lawson, son of the murdered James Lawson, was himself murdered by his brother-in-law John Bille in 1564. The family feud was a complicated and extended affair that indicates that feuding was not limited to clans and rural families, but extended to the urban setting as well.)

The murder of James Lawson was not the only act of violence one might have witnessed on Watergate. Had we been here in September 1549 we might have seen a group of eight men (three burgesses, three lairds and two of the bailies of the burgh) breaking into Nicoll Ramsay's house from whence they allegedly stole goods and furnishings ranging from gold rings and silver spoons to feather beds, linens and household utensils. They then set fire to the house.[21] Perhaps this raid was justified in some way for Nicoll Ramsay seems to have been an argumentative fellow. He borrowed money frequently, had an extended dispute with his mother over her heirship goods and her handling of his father's estate. In the end, he was convicted of the murder of Patrick Henry and was sentenced to death in February 1555.[22]

Nicoll Ramsay's father John had been the hereditary keeper of the Abbott of Lindores hospice located at the junction of Watergate with Northgate. A few doors to the west on the same side of Northgate was another hospice, namely that of the Abbot of Scone. Hospices were town houses belonging to various religious foundations that were kept in readiness by a tenant for the superior's visits to Perth. Besides Scone and Lindores, the abbots of Coupar Angus and Inchaffray maintained hospices in Perth prior to the Reformation. The Scone hospice is well documented and thus provides an example of what comprised an abbot/bishop's lodging in the mid-1500s.

The foreland (the part of the property fronting on street) was occupied by several booths, a wine cellar and a fore lodging. The inner and backland were built up with cellars, a lower house, a hall, kitchen and a wine cellar. There is at least one reference to an oratory on the property and one to a tavern. In 1555 the abbot granted a license to Andrew Moncreiffe (his loved servant and factor) and his wife to build a house for themselves at the extreme south edge of the rig, adjacent to the kirk yard, where there was some vacant land. This house they were to enjoy rent free in exchange for their services.[23] When Andrew died about three years later his widow subsequently married James Hepburn, a kinsman and possibly a son of the abbot (Patrick Hepburn). Their new lease of the property, dated 23 September 1559, just three months after the burning of Scone Abbey, suggests that the abbot may have proposed the union in the interests of keeping the property in the family. This couple do not appear to have been very conscientious about maintenance, for a mere three and a half years later the hospice was described as being badly in need of repair from the sub-structure up. The walls were crumbling, support beams broken and the kitchen in need of total rebuilding. Repairs were commissioned by the abbot, now commendator of Scone, but by 1567 a reference to this property, which for generations had been the Scone hospice, simply identified it as James Hepburn's house.[24]

Besides keeping up the property, the factor had to maintain the house in readiness for the superior's visits. An altercation between the abbot of Lindores and his tenant in 1557 informs us that the principal hall and chambers were to be readied with bed furnishings at hand. Use of the kitchen and cellars was expected along with stabling for horses. Servants to attend to the various needs of the visitors were to be provided. An Inchaffray document adds the following specifics: twelve suitable pewter vessels and measures along with three feather beds with stoops decked in a becoming manner.[25]

Commercial use of strategically located lands, as were many of these properties granted to religious houses, was inevitable. A goldsmith, a saddler and a merchant, along with others unnamed were ordered to flit from the Scone foreland in 1552, suggesting more than three booths located there. The Coupar Angus land was situated on the north-west corner of Northgate at Castlegavel, right at the commercial heart of the burgh. A rental of 1542 indicates that there were six booths on the Northgate facing side of the property and a further four on the Castlegavel front. The Northgate booths were all occupied by merchants. Above these booths were living quarters (flats maybe?) inhabited by various tenants paying between twelve and 21.5 shillings for rent. John Marshall, skinner, leased all four booths located 'below the steps' on the Castlegavel side, and the 'dwelling house' above his booths. Meanwhile, the abbot kept a town house in Speygate, next door to the King's lodging, for his convenience.[26]

The Inchaffray land and hospice was also located on Northgate, but at some distance from the commercial hub. Its chief claim to fame in the sixteenth century may have been the notoriety of its occupants. The principal tenants in 1543 were James Rannaldson, his wife Helen Stirk and their three children. This couple were put to death in January 1544, along with Robert Lamb and the others mentioned above. Rannaldson's orphaned children and their grandparents were eventually unable to maintain the property suitably or to pay the rent to the superior Alexander Gordon, commendator of the abbey and later Bishop of Galloway. In 1556 the house and land were repossessed by the abbey and shortly thereafter, Gordon installed his mistress Barbara Logy and her five children in the house where they lived well into the latter half of the century.[27] Logy, it turned out, was not merely Gordon's mistress, but was in fact his wife, they having been married before he entered the service of the old church. This confession came from Gordon, and was confirmed by Barbara, before the 'whole congregation of the burgh of Perth convened for the hearing of God's word' on Sunday 21 April 1560. The Instrument taken on that day indicates that discussion of the subject (gossip?) had been booted about and that the declaration was made to clarify the issue and possibly to ensure the legitimatisation of their children.[28]

Before heading above the Cross on Northgate, we must pause to take in the Tay Bridge and the Tolbooth. The latter served as administrative and judicial centre of the burgh and was located immediately west of the bridge. It served as a meeting place for the burgh council, the burgh, sheriff and guild courts. Little is known of its dimensions and adornments, but it contained a 'council house therein', a courtroom and a prison. A window overlooking the street was another designated spot for making public proclamations while a vault or cellar under the building served as an assay house for goods being exported or imported by the merchants.[29] Had we been in the vicinity of the Tolbooth on 10 October 1547 we may have seen James Cristeson bringing the hide of an allegedly stolen cow into the court to present as evidence in the suit brought against him by Margaret Blair, the widow of John Blair in Melginch.[30] The condition of the bridge was a constant source of worry throughout most of the century until its eventual collapse in 1583. There are many stories associated with this structure, but I must leave those for another day. Suffice it to mention that the tron or burgh scale was to be found immediately south of the bridge on a site identified as the 'wayt house land beside the bridge'.[31]

We will head back up through the salmon market taking a quick look down Castlegavel as we pass. The records indicate very intense use of the land on both sides of the street with booths on almost every rig and with merchants and skinners being the chief tenants. David Schang, a wright burgess who appeared quite frequently in the burgh court, was the occupant of a backland on the east side of the street. On one occasion he sought payment for a rowing boat used for salmon fishing that he had made for Andrew Murray and on another occasion his ownership of an English New Testament (in 1547!) was challenged by the son and heir of the late John Chalmer who wanted it back.[32]

When we pass the Cross it is not long before we spy a house on the north side of the street just west of Bunche's Vennel that was inhabited by Patrick, Lord Ruthven, provost of Perth almost continuously from 1547 to 1566 and a champion of religious reform.[33] Ruthven's neighbour to the east was James Rind, who had taken part in the intrusion into the Blackfriars kitchen in 1543 and who shortly thereafter had fled from Perth. Rind was later to be found in Danzig where he borrowed money from a fellow Perth burgess Martin Murdeson, subsequently the owner of a Coverdale Bible published in Zurich in 1550. To the west of Lord Ruthven's house was that of Robert Cameron and Margaret Whitson. They were the parents of John Cameron, a baxter burgess of Perth who was accused of heresy and forfeited in May 1539.[34] Did the three neighbours know one another and did they share their interest in challenging the teachings of the old church?[35] As a historian who has long been preoccupied with the religious reformation and its outbreak in Perth in 1559, I am always looking for clues as to who knew whom and to how their lives intersected.

Helen Stirk and James Rannaldson, two of the alleged heretics of 1544, lived on the north side of Northgate, although at some distance west of the three mentioned above. James Hunter, flesher, and another of those executed in the same purge of that year, occupied some land on the south side of Northgate close to Meal Vennel. He was married to Christine Piper whose family were prominent landowners on Southgate. Their daughter Violet was first married to Robert Cristeson who, quite likely, is the same Robert Cristeson who factored for several Perth merchants in Flanders in the 1540s. I have not found any evidence that might suggest his religious outlook, but it is worthy of note that he was a merchant who travelled overseas, making him one of those most likely to be exposed to the religious currents sweeping the continent by mid-century and possibly sending books and pamphlets back to Scotland in his shipments. It is also interesting that when Cristeson died, in 1557, James Rind became tutor to his children. Violet Hunter seems to have followed in her father's footsteps. She and her second husband John Maxton claimed to be 'of the Congregation' and unwilling to set foot in Edinburgh in the winter of 1559 when they were summoned to appear before the lords of council and session.[36]

But, I digress... We were heading west on Northgate towards the Turret Brig Port. The properties on the south side of the street, as far west as Meal Vennel, are extremely well documented and most were occupied by baxters. At the Meal Vennel a cluster of smiddy booths populated the area around the junction with Northgate, while several litsters (dyers) congregated at the Southgate end of the vennel. The west end of Northgate was built-up all the way to the Turret Brig Port, but the density of houses and booths gave way to yards, barns, kilns and bark pots in the inner and backlands. Beyond the port the road led west towards the Carmelite friary at Tullilum. Bishop Brown of Dunkeld, in whose diocese the friary lay (Perth itself came under the jurisdiction of St Andrews), was a very generous benefactor to the Carmelites. In the first decades of the sixteenth century (Brown died in 1515) he re-roofed and restored the chapel at Tullilum, ordering 14,000 slates to be brought from Caithness and wood for the fabric of the church from Rannoch. The latter was towed across the loch and hauled to Perth where sawyers went to work for fees of between eight and twelve pence a day.[37]

Between the four neighbouring religious houses and the numerous chapels situated within the parish church the presence of clerics and clergy would not go unnoticed as we walked along. However, this demographic would alter in the latter half of the century with the advent of the Reformation and the changes in religious practices. Furthermore, one should not forget that at least half of the people who lived in Perth in the sixteenth century must have been women. Women did not receive a great deal of attention in my study of politics and religion, so to redress this imbalance, I will conclude our tour of sixteenth century Perth by introducing you to just a few of the women we might have met as we walked along.

Perth's women

It is generally accepted that in the sixteenth century most businesses, be they urban or rural, involved not just a 'breadwinner' but a whole family. Wives fulfilled the dual role of helpmate and caregiver. Furthermore, single women, especially widows, enjoyed opportunities for independent action in the world of commerce. They could inherit property when no male heirs survived and they were at liberty to pursue and to be pursued in the burgh court without any particular pre-amble or formality. For example; James Young was called upon to pay Robert Salmond's wife for wine he had received. The alcohol had certainly been procured by Salmond, who in the mid-1550s shipped twenty-six barrels of salmon to France, the profits of which were to be spent on the purchase of wine in Rouen, but the court order makes it clear that the wine had been sold to Young by Salmond's wife. In another case Bessie Blair sought £15 from John Bonar and his wife for cloth that Bessie had dyed for them, indicating that she had done the work herself and was her own bookkeeper. She did, in fact, produce an account book in court on another occasion. Women might also act on behalf of their husbands. When Henry Burrocht was 'absent from the realm' his wife leased his booth to a tenant for another term and when Alexander Lindsay died in the office of master of work and treasurer during the 1548–49 fiscal year, his wife, Jonet Bunche, rendered his accounts in his name.[38]

The most prominent and the most enterprising group of women were those who were widowed and who were then at liberty to manage their late husbands' affairs and the affairs of the children of the marriage. Margaret Whitson, the mother of John Cameron, provides an interesting example. Her husband Robert died before 1528 leaving her to manage their property on Northgate. The following year she became heir to her brother who owned land on Southgate. Margaret used the properties as a source of income renting out booths, rooms and living spaces to various tenants and as often as not having to pursue them in burgh court for delinquent rent payments or even having to evict some.[39]

The ownership of property also gave single women a negotiable asset. In this vein Agnes Brown gave a booth she owned to a widow and her children so that they might have some means of support. Elizabeth Murray gave some property to her sister Margaret, to help Margaret in her marriage to Adam Pryll.[40] On the other hand, economic necessity may have persuaded Christine Loutfut to alienate to John Moncur her right and title to her portion of the land she had inherited, Moncur having lent her 'a certain sum of money in her great and urgent necessity'.[41]

And finally, let us greet Marione Dundas and Christine Piper, two of the most enterprising women I met in mid-sixteenth century Perth. On becoming widowed each took a very active part in the commercial life of the town. Amongst other undertakings, both these women had the initiative and the means to become involved in the salmon fishing 'industry' – one of Perth's more lucrative commercial enterprises. The records show that in 1547 Marione leased one net on the Tay from James Campbell of Lawers for a fee of £24 Scots plus twelve fish. Two years later she took two nets from Campbell, which she then sublet at a considerable profit to herself.[42]

Christine Piper leased one of the twelve nets owned by the town that were put to 'roup and tack' annually, no doubt as a means of raising revenue. Whereas some of the male burgesses and corporations only managed to lease one third, or one fourth part of a net, Christine took a whole net to herself. One assumes that she hired fishers or sub-leased the net as Marione Dundas had done; however, it is evident that she managed her business for on one occasion she appeared in burgh court in pursuit of Andrew Murray from whom she asked the court to award her 'the dearest price salmon is being sold for this year and costs' to cover Murray's obligation to her.[43] Note: Andrew Murray was the man for whom David Schang built the boat! Perhaps this altercation gives some suggestion as to just how small the town was in the sixteenth century and how closely people's lives intertwined.

Conclusion

Perth's situation at a crossroads, rather than on an estuary or coast, certainly made it unlike Dundee or Aberdeen. It was neither an administrative centre as Edinburgh was becoming, nor a university town. But, manufacture and craft work flourished in Perth (alongside overseas trade) and the town's prosperity was built on domestic manufacture to a larger extent than the economies of the other 'great burghs'. Perth's craftsmen made spears, knives and helmets, gloves, saddles and ladders, barrels, boats and all manner of ironwork. In these ways, Perth was probably not like other burghs, as the craftsmen complained in 1560. They comprised a larger segment of the population and their comparatively greater wealth meant that the tax burden did fall more heavily on them than it may have done on craftsmen in other burghs. However, the conditions under which all the inhabitants dwelt were almost certainly similar to those in most other sixteenth century towns. People lived in close proximity that afforded little privacy thus making social interaction unavoidable. Affability and good neighbourhood, heated exchanges and violent confrontations, all were characteristic of town life and the life of the town. Our walk has been brief but we have seen a number of significant landmarks, covered quite a bit of ground and have met a number of interesting people along the way. There are many others I know quite well, but space precludes my introducing them to you here. I hope that at least this paper has offered a taste of town life in the sixteenth century.

End Notes

1 A. K. Bell Library. Perth (hereafter AKBL) Perth Burgh Records, Register of Decreets 1547–1552, B59/12/3 fo. 107r (Small), fo. 162r (Frew).
2 Ibid fo. 188r.
3 National Archives of Scotland (NAS), Muniments of King James VI Hospital, Perth, GD79/6/47. *The Chronicle of Perth*, J. Engles (ed), (Felinfach, 1996) p. 7. There is a MS copy of The Chronicle in the National Library of Scotland (NLS), Adv. 35/4/4 and numerous transcriptions have appeared in print over the years.
4 AKBL, Perth Burgh Records, Court Minute Book 1560–1562, B59/12/4 fo. 7r, fo. 20v. Fos. 31r -140v *passim* records a lengthy dispute between Robert Salmond and Blaise Colt over 26 barrels of salmon that Salmond sent to be sold in France. The profits from the sale were to be spent on wine to be returned to Perth. Register of Decreets B59/12/3 fo. 107r. *The Protocol Book of Sir Robert Rollok 1534–1552*, W. Angus (ed), Edinburgh, SRS, (1931) no. 36.
5 NAS, Acts and Decreets of the Lords of Council and Session, Processes, CS15/Box 1556.
6 AKBL, Perth Burgh Records, Court and Council Records 1507–1543 (1554), B59/12/1 fo. 33r.
7 NAS, Perth Kirk Session Records, vol. 1 (1577–1586) CH2/521/1 fo. 50r.
8 M. Verschuur, *Politics or Religion? The Reformation in Perth 1540–1570*, (Edinburgh, 2006).
9 J. Foxe, *The Acts and Monuments of John Foxe*, G. Townsend (ed), 8 vols. (New York, 1965 edition cited) vol. 5, p. 623.
10 bid. pp. 624-625. Verschuur, *Politics or Religion?* pp. 74-78.
11 AKBL, Register of Decreets B59/12/3 fo. 105v.
12 Ibid fo. 188r. NAS, Perth Kirk Session, CH2/521/1 fos. 16r, 79r, 88r, 94r.
13 *Rental Book of King James VI Hospital, Perth*, R. Milne (ed) (Perth, 1891) p. 3. NAS, *The Protocol Books of Sir Henry Elder*, 3 vols. B59/1/1 fo. 158r.
14 Ibid. fo, 75v. NAS, Muniments of King James VI Hospital, Perth, GD79/4/18 for schoolmaster's house.
15 *RMS*, iii no. 722, iv no. 1729. *Protocol Book of Sir Robert Rollok*, no. 35. *RSS*, v no. 2927.
16 *RPC*, i p. 340. *RMS*, iv no. 522.
17 *The Perth Guildry Book 1452–1601*, M. Stavert (ed), (Edinburgh, 1993), no. 329. *Accounts of the Masters of Works for Works for Building and Repairing Royal Palaces and Castles*, 2 vols. Henry M. Paton (ed), (Edinburgh, 1957) i p. 111. Perth Museum and Art Gallery, The Convenor Court Book of Perth: original letters and papers produced by the craftsmen of Perth in defence of their ancient rights and privileges, 1365–1717, 2/1/31.
18 *RMS*, iv no. 5 (grant to Lord Ruthven). It had been given into their custody in 1528, then had changed hands in the fitful 1530s but it had reverted to the Ruthvens in a 1546 grant. Numerous accounts of the Gowrie Conspiracy have been related over the centuries.
19 NAS, Register House Charters, RH6/1763.
20 AKBL, Register of Decreets B59/12/3 fo. 22r.
21 NAS, Register of the Acts and Decreets of the Lords of Council and Session, 1542–1659, 607 vols. (Heresfter ADCS) CS7/3 fos. 183r, 212r, 283r and CS7/4 fos. 84r, 153v-155r.
22 AKBL, Register of Decreets B59/12/3 fos. 9r, 15r, 87r, 101r, etc. R. Pitcairn (ed),. *Ancient Criminal Trials in Scotland*, 3 vols. (Edinburgh, 1833) i, pp. 374-375.
23 Scone Palace, Scone Cartulary, ii fos. 134v-135r. AKBL, Register of Decreets, B59/12/3 fo. 192r (tavern). NAS Register of Deeds RD6/i, fo. 30r-31r (oratory).
24 Ibid. Scone Cartulary, ii fos. 180v-181r. NAS, *Protocol Book of Sir Henry Elder*, B59/1/1 fo. 220v.
25 NAS, ADCS, CS7/14 fos. 53v-54r. NLS, Manuscript notes by Rev James Scott in his Transcription of the Baptismal Register NLS, Adv. 31-1-1 pp. 46-48.
26 AKBL, Register of Decreets, B59/12/3 fo. 192r. (Order to flit). NAS, Liber Compositionum B. Marie de Cupro 1543–1562 and Rentale 1542, CH6/2/3 fo. 105r. (Booths and dwellings)
27 NAS, *Protocol Book of Sir Henry Elder*, B59/1/1 fo. 156v. ADCS, CS7/15 fos. 133v-134v. Muniments King James VI Hospital, Perth GD79/6/77.
28 NAS, *Protocol Book of Sir Henry Elder*, B59/1/1 fo. 184r.
29 AKBL, Court Minute Book 1564–1565, B59/12/5 p. 133, Register of Decreets, B59/12/3 fo. 86r, Court Minute Book, B59/12/4 fo 23r. *Perth Guildry Book* Stavert (ed) (intro) p xvii.
30 AKBL, Register of Decreets, B59/12/3 fos. 23v – 26v *passim*.
31 NAS, Coupar Angus Rentale, CH6/2/3 p. 133.
32 AKBL, Register of Decreets B59/12/3 fos. 14r, 16r, 45r, 106v.
33 NAS, *Protocol Book of Sir Henry Elder*, B59/1/1 fo. 164v. Later this alley became known as Parliament Close, a section of which was included in the Perth High Street Excavation of 1975–76.
34 *RSS*, iii, no. 3033.
35 For a fuller description of the pre-reformation religious climate in Perth see Verschuur, *Politics or Religion?* Esp. Chapter 5
36 NAS, *Protocol Book of Sir Henry Elder*, B59/1/1 fos. 16v, 101r. Register of Deeds RD1/4 fos 469r-469v. ADCS CS7/19 fos. 157v, 215v, 285r and continued in vols 20 and 22. Christine Piper's burial is recorded in *The Blackfriars of Perth. Their Cartulary and Other Papers*, R. Milne (ed), (Edinburgh 1893) p. 247. Robert Cristeson was abroad in the 1540s.See NAS, *Protocol Book of Sir Henry Elder*, B59/1/1 fo. 16r, or ALBL, Register of Decreets, B59/12/3 fos. 39r-70r passim, fo. 127r).
37 *Rentale Dunkeldense*,ed. R. K. Hannay (Edinburgh, 1915) pp. 194-282 passim.
38 AKBL, Register of Decreets, B59/12/3 fo. 64v, 69r, 102v-107v (Blair/Bonar), fo. 129r (account book). Jonet Bunch's rendering of the account is in *Perth Guildry Book*, Stavert (ed) no. 402.
39 AKBL, Court and Council Records, B59/12/1 fo. 63r. Register of Decreets, B59/12/3 fos. 12r, 41v, 71r, 85r, 94r, 162r, 199v, 204r. NAS, *Protocol Book of Sir Henry Elder*, B59/1/1 fo. 48r.
40 NAS, *Protocol Book of Sir Henry Elder*, B59/1/1 fos. 185r, 97r, 147r.
41 Ibid, fos. 30v, 134v.
42 Ibid. fos. 29r, 112r.
43 *Perth Guildry Book*, Stavert (ed), no. 1056. AKBL, Register of Decreets, B59/12/3 fo. 27r.

Perth in the Era of the Enlightenment[1]

Christopher A Whatley

Introduction

The eighteenth-century Enlightenment was a Europe-wide phenomenon, but it manifested itself in Scotland too – notably in Edinburgh, the so-called 'Hotbed of Genius'.[2] Here, philosophers, lawyers, economists, scientists as well as artists worked, talked and combined to make their contribution to the intellectual foundation of the modern world.[3] The concerns of men like David Hume, Adam Smith and the others weren't just theoretical, although they did their fair share of theorising; the Enlightenment in Scotland was always practical, connected to the real world and focused on issues like economic growth, invention and innovation in manufacturing and in agriculture and the social consequences of change.[4] They thought a lot about how society should be ordered, and about human happiness.[5] The term Enlightenment wasn't used at the time, it was devised much later, and it can mean different things to different people. For the purposes of what follows however I'm defining the era of the Enlightenment as an age of reason, rationality and order, but also of improvement, broadly conceived. In the urban context the best-known example of these several characteristics in practice was Edinburgh's New Town, a conscious attempt to discard the past and create a new kind of place, characterised by a more orderly, regular way of living.[6] But in Scotland Edinburgh was not alone in being influenced by the Enlightenment zeitgeist: Glasgow and Aberdeen were prominent in this regard, as indeed in a less obvious way was Dundee.[7] But to what extent – if at all – did the Enlightenment affect Perth?

Apart from a handful of rather slight forays, including David Graham-Campbell's interesting account, *Thomas Hay Marshall and the making of Georgian Perth,* Perth has been surprisingly little studied in this period – which begins in the early eighteenth century and draws to a close in the 1820s.[8] By this time Perth could boast not one but two new towns, albeit incomplete. One was located at the northern edge of the medieval burgh, with Charlotte Street and Rose Terrace facing onto the much expanded and part-gentrified North Inch, the other to the south, with Marshall Place providing the backdrop for the South Inch. Yet there is no good reason why eighteenth-century Perth shouldn't be

South Inch, Perth, 1830s. Seen in the background is Marshall Place, the most prominent element of the vision for Perth's southern new town devised by the Perth's lord provost Thomas Hay Marshall and the architect Robert Reid. In the distance is the chimney stack of Adam Anderson's much-needed water works, opened in 1834 (courtesy of Perth Museum and Art Gallery).

as well known by historians and their readers as the other leading Scottish towns.[9] Not only are there invaluable published primary sources such as George Penny's first-hand account of the period from around 1770 through to 1830, *Traditions of Perth* (1836), but Perth also possesses one of the richest and most user-friendly local authority archives in Scotland, housed in the A K Bell Library.

To make a start in understanding better something of the character of Perth in the eighteenth century it makes sense to establish the size of the town and its place in Scotland's urban hierarchy. At the end of the seventeenth century Perth was probably Scotland's eighth largest burgh. With a population of just under 4,000 it was roughly similar in size to places like Inverness and Stirling – but a long way behind Edinburgh and Glasgow.[10] During the first half of the eighteenth century however Perth experienced a marked surge in the number of its inhabitants, with the town's population more than doubling to 9,000 people, which lifted Perth into sixth place in Scotland. But despite substantial growth thereafter Perth never became one of Scotland's 'big four'. The rate of increase between 1755 and 1821 was nowhere near as spectacular as that of Paisley, even though in the early 1790s both places accommodated around 19,000 people. Perth's more modest rate of growth was closer to the average; slower than Dundee or Montrose but faster than the border towns. Consequently, throughout the Enlightenment period Perth continued to be one of Scotland's larger towns, one of only sixteen with populations of over 5,000 at the end of the eighteenth century.

Accounting for the growth that did take place is relatively straightforward. Unlike England, where towns tended to grow in accordance with their function such as county towns, spa towns, port towns, and industrial centres, the expansion of Perth, as in much of the rest of urbanising Scotland, was largely due to the rise of manufacturing. Generally speaking, it was towns in which manufacturing was most concentrated that grew fastest.[11] Perth was a royal burgh with a notable place in Scotland's religious history; it was a county town and an important legal and administrative centre; its geographical location at the Lowland–Highland border and between east central Scotland and the west allotted to Perth a major military function in the civil wars of the later seventeenth and eighteenth centuries. But in the eighteenth century it was also a place of production. 'Here [in Perth]' wrote David Loch on his tour through Scotland in the later 1770s, 'the true spirit of industry prevails among all ranks of people'. Indeed Scotland's towns were first and foremost places of work, whether in commerce or industry. Underlining this point in relation to Perth was the remark of one local commentator in the early nineteenth century who regretted the fact that even if the town's Inches were turned into the places of leisure he longed to see, with walkways, arbours, groves, flower pots, shrubbery, and seats, people were so busy working there would be little time for them to enjoy such facilities.

The Linen Trade

In Perth as in so many other Lowland towns in Scotland, notably the nearby Angus towns of Arbroath, Brechin, Dundee, Forfar and Montrose, the engine of growth was linen cloth.[12] Linen, which had become Scotland's single most important manufactured export over the course of the seventeenth century, continued to flourish in the eighteenth century. Driven in part by patriotic zeal both before and after the parliamentary union of 1707, and with the support of the Hanoverian state which was intent on creating work as a means of deflecting support on the part of un- and under-employed Scots from the Jacobites in the aftermath of the failed rising of 1715, linen led Scotland's march towards what would become the foothills of industrialisation.[13] Long mixed with cotton, but on a small scale only, linen manufacturing flourished from the 1730s but was eventually overtaken but not altogether supplanted by cotton. It was the opportunities in linen that attracted to Perth men such as David Sandeman, founder of the Sandeman textile dynasty, a pioneer who established a linen manufactory at Milnwynd in the early eighteenth century.[14] One of David Sandeman's sons, William, laid out the well-known bleachfield at Luncarty, which further enhanced the reputation of Perth linen.[15] It was possibly through linen that John Pullar, founder of Pullars of Perth, was first drawn to the town, as a handloom weaver. He was certainly working at this trade when he married in Perth, in 1773.[16]

Without linen, Perth's development in the eighteenth century would have been very different. At the turn of the eighteenth century the burgh was struggling economically. In a petition sent to the Scottish parliament in 1700 it was claimed that in addition to the several years of war and famine that had affected Scotland as a whole during much of the 1690s, Perth was particularly hard hit. In part this was due to the town's location, referred to earlier, 'being the place where greatest confluence of his majesties forces did meet and lye for reducing the Highlands and maintain the peace of the country', a reference to the civil war that had followed the Revolution of 1688–9 which had led to James VII's flight to France. Exacerbating the townspeople's woes was an apparent decline in trade – including the export of salmon which had happened as a result of King William's and Mary's government's prohibition of commerce with France, although Perth was not the only Scottish town adversely affected by this measure.[17] There may have been a degree of exaggeration in this; Scottish burghs had become adept at complaining about their circumstances as a means of reducing their tax burden. In 1701 the burgh's Dean of Guild, Robert Robertson, claimed that he had for eighteen years, at his own 'vast' expense, been 'gracing' and improving the town 'in its most publick and auspicious pairts and streets'.[18] Yet the impression given of a town in difficulty is supported by another petition (from 1709) and sent to the provost, baillies and council of Perth by the 'heritors and proprietors of the several tenements of land lying on both sides of the Southgate above the [Perth] meal mercat'. In this the petitioners referred to 'the want of trade and traffick in that part of the town these many years bygone', and to the houses and tenements in the vicinity that 'for the most part [had] become altogether void and ruinous'. Nevertheless what this same petition also reveals is that even this early there was a preparedness to do something, with the petitioners declaring their resolve to 'build and repair these ruinous tenements for policy and decoration of the burgh and rendering accommodation to those resorting to it'. This was new – although as we have just seen, not unprecedented. There was no master plan, but even so, what we have are straws in the wind that would later become what in the context of Scottish urban change was a full-blown process of town improvement.

Perth's population

Rapid population growth created by substantial in-migration is testimony to the attractions of Perth as a place in which to find work and wages. In part this is evident from census data. Unusually, the town council in Perth commissioned two censuses of the town's population – in 1766 and 1773. From the second

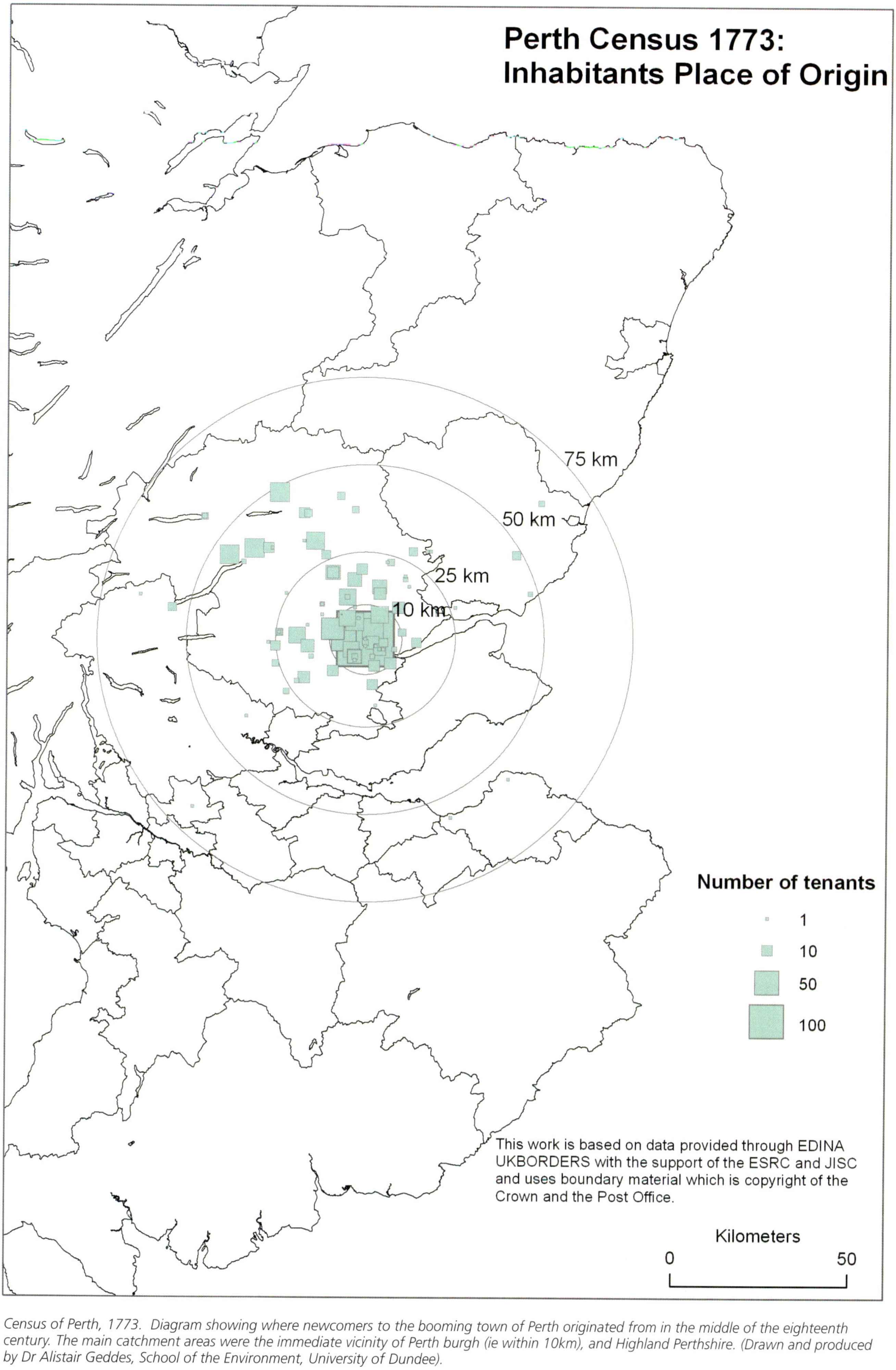

Census of Perth, 1773. Diagram showing where newcomers to the booming town of Perth originated from in the middle of the eighteenth century. The main catchment areas were the immediate vicinity of Perth burgh (ie within 10km), and Highland Perthshire. (Drawn and produced by Dr Alistair Geddes, School of the Environment, University of Dundee).

of these we can learn who the burgh's inhabitants were, where they had come from, where and with whom they lived, and who they worked for. The fact that the censuses were undertaken at all suggests that at least some aspects of Enlightenment thinking had pervaded the burgh's town council; they reflect an interest in statistics and quantification, the application of rational thinking to the organisation and ordering of society. They were also in keeping with the long-standing policy of the town council to keep a close watch over incomers. Landlords and others had to be reminded periodically that they could not let rooms to 'strangers' without first acquiring a licence from the magistrates. Burgh authorities in Perth and elsewhere were wary of various categories of incomer, including Jacobite sympathisers, 'loose women' and poor people without any obvious means of support. Expansion was to be orderly.

What the data from the 1773 census reveals is that of the town's tenants and sub-tenants where a place of origin was recorded, not far short of eighty per cent appear to have been incomers.[19] In this sense Perth was a town in which newcomers formed a large proportion of the population. The migrants had not come far however, the vast bulk of them having been born within a radius of less than 10km, with most of the rest coming from Highland Perthshire, and only a few people from other parts of Scotland – although there were large enough numbers to justify the opening of a Gaelic chapel in 1787.[20] The concentration of incomers from Perthshire itself is to be seen in the following census entry made by Margaret Wilson, wife of the deceased Thomas Willets:

> Perth 29th January 1773 By order of the Honourable Magistrates and Town Council of Perth: A list of the tenants in the deceased Thomas Willets land: viz Andrew Millar Tiree Meason his wife and daughter he came from Methven Parish has been six years in this land. Katharine Robertson came from parish of Little Dunkeld has been nine years in this land her son Thomas Dow and apprentice to Mr Forsyth Couper. James Fores a fisher has been her lodger three years he came from the parish of Little Dunkeld. James Craigie his wife became from the parish of Kinnoull has been thirteen years in this land: Katharine Rankine came from Methven parish has been three years in this land: Jannet Buchannan and one little girl she came from the parish of Fortingall has been nine years in this place: Mary Elder and her daughter she came from the parish of Aughtergen [sic] has been one year in this place: Margaret Drummond and one child she came from the parish of Mullion in Atholl and has been eight years in this place. This given by Margaret Wilson Relect of the deceased Thomas Willets.[21]

The single most important occupation in Perth was handloom weaving, although as the *Statistical Account* from the 1790s makes clear, skinners and glovers as well as the usual mix of urban tradesmen were also much in evidence. Much of the weaving work was undertaken in outhouses and weaving sheds in the area near to New Row. The town council had had high hopes when it first planned this street around 1750 but by 1773 New Row housed hardly anybody else but handloom weavers. At this point in time, however, large numbers of (but not all) handloom weavers were relatively well-off skilled artisans and not the desperately poor group of workers clinging on to the vestiges of their former status. By the 1790s they had a relatively comfortable lifestyle.[22]

Civic Improvement

But while the town council was keen to promote linen, this was part of a grander mission (but never a co-ordinated plan) to enhance Perth's attractiveness as a commercial centre. Following the lead taken by Edinburgh, and in common with many other towns, the authorities in Perth engaged enthusiastically – albeit far from systematically and in a series of uneven steps – with the 'improvement' agenda of the time, at the heart of which were enhancement of the built environment and the provision of 'luxury' services.[23] Indeed the indications are that Perth set in train its improvement process a few years earlier than most of the other smaller Scottish towns; in this respect its nearest comparators seem to have been Dumfries and Montrose. The process began around 1734 with a scheme to widen the Skinnergate, then the only route into the town from the north, whilst at the same time plans were laid to improve the Watergate, the main route from the south. Recognising the importance of opportunities to the north, in 1752 the town council agreed to support the county commissioners in making a 'highway' through the carse of Gowrie to Dundee and thence to 'the whole Burrows and Countys on the North and Northwest Sea Coasts' a measure that would tend 'greatly to the Encouragement of Trade & Commerce'.[24] By removing impediments to the movement of goods and people, straightening and widening roads so that wheeled traffic could pass through, and from 1764 supporting the campaign for the new bridge over the Tay, a greater degree of commercial efficiency was to be achieved.[25]

The Tay bridge project was a major civil engineering undertaking, so much so that when construction began in February 1766 it was feared that such would be the demand for labour that there would be a shortage of workers in and around Perth; accordingly, two companies of foot soldiers were employed to work on the bridge instead – initially at least. They were after all, used to building military roads and John Smeaton's bridge over the Tay was, like the military roads, seen as a project that was of major national strategic importance, not least as a means of making it easier for troops from the south to move north and thereby assist in 'improving and civilising' the Highlands. Accordingly the government provided around forty per cent of the funds to build it (£9,000/£24,000).[26] Improvement entailed not only majestic new structures like the Tay bridge, but also a sustained assault on the old where this inhibited commercial progress. Thus in 1765, the market cross was judged by the town council to be 'the great impediment' to the passage of what were called 'wheeled machines' through North Street and into the Kirkgate and the Skinnergate. Consequently the magistrates were authorised 'to remove the same and to dispose thereof by public sale'.[27] This was a hugely significant step, as the market cross was customarily the ceremonial focal point for Scotland's burghs, an important symbol of the town's function and authority, from where official proclamations were made for instance and often the place at which transgressors of burgh laws were made to stand in chains in full view of the community.[28] The removal of the cross in Perth therefore represented a preparedness to break with the past – to abandon the world of custom and tradition – and a declaration that in progress was the creation of a modern town.

Civic improvement was not solely about function. As noted already, as important was what contemporaries often referred to as 'ornamentation', along with neo-classical elegance and order. Function and form were not always mutually compatible.

A View of Perth from the north, 1774. Drawn from the North Inch either by Andrew or Archibald Rutherford, the centrepiece of this illustration is John Smeaton's new bridge over the Tay, first opened in 1770. (courtesy of Perth Museum and Art Gallery).

Throughout the period there was a tension, sometimes resolved and at other times not, between on the one hand the need to encourage industry and commerce, and on the other the enhancement of the appearance of the town. Another complication of course was lack of money, something which periodically caused the town to abandon or scale down its more ambitious proposals for improvement.

Yet for all of the limitations of its individual members and a studied refusal to separate private gain from the public good, it has to be acknowledged that town council initiative was critical in reshaping the burgh. The trick was to provide low-cost inducements to individuals who, and businesses which, in serving their own private interests, would also benefit the burgh. For example, in the 1750s, apparently there was some reluctance on the part of private builders to invest, the cause alleged being lower than anticipated house rents. Thus in order to encourage the building of new tenements, including those in South Street, the council during the summer months provided stone from the town's quarry at no cost to the builder.[29] In fact the opening up of the town's stone quarry in the early 1730s was an important factor in the transformation of Perth. Previously, building stone had been scarce, and expensive, and possibly as a consequence there were a large number of wooden buildings – anathema to urban improvers in the eighteenth century not least as they were a major fire risk. It was for this reason that in 1748 the council ordered that flax dressing should be confined to the outskirts of the burgh and in 1749 purchased a fire engine – one of the first burghs in Scotland to do so.[30] But whilst there was enough water for a fire engine, there was too little to drink, at least of a decent quality, with the result according to an understated complaint made in 1761, that the 'lives of the inhabitants', as well as strangers, were exposed to 'many inveterate maladies'.[31]

It was concern about fire (with the burgh's first fire engine being purchased in 1749, and a 'new' one in 1751), but also for the appearance of the town that the authorities paid increasing attention to roofs, with the preference being for slate rather than the more traditional thatch. This was important: a telling indicator for contemporary observers of how far a town could be considered as 'improved' in the late eighteenth and early nineteenth century was the extent to which its roofs were slated. Other markers of urban rationality that met with approval were stone-built housing (from November 1751 all new tenements in Perth were to be stone-built, with lime mortar, with old timber structures ordered to be demolished), regularly laid out.[32] Essential too were sash windows – introduced to Perth at least as early as 1753, as well as wide straight paved streets, and night lighting. Indeed nothing else would do: when in 1773 there was a suggestion that the houses in South Street were being rebuilt but not in a straight line, John Buchan, a lawyer, wrote in horror to the town council that if there was to be any deviation, the 'publick decoration of the street would not be answered'. Such houses, he went on, 'would stand with their fronts zig zag to one another'. This, concluded Buchan, 'is the most unseemly and barbarous like thing that can be'.[33]

In order to improve the amenity of the burgh, the town council had to exercise a strong degree of social control, or at least to attempt so to do. A series of proclamations were made and acts passed, listing rules and regulations designed to alter and improve the behaviour of the town's inhabitants as well as to outlaw those practices deemed altogether unacceptable, all of which were publicly announced and usually displayed on posters pasted up throughout the burgh.

But what the proliferation of local regulations reveals, albeit unwittingly, is how unpleasant and in some senses chaotic Perth must have been beforehand. Petitions to the council from inhabitants complaining about the activities of their neighbours provide colourful but also telling insights into the nature of eighteenth century Perth and the scale of the challenge faced by the improvers. An example from 1749 is the case of Mr William Thomson who lived on the middle storey of a three-storey house near the river. Living above him was what nowadays would in popular parlance be described as 'the neighbours from hell' – the Goodmans. Mr and Mrs Goodman, according to Thomson, had for many years kept what he called a 'sort of publick house, or ale house', which was now attracting 'great companies of soldiers and…disorderly persons'. Sundays were no different, with the Goodmans and their customers allegedly cursing and swearing and 'prophaning the Lords day', even during the hours of divine worship. This was bad enough but not unusual anywhere in urban Scotland; indeed it was what caused the greatest consternation for kirk sessions and even town councils, arguably as much or even more so in Perth than most places.[34] What caused the greatest offence was Mrs Goodman's daily habit, 'of throweing down foul water and other nasty stuff through the floor of said house upon your petitioners's furniture'.[35] A second but equally distressing nuisance was that allegedly caused by James Cuthbert – a hammerman. In Cuthbert's case this meant – apparently – that he was a joiner or carpenter who was also practising as a part-time, unregulated surgeon. This came to light in 1773 when his neighbour James Robertson, a staymaker who lived on the floor beneath him complained that Cuthbert was in the practice of accommodating 'distressed and infirm people' who were treated for conditions such as kidney stones or who required a limb to be amputated. This however was not the immediate focus of Robertson's concern. His complaint was about the noise, namely that he and his family were 'often keept from sleep for several whole nights together by the moaning cries and groans of these distressed people and sometimes the said James Cuthbert has two beds at one time occupied by such distressed persons.'[36]

In tackling the challenges associated with the creation of an improved town the authorities in Perth seem to have been more than usually successful, albeit that progress was slow and patchy and strewn with obstacles. Perth for example was in the forefront in the provision of street lighting in Scotland: of the provincial towns Perth was the first to provide street lamps, fuelled by oil, at least as early as 1746.[37] Dumfries, in many ways similar to Perth, was ten years later. Indeed in terms of street lighting – essential for the maintenance of law and order and the safety of the citizenry after dark – Perth's record continued to be one of the most impressive in comparison to most towns, where progress was slow and patchy.[38] A

George Street, Perth, c1825. George Street was one of Perth's new, wider, impediment-free thoroughfares, which facilitated the movement of traffic and people from the south and across the new Tay bridge. Of particular note here are the Georgian buildings – some of the first in Perth – but also street lamps. Street lighting was an important marker of urban improvement (courtesy of Perth Museum and Art Gallery).

series of attempts was made over the following decades to improve the quality of lighting as well as to illuminate more streets; in 1788 for example twenty lamps were put up on the parapet of the bridge, while both George Street and Charlotte Street were enhanced by the provision of what were called 'christall globular lamps'.[39] Even these however had their limitations, with the Greenland whale oil that they burned offering 'minimal illumination'.[40]

Education and learning

There were other respects too in which we can reasonably conclude that Perth's municipal elite seem to have been amongst the more ambitious in provincial Scotland, even if their actions were often in response to public pressure, stemming mainly from the burgh's better-off inhabitants. There was a competitive aspect to this. Inter-town rivalry was as prevalent in the eighteenth and early nineteenth centuries as it is today. Thus in September 1760 when the magistrates and town council considered 'the great utility it would be to the youth of this place and neighbourhood that an academy for literature & the sciences should be established here', they agreed to proceed on the basis of looking at what was provided elsewhere but also to seek the advice of people 'from different parts of Britain' – surely a measure of the town's elevated ambition.[41] And to get the new academy moving the Perth councillors head-hunted who they judged to be the best man for the post – and invited John Mair, a graduate of St Andrews and one of most innovative teachers of his era, to join them from the recently-established 'sort of academy' at Ayr, as a teacher of book-keeping (accountancy), mathematics and natural philosophy.[42]

But if boys and youths in Perth and from other places, if they could be persuaded to come, were to be taught philosophy, literature, logic and the history of the British constitution, the town's girls had to make do with something rather more mundane. Thus in August 1763 the council thought that it would be useful to the town's young ladies if they could recruit a 'gentlewoman' who could teach sewing and stitching, cookery including pastry making, confectionery making, embroidery and drawing and painting on silk, gauze, paper and glass.[43] Mrs Hanna Swan, wife of Robert Robertson, a merchant, was appointed to the post. It was not until 1788 that what was called a 'proper school' was opened for teaching 'female education', although as in the case of the Academy, the hope was that such an institution would attract boarding scholars to the town and so add to its prosperity and enrich its cultural life.[44]

Indeed by 1820 Perth had become one of the more genteel of Scotland's provincial towns, with once again its main rival in this regard probably being Dumfries. A difference perhaps was that Perth's gentility was long-standing, with a volunteer soldier who came to Scotland with the Duke of Cumberland's forces and who passed through Perth in February 1746 noting the 'great Manufacture' of linen and the bleaching greens on the Inches but at the same time describing (without explanation) the burgh as the 'second town in Scotland for Dignity'.[45] By the end of the century the town could boast its coffee house, reading rooms, assemblies, and a theatre in Glovers' Hall. Around 1820 both Perth and Dumfries had thirty-three writers (or lawyers) and not dissimilar numbers of surgeons and physicians – the first and the last being occupations which provided services to the middle and upper classes. There were a few provincial towns in Scotland which could boast a higher number of providers of high class services – hairdressers, perfumers, jewellers, coach-makers and the like – but in not many other places was there such a high proportion of well-heeled (or 'genteel') residents, including widows and spinsters.[46]

But where Perth stands out in terms of the Enlightenment is in its literary and intellectual interests. In fact what distinguished Scotland's towns in the century or so after the defeat of the Jacobites at Culloden in 1746 was the rise in the number and extent of subscription libraries – where like-minded individuals paid a subscription to buy, collectively, books they could then borrow.[47] Distinctive too was the nature of much of the reading material. History featured strongly, as did treatises on religion and philosophy but popular too were works with a strong utilitarian dimension. In fact the range of readers' interests, as measured by publications, numbers of editions and sales, was remarkably wide.[48] But what is important here is that in its enthusiasm for reading and serious enquiry Perth was in the forefront. After Edinburgh, Perth was the first place in Scotland to have a circulating library (1752), under Robert Morison. This was followed in December 1784 by the establishment of a Literary and Antiquarian Society, modelled on Edinburgh's Select Society and, a fortnight later, Perth Library.[49]

Between them the two Perth institutions founded in the 1780s drew on most of the leading members of Perth's respectable and educated elite. This included Adam Peebles, the town's Episcopalian minister, the Rev James Scott (the Literary and Antiquarian Society's prime mover) of St John's Kirk, David Black, with other clergymen from the surrounding county, a lawyer, John Duff, a Presbyterian clergyman, along with others including schoolmasters from the Academy, two surgeons, one of the town's customs officers and a sprinkling of businessmen representing mercantile, banking and manufacturing interests. In common with many subscription libraries elsewhere, proprietors of landed estates joined Perth Library, neatly linking town and country; in the Literary and Antiquarian Society too there were local lairds amongst the members. Town councillors, some of whom such as John Caw would later hold prominent positions – Caw became a provost for example – were also involved. Perth's subscription library was the major channel through which the town's leading citizens engaged with the Enlightenment. Many of the core Enlightenment texts were purchased, including the works of leading figures from the Scottish Enlightenment – Adam Smith, David Hume, William Robertson, Hugh Blair, John Millar and Lord Kames. Significant too is the concentration of books on trade and commerce and manufactures – underlining the very practical nature of Enlightenment culture in Scotland, Perth included.[50] The pragmatism of Perth's middling and upper class associational culture is further reinforced by the decision of the Literary and Antiquarian Society in 1786 to commission a report into the price of labour as far back in time as was possible, while the Perth Library subscribers made it their business to purchase books on recent economic history.[51]

There was also a powerful patriotic dimension to both of Perth's late eighteenth century learned institutions. This had two strands, the first being national (Scottish), while the second was local, that is Perth-centred. A high proportion of the books purchased for the Library were about the history and topography of Scotland. But whereas in Edinburgh the inclination of Enlightenment writers like William Robertson was to dismiss Scotland's pre-Union culture as backward, Perth's Literary and Antiquarian Society – strongly influenced by its principal patron the Scottish cultural patriot David Steuart Erskine, eleventh earl of Buchan –

Conversation and evening walk, the North Inch, 1794. Illustrated in William Kay's engraving is a representative cross section of the burgh's social elite perambulating on the North Inch. In the forefront is John Caw, the then provost (numbered 1), Lord and Lady Breadalbane (4), Majors Dalton and Hooper (5 and 6), and others including the lawyer Andrew Davidson (3), a merchant, John Skane (10) and the cotton manufacturer, John Stewart (9). From the fashion trade was Beau Watt, a haberdasher (7), and Miss McIntyre, a milliner (8) (courtesy of Perth Museum and Art Gallery).

consciously supported the publication by the local printer James Morison of older Scottish poems and ballads as well as a history of William Wallace, celebrating thereby Scotland's independence and literary accomplishments prior to the Union.[52] Underlining the point about the passion there was for the local, the provincial and the pragmatic was the decision of the Literary and Antiquarian Society to have an enquiry into 'The foundation and rise of the principal towns of Scotland'.

In short, evidently shared by the members of both societies was not only a desire to engage with the Enlightenment and indeed to keep up with the latest literary fashions, but also to ensure that in Perth the Enlightenment was firmly grounded in Scotland, in Scottish history and Scottish society – including the provinces. There was a clear concern on the part of the leading lights in the Perth societies to distance themselves from abstract philosophising – in the manner of the French *philosophes* and even closer to home in Edinburgh – and to position and ground Perth not only as a Scottish town whose recent success was part of Scotland's advance through the eighteenth century, but also as a provincial centre that was determined not to be dominated by Edinburgh.

Order

But there was another side to Perth. It was one thing to create an elegant, ordered town in stone and slate; rather more difficult to accomplish was the creation of an orderly urban community.[53] Improvement which was driven primarily by and in the interests of the town's better-off inhabitants – with merchants being seen as the main beneficiaries, backed by the town council – was sometimes resented and resisted by the lower orders. Even more respectable members of the community could take umbrage when, for example, they were required to alter or even abandon properties deemed to be in the way of new street layouts. When livelihoods were affected, protest was invariably the result. In 1770, just prior to the opening of the Perth bridge to traffic, the shoemaker inhabitants of the Watergate objected that as a result of road re-routing associated with the bridge they would be denied 'the East country people's business as crossed the river at the Venals', while the residents of Castlegavel complained that the new street planned from George Street to the Skinnergate would deprive them not only of 'east country' trade but also customers from the north. Opposition to the changes necessitated by the new bridge took on a more malevolent character in December 1771 when it was reported that during the hours of darkness, 'some ill Getted persons throu down the Lodge One the Bridge that was Set their for to uplouft the Custom In & has Brok part of it', presumably as a mark of protest against the bridge tolls – or perhaps the very existence of the bridge.[54] Elsewhere others simply ignored the orders of the council, as for example the demand that forestairs projecting onto the streets should be removed. Early one morning in 1768 for example, David Scott, a mason, and John Menzies, a wright, rose and built just such a stair in front of a property in the Skinnergate.[55] The repeated issuing by the authorities of lists of regulations for the better order of the everyday life of the burgh suggests that Scott and Menzies were not alone in turning a blind eye to the blandishments of their local rulers.

There was a downside too to the successful policy of attracting large numbers of migrants to the town. People who worked for wages needed to be able to buy food to eat and fuel for cooking and heating. Grumbling over the availability of oats and oatmeal and other grains, as well as over fuel became much more commonplace as the town's population grew. In order to maintain the public peace and prevent disturbances the magistrates and town council had to be on constant alert for grain shortages, and to intervene if they threatened.[56] Although attempts were made to find coal locally (the council in 1723 employed an Englishman to sink a mine), Perth had no workable supply of its own and relied on coal being shipped in from the coal mines of Fife and the Lothians, so sufficiency of coal was an issue too, as for instance in the troubled year of 1792. More frequent too were complaints about the practice of the town's poorer inhabitants during periods of shortage to raid gardens and farmers' fields for food, and to break into plantations and steal wood.

Indeed in the second half of the eighteenth century one of the biggest challenges the authorities faced in Perth was the threat and on occasion the reality of food rioting – when local suppliers were unable to satisfy the demand there was for staple commodities like oats, peas and wheat that had been generated by the expanding population. In Perth there were serious disturbances over food between 1771 and 1773, in 1778, 1796, 1799 and 1800, and in 1811 and 1815.[57] With the surrounding districts struggling to meet the town's burgeoning demand for staple foodstuffs, any shipments outwards during periods of shortage were subject to the intervention of the crowd, whose leaders objected to what was perceived to be profiteering on the part of farmers and merchants who sold their produce in bulk to the highest bidders. This applied primarily to oats and oatmeal but in 1774 even shipments outwards of salmon, a major export from Perth, were subject to close scrutiny on the part of the inhabitants – as a new tack of the town's fishings had been granted by the town council, but without any requirement on the part of the tacksmen to ensure that the townspeople's needs were supplied first.[58]

And in spite of – perhaps because of – the increased regimentation of work and the attempts of the town council and magistrates to create a more orderly urban environment, there was amongst the lower orders a marked propensity to engage in excessive drinking, fighting, and in some circumstances rioting. Particularly noticeable in this respect was the King's Birthday, an annual celebration held on 4 June. Although the day had been one of heavy drinking, for many decades the celebrations had served to unify the town. But as in much of the rest of early modern Europe, the classes were drawing apart and by the 1790s, 4 June had been seized as an opportunity for the labouring classes to hurl abuse, as well as mud and dead cats and dogs, at the magistrates and other unpopular members of the town's elite.[59] Disaffection manifested itself in other ways and at other times too, as in 1789 when there was a bout of lamp breaking.[60] Former strangers to Perth, working at the same trade and living in the same properties and neighbourhoods developed over time a sense of group identity, and sought to promote and protect their interests. Thus in 1779 was formed the New Row Friendly Society, comprising in the main journeymen handloom weavers – who advertised their collective presence by processing through town, with sashes and other identifying marks.[61] In itself this was harmless enough, but in certain circumstances friendly societies could take on the role of combinations, or early trade unions, and adopt a more aggressive stance within and even beyond the workplace.[62] With its large population of handloom weavers – who elsewhere in Lowland Scotland tended to be in the vanguard of radical and at times revolutionary politics – Perth in the 1790s and early years of the nineteenth century was somewhat at odds

The King's Birthday in Perth, 1819. Illustrated here, by D.O. Hill, is an impression of the scenes which accompanied the King's birthday celebrations in Perth. The disorder associated with the occasion – very much the antithesis of the orderly environment the burgh's elite was trying to create - led the provost and town councillors to withdraw from the public celebrations. What this picture reveals, however, is that old habits died hard (Samuel Cowan, The Ancient Capital of Scotland 2nd volume, London, 1904).

Thomas Luke (1776–1832). Thomas Luke was a glover (one of Perth's oldest trades) and an auctioneer. He was also a baillie and police superintendent. Maintaining order amongst a population prone to disorder and periodic riot was a major challenge for the authorities in Perth in the Enlightenment era. Luke – being of medium height and ample girth – may have been 'the butt of wags', but he also earned himself a reputation as 'the terror of evil doers' (courtesy of Perth Museum and Art Gallery).

with the image of the town which the town's elite was intent on creating. There were charismatic individuals too from the lower classes – women as well as men – who were able to galvanise their neighbours and raise a mob. One of these was Blair Flight, a clockmaker, who was described as 'an odd-looking figure' with a countenance 'which indicates a mind capable of any mean action'.[63] If there is a catch-all term that encapsulates what men like this stood for, it is custom, in defence of an older, pre-Enlightenment set of values. They were enforcers, so to speak, of what Edward Thompson has called the moral economy.[64] They were not unique to Perth but part of the hidden – or less easily accessible – histories of most places.

It may seem paradoxical, but the presence in Perth of a number of dissenting religious sects probably exacerbated the situation; religious dissent in Scotland with its Covenanting roots often went hand in hand with political radicalism during the 1790s. Indeed Enlightenment Perth was one of Scotland's simmering centres of radicalism during the French Revolution.[65] And contrary to what might be expected, Perth's radical leaders were not all, or even mainly, working class hot-heads but included men such as George Mellis, a cotton manufacturer and merchant – of Cromwell works – who lived in Rosemount villa, on the north side of the Tay. Amongst the many books that were being read in and around what was a town of avid readers, were multiple copies of Tom Paine *The Rights of Man;* it is not so surprising then that on a morning in April 1794 anyone walking across the Tay bridge would have come across a prominent bit of graffiti announcing, 'Britain must be a republic, liberty and equality'.[66]

Adding to the authorities' difficulties was Perth's military importance and that after the last Jacobite rising of 1745–46 it became a garrison town. The upside of this was the business opportunities created in the provisioning trades, for tailors, milliners and alehouse keepers – and even a few women of ill repute. A considerable drawback was that large numbers of soldiers in town led to jealousies and tensions between them and the townspeople, and ultimately to fights and disturbances. So too did attempts by soldiers to recruit Perth males into the army – when they were drunk and overly eager to claim their 'king's shilling'. Squabbles of this kind with the military and serious attacks on customs and excise officers were reported as early as the 1720s.[67] There is little to suggest that the incidence of violent disorder was much reduced in the subsequent decades.[68] In short, Perth was a fairly turbulent town, probably more so than its near neighbour Dundee.[69]

Conclusion

In conclusion, the Enlightenment zeitgeist clearly left its mark on Perth. But despite the burgh's refinement there was also a rough side to Perth. But also in evidence was a proud provincialism. Allied to this was a desire too to place Perth at the forefront of provincial Scotland, and a well-founded belief that Perth had its own distinctive place in Scottish society and therefore in Scottish history.

End Notes

1 Much of the research for this chapter was carried out as part of an Arts and Humanities Research Council (AHRC) funded project on the smaller Scottish towns in the era of the Enlightenment. Apart from my own material, I have drawn heavily on transcriptions of documents from Perth and Kinross Council Archives provided by Dr Nathalie Rosset as well as draft articles written by Dr Bob Harris, of Worcester College, University of Oxford. For their assistance in making available source materials for this chapter I am grateful to Steve Connelly and Dr Jan Merchant of Perth and Kinross Council Archives, and for help in identifying illustrations, Maria Devaney of Perth Museum & Art Gallery.

2 D. Daiches, P. Jones and J. Jones (eds), *A Hotbed of Genius: The Scottish Enlightenment, 1730–1790* (Edinburgh, 1986).

3 A. Herman, *The Scottish Enlightenment: The Scots' Invention of the Modern World* (London, 2002).

4 See, for example, J. Robertson, *The Case for the Enlightenment. Scotland and Naples, 1680–1760* (Cambridge, 2005).

5 See J. Dwyer, The Age of the Passions: *An Interpretation of Adam Smith and Scottish Enlightenment Culture* (East Linton, 1998).

6 T. C. Smout, *A History of the Scottish People, 1560–1830* (London, 1969, 1981 ed.), pp.342-3; M. Glendinning, R. MacInnes and A. Mackenzie, *A History of Scottish Architecture: From the Renaissance to the Present Day* (Edinburgh, 1996), pp.169-76.

7 A. Hook and R. B. Sher (eds), *The Glasgow Enlightenment* (East Linton, 1995); J. J. Carter and J. Pittock (eds), *Aberdeen and the Enlightenment* (Aberdeen, 1987); M. G. H. Pittock, 'Contrasting Cultures: Town and Country', in E. P. Dennison, D. Ditchburn and M. Lynch (eds), *Aberdeen Before 1800: A New History* (East Linton, 2002), pp.365-73; C. McKean, Bob Harris and C. A. Whatley (eds), *Dundee: Renaissance to Enlightenment* (Dundee, 2009).

8 This is not to overlook some recent work that has been published, such as V. Linacre, *The Marshall Place Conspiracy* (Perth, 2008), C. D. Waterston, *Perth Entrepreneurs: the Sandemans of Springland* (Perth, 2008), and there are also the occasional publications of local learned societies in both Perth and Dundee.

9 For a model study of Scottish towns like Perth in this period, see Bob Harris, 'Towns, improvement and cultural change in Georgian Scotland: the evidence of the Angus burghs, c.1760–1820', *Urban History,* 33, 2 (2006), pp.195-212.

10 I. D. Whyte, 'Scottish and Irish urbanisation in the seventeenth and eighteenth centuries: a comparative perspective', in S. J. Connolly, R. A. Houston and R. J. Morris (eds), *Conflict, Identity and Economic Development: Ireland and Scotland, 1600–1939* (Preston, 1995), p.24.

11 T. M. Devine, 'Scotland', in P. Clark (ed), *The Cambridge Urban History of Britain, Volume II,* 1540–1840 (Cambridge, 2000), p.159.

12 Harris, 'Towns', pp.197-8.

13 C. A. Whatley, *Scottish Society, 1707–1830: Beyond Jacobitism, Towards Industrialisation* (Manchester, 2000), pp. 64-5, 219-21; A. J. Durie, *The Scottish Linen Industry in the Eighteenth Century* (Edinburgh, 1979).

14 Waterston, *Perth Entrepreneurs,* pp.16-17.

15 Durie, *Linen Industry,* p.85.

16 A. W. Harding, *Pullars of Perth* (Perth, 1991), 16.

17 C. A. Whatley, *The Scots and the Union* (Edinburgh, 2006), pp.159-60.

18 PKCA, Perth Burgh Petitions, B59/26/4/1.

19 For the individual records completed by householders, see PKCA, Perth Burgh Records, B59/24/1/40/1-135.

20 C. W. J. Withers, *Highland Communities in Dundee and Perth 1787–1891* (Dundee, 1986), p.11.

21 PKCA, B59/24/1/40/8a; for transcribing the census records of 1773 I am grateful to Katherine McBay of the University of Dundee, and for preparing the map showing the places of origins of Perth's migrants I am indebted to Dr Alistair Geddes, School of the Environment, University of Dundee.

22 N. Murray, *The Scottish Hand Loom Weavers 1790–1850: A Social History* (Edinburgh, 1978), pp.40-2; J. H. Treble,'The Standard of Living of the Working Class', in T. M. Devine and R. Mitchison (eds), *People and Society in Scotland, Volume I,* 1760–1830 (Edinburgh, 1988), p.197.

23 Harris, 'Towns', p.196.

24 PKCA, Perth Town Council Minutes, PE1/1/1, 21 September 1752.

25 PKCA, Perth Town Council Minutes, PE1/1/1, 2 July 1764.

26 For information on the building of the bridge, see PKCA, Records of the Perth Bridge Commissioners, 1765–1770, PE23, Bundle 2, Scroll minutes of the Trustees; PE23, Bundle 4, State of the Funds for Building the Bridge of Perth, 22 January 1770.

27 PKCA, Perth Town Council Minutes, PE1/1/1, 1 April, 1 July 1765; PE1/1/2, 3 March, 7 April 1766.

28 For a splendid study of the place of the market-place in early modern England, see E. Griffin, 'The "urban renaissance" and the mob: rethinking civic improvement over the long eighteenth century', in D. Feldman and J. Lawrence (eds), *Structures and Transformations in Modern British History* (Cambridge, 2010), pp.54-73.

29 PKCA, Perth Burgh Petitions, B59/26/4/3, Petition of Baillie Pat Coupar and William Lindsay, 8 October 1755.
30 PKCA, Perth Town Council Minutes, B59/16/14, 10 October 1748, 20 March 1749.
31 PKCA, Perth Burgh Petitions, B59/26/4/4, Petition of Patrick McGilliwie, 1761.
32 PKCA, Perth Town Council Minutes, B59/16/14, 18 November 1751.
33 PKCA, Perth Burgh Petitions, B59/26/4/7, Petition of John Buchan, writer, 12 August 1773.
34 L. Leneman and R. Mitchison, *Sin in the City: Sexuality & Social Control in Urban Scotland, 1660–1780* (Edinburgh, 1998), pp.43-9; PKCA, B59/24/11/13, Instructions for the constables appointed by the magistrates, 8 January 1748; see too PKCA, B59/24/1/24/5, Immorality bank, 15 October 1753.
35 PKCA, Perth Burgh petitions, B59/26/4/2, William Thompson against Thomas Goodman and spouse, 1761,
36 PKCA, B59/26/4/8, Petition of James Robertson, staymaker, 1773
37 PKCA, Perth Town Council Minutes, B59/16/14, 6 October. There is a suggestion that lamps may have been provided even earlier, in 1723.
38 Harris, 'Towns', pp.201-2; on lighting generally, see R. Sweet, *The English Town, 1680–1840: Government, Society and Culture* (Harlow, 1999), pp.81-3.
39 PKCA, PE1/1/4, Perth Town Council Minutes, 6 October 1788.
40 K. J. Cameron, *The Schoolmaster Engineer: Adam Anderson of Perth and St Andrews, c.1780–1846* (Dundee, 1988), p.17.
41 PKCA, Perth Town Council Minutes. PE1/1/1, 24 September, 7 October 1760.
42 PKCA, Perth Town Council Minutes, PE1/1/1, 23 February 1761; J. Strawhorn, *The History of Ayr: Royal Burgh and County Town* (Edinburgh, 1989), p.127.
43 PKCA, PE1/1/1, 1 August 1763.
44 PKCA, PE1/1/4, Perth Town Council Minutes, 7 January 1788.
45 *A Journey Through Part of England and Scotland Along with the Army Under the Command of His Royal Highness the Duke of Cumberland, By a Volunteer* (London, 1747), pp.110-11.
46 Bob Harris, 'Cultural Change in Provincial Scotttish Towns, c.1700–1820', *The Historical Journal,* 54, 1 (2011), pp.124-5, 133.
47 K. A. Manley, 'Scottish circulating and subscription libraries as community libraries', *Library History,* 19 (Nov. 2003), pp.185-94; see too, M. R. M. Towsey, '"All partners may be enlightened and improved by them": the distribution of enlightenment books in Scottish subscription libraries, 1750–c.1820', *Journal of Scottish Historical Studies,* 28 (2008), pp.20-43.
48 For a monumental study, see R. B. Sher, *The Enlightenment & the Book: Scottish Authors & Their Publishers in Eighteenth-Century Britain, Ireland & America* (Chicago and London, 2006).
49 D. Allan, 'The Scottish Enlightenment and the Politics of Provincial Culture: The Perth Literary and Antiquarian Society, ca.1784–1790', *Eighteenth Century Life,* 27 (2003), pp.1-30.
50 D. Allan, 'Provincial Readers and Book Culture in the Scottish Enlightenment: The Perth Library, 1784–c.1800', The Library, 3, 4 (December 2002), pp.375-80.
51 Allan, 'The Scottish Enlightenment and the Politics of Provincial Culture', p.7; Allan, 'Provincial Readers', pp.388-9.
52 Allan, 'The Scottish Enlightenment and the Politics of Provincial Culture', pp.8-20.
53 This is the main thrust of Griffin, 'The "urban renaissance" and the mob'.
54 PKCA, Perth Burgh Petitions, B59/26/4/6, Petitions, The inhabitants of the Watergate and Castlegavel, 1770.
55 PKCA, Perth Burgh Petitions, B59/26/4/6, Procurator fiscal versus David Scot, mason, & John Menzies, wright, 1768.
56 PKCA, Perth Town Council Minutes, PE1/1/1, 31 January 1757; PE1/1/3, 6 January 1783.
57 These have been little investigated but see S. G. E. Lythe, 'The Tayside meal mobs, 1772–3', *Scottish Historical Review,* xlvi (1967), pp.26-36; K. J. Logue, *Popular Disturbances in Scotland 1780–1815* (Edinburgh, 1979).
58 PKCA, Perth Town Council Minutes, PE1/1/2, 9 August 1774.
59 C. A. Whatley, 'Royal Day, People's Day: The Monarch's Birthday in Scotland, c.1660–1860', in R. Mason and N. Macdougall (eds), *People and Power in Scotland: Essays in Honour of T. C. Smout* (Edinburgh, 1992), pp.170-88.
60 PKCA, Perth Town Council Minutes, PE1/1/4, 5 January 1789.
61 PKCA, Perth Burgh Petitions, B59/26/4/10, John Duncan & Alexander Scobie & others, journeymen weavers, 1779.
62 See W. H. Fraser, *Conflict and Class: Scottish Workers 1700–1838* (Edinburgh, 1988).
63 G. Penny, *Traditions of Perth* (Perth, 1836), p.47.
64 E. P. Thompson, 'The moral economy of the English crowd in the eighteenth century', *Past and Present,* 50 (1971); for a more recent survey of the debate about markets and popular protest, see A. Randall, A. Charlesworth, R. Sheldon and D. Walsh, 'Markets, Market Culture and Popular Protest in Eighteenth-Century Britain and Ireland', in A. Randall and A. Charlesworth (eds), *Markets, Market Culture and Popular Protest in Eighteenth-Century Britain and Ireland* (Liverpool, 1996), pp.1-24.
65 Whatley, Scottish Society, p.303.
66 Bob Harris, *The Scottish People and the French Revolution* (London, 2008), pp. 83, 103.
67 PKCA, B59/32/31/2, Memorial and Queries for the Magistrates of Perth, 12 January 1726; Whatley, *Scottish Society,* p.172.
68 See, for example, Penny, *Traditions,* pp.61-86, 97-103
69 Crime and disorder in Perth have not been seriously investigated but for Dundee see D. G. Barrie, 'Urban Order in Georgian Dundee, c.1770–1820', in McKean, Harris and Whatley, *Dundee: Renaissance to Enlightenment,* pp.216-42.

Perth on the map – a cartographic voyage through time

Chris Fleet

Maps of Perth over the centuries provide an instant graphic insight into the nature of the city at particular moments in its history, and taken together, they provide a detailed visual chronology of its development. Those interested in the history of Perth's maps are indebted to the splendid carto-bibliography by Jeremy Duncan,[1] updating the work of Thomas McLaren.[2] Over twenty-five detailed maps of the city, dating from c1600 to c1900 are described and illustrated, particularly noting the new streets, buildings and developments shown on each map. There is also a list of over eighty maps destroyed in 1895 when the Municipal Buildings were burned down.

This chapter does not intend to duplicate this carto-bibliography, but rather to summarise the significant features of these maps in terms of their own history, production and purpose. Whilst a few additional maps besides those in the carto-bibliography are discussed, its main aim is to examine the cartographic background to the mapping of Perth, asking several related questions. Who made these maps and why? How did the background and purpose influence the maps? And how did this change over time?

Maps of Perth do not reflect a steady, progressive trend towards ever increasing accuracy or detail, but rather, show more interesting processes, reflecting the societal values and time periods to which they relate. Creating maps necessarily involves selection from the real world, and conscious or unconscious decisions to show some features rather than others, so the personal values of the map maker and their context inevitably show through. For example, we can see Pont's concern to sketch the general nature of the country as part of a wider regional description, the military map makers' concern to protect forts and towns from future Jacobite control, and estate surveyors' concern to promote the interests of major landowners or the gentry. We similarly see contrasts between the Town Council's attempt to promote new development and improve the town, and the state funded, immensely detailed and authoritative work of Ordnance Survey. Assessing the value of these maps becomes inseparable from their purpose and audiences, and accuracy can be often less important and interesting than their misrepresentations and absences.

Allied to these social changes, and in part driving them, came practical changes in the technologies of map production; moving from manuscript, pen and ink (particularly up to the mid-eighteenth century), to engraved copper plates thereafter, overlapping with the use of lithographic stones and photographic work in the nineteenth and twentieth centuries. These changes created not just a different aesthetic to maps of Perth, but, in association with the rise in literacy, and spread of printing, helped to create new, largely urban, markets for maps and encourage new sorts of maps altogether. Digital technologies from the 1990s allow a further perspective on the nature of Perth in recent times.

From symbols to pictures

In the earliest maps of Scotland such as those by Matthew Paris[3] in the thirteenth century or in the Gough map[4] of the fourteenth century, the country's settlements including Perth simply appear as rather roughly done symbols. Over time, however, in Europe, there is an evident trend from the use of symbols, to pictures, to plan-view surveys in the depiction of urban centres, and we see this for Perth too.

We know that Perth was an important medieval burgh, with extensive trading links, and therefore it is usually named on all the earliest maps of Scotland. Before the late sixteenth century, there is usually no detail shown of the city itself, and the maps were not based on any direct survey on the ground. For example, Paulo Forlani's *Scotia* (c1560) was based on a copy of George Lily's *Scotia* map of the 1540s, but neither Forlani nor Lily had visited Scotland. Lily was an English exile based in Rome, and his main geographic information was taken from historical narratives, such as John Major's *History of Great Britain* (1521) and Hector Boece's *History of Scotland* (1526); ecclesiastical centres, rivers, mountain ranges, islands and elements of mythology and fable all appear on the map.

Timothy Pont (c1565–1614) provides a major contrast to all these earlier map-makers, in deliberately setting out on foot or horseback to record the landscape first hand. There were several reasons why more detailed maps of Scotland were needed. For James VI, seeking greater political control, especially of the Highlands, maps were needed for state integration, prestige and defence. There were economic motives too, with merchants and burgesses keen to explore potential sources of wealth from the land. In addition, following the Scottish Reformation, from 1560 onwards an emerging but still relatively small body of ministers, lawyers, teachers and lairds were coming to appreciate the value of detailed, historically grounded descriptions of their country in maps and texts.

Pont's mapping can only be approximately dated to sometime between his graduation from St Andrews in 1583 until his death, by 1614. Without his having employed trigonometry or accurate measurement, his sketch maps are better regarded as a qualitative representation of what was where, and naming or illustrating an immense breadth of features. Pont's depiction of Perth is very much on the edge of his large map of Angus (Pont 26), and incomplete, but still very useful to us. It shows St John's

Timothy Pont's bird's eye view of Perth c1583–1614.

Church, dominating the skyline, the buildings of the city to the north and south of the High Street along the west bank of the River Tay. Perhaps the bridge shown was the medieval four-pier timber bridge, soon to be upgraded to a ten-arch stone bridge by 1617, but then washed away in the floods of 1621. The city's walls are also shown, as a two-ringed enclosure, on three sides of the city, the Tay providing defence from the east. The city walls date from the twelfth century and survived in places until the 1760s. Pont's portrayal of the town reflects Perth's burgh status and its privileges, as well as signalling its central place in the local area. In word and in symbol, what Pont shows is a simple relative settlement hierarchy as well as a location and a pictorial view.[5]

From the 1680s onwards, Scotland's second major map-maker, John Adair, created county maps and sea charts for many parts of Scotland, and fortunately, these have survived well for the lowland parts of Perthshire. Adair was commissioned by the Privy Council from 1681 to map counties of Scotland, particularly to assist Sir Robert Sibbald who was hoping to publish a revised *Scotch Atlas* to update the Blaeu Atlas of 1654. Funds were never sufficient for Adair's work and he disputed seriously with Sibbald, and the *Scotch Atlas* project never materialised. Adair's maps reveal an attempt to update and improve upon Pont, but were often

Detail from 'The Mappe of Straithern, Stormont, & Cars of Gourie with the rivers Tay and Ern / surveighed & designed [by] John Adair (1683)'.

more selective of features on the ground, and reduced Pont's exuberance in portraying landscape detail to a more standardised and simplified geometry. Adair gives a stylistic but arguably more complete depiction of Perth's environs than Pont and the first depiction of routeways – radiating outwards in all directions to Dunkeld, Forfar, Dundee, Edinburgh and Glasgow.

Pont and Adair's maps are best regarded as part of a longer and older chorographic tradition of regional description, where maps were intended to accompany texts describing the history, geography, antiquity and genealogy of an area. We quickly see the contrast between these and the maps made by the engineers of the Board of Ordnance which followed them, being chiefly compiled for the purposes of military conquest and control.

Military mapping

One of the primary motivations behind cartography in the world has always been warfare, and during the early eighteenth century, we find several maps of Perth associated with the Jacobite Rebellions, and the construction of forts, defences and roads. Internationally, there was a steady militarisation of cartography at this time, with new state-funded military academies in several European states, and a growing military appreciation of the value of maps.

The Board of Ordnance had existed since the Middle Ages, and although a civil organisation, its chief responsibilities were as the principal supplier of munitions and equipment to the Army and Navy, and as custodian of lands, depots and forts for the defence of the realm at home and overseas. By the late seventeenth century, Board of Ordnance engineers were expected to be polymaths, skilled in mathematics, geodesy, trigonometry, and engineering, carrying these skills into practice too by estimating charges for all proposed fortifications, supervising the building and design of fortifications and conducting sieges. Many of these engineers were from the Continent, and brought with them very distinctive cartographic practices, particularly in colour, style and scale.

John Slezer was the first Chief Engineer in Scotland, and an expert military draughtsman of forts and castles. In 1693 he brought together fifty-seven drawings and views of towns, abbeys, castles, and country houses in a volume, the *Theatrum Scotiae,* and included a fine *Prospect of ye Town of Perth* from the east. Although the volume did not sell well, and effectively bankrupted Slezer, it was reprinted several times in the eighteenth century with additions.

Perth was mapped in greater detail by the French Huguenot military engineer in the Board of Ordnance, Lewis Petit – this was the first overhead or ichnographic depiction of the city.[6] Petit had seen major action in the War of the Spanish Succession, and in the British takeover of Minorca in 1707. In 1714, he was commissioned to travel to Scotland to report on castles around Fort William, and through this experience he was then commanded to lead an artillery train in late 1715/early 1716 into Scotland by the Duke of Argyll. After Perth was recaptured from the Jacobites he drafted this earliest surviving plan of Perth. In terms of detail, features of military value are shown, including the V-shaped revetments or redans that were rapidly assembled by Jacobite forces during its occupation. The old Cromwellian citadel built in 1652 on South Inch with its earthen ramparts and deep moat is also well portrayed, with moving water supplied by canal from the Craigie Burn.[7] The King's Lade or Town Lade that supplied the fosse around the city walls appears as an important

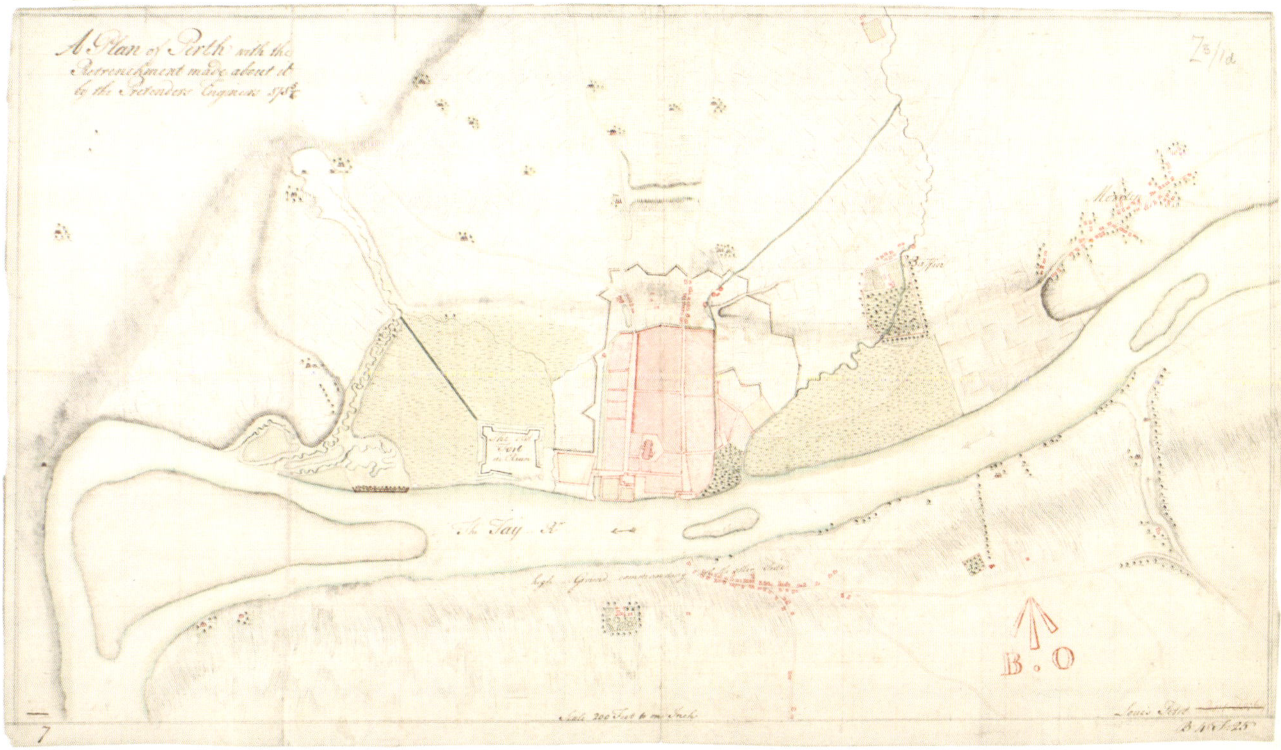

'Plan of Perth with the retrenchment made about it by the Pretenders Engineers', by Lewis Petit 1716.

barrier, bridged only opposite the ports or gateways, with the old quay at the end of Canal Street shown too, a feature of practical military value. The date 1715/6 on the plan suggests that it was drafted before 25 March 1716, when England officially moved to the new year. The standard training for engineers involved copying the plans of earlier engineers, and William Horneck's plans,[8] although employing an elaborate but slightly later military conventional style for gardens, are in essence a copy of Petit's plan, not an independent survey.

The cheapest and most effective means of demonstrating Hanoverian military prowess and creating a defensible fortress at Perth was through the construction of a new fort, with clear ground between it and the city. This conception and its cartographic depiction[9] perhaps

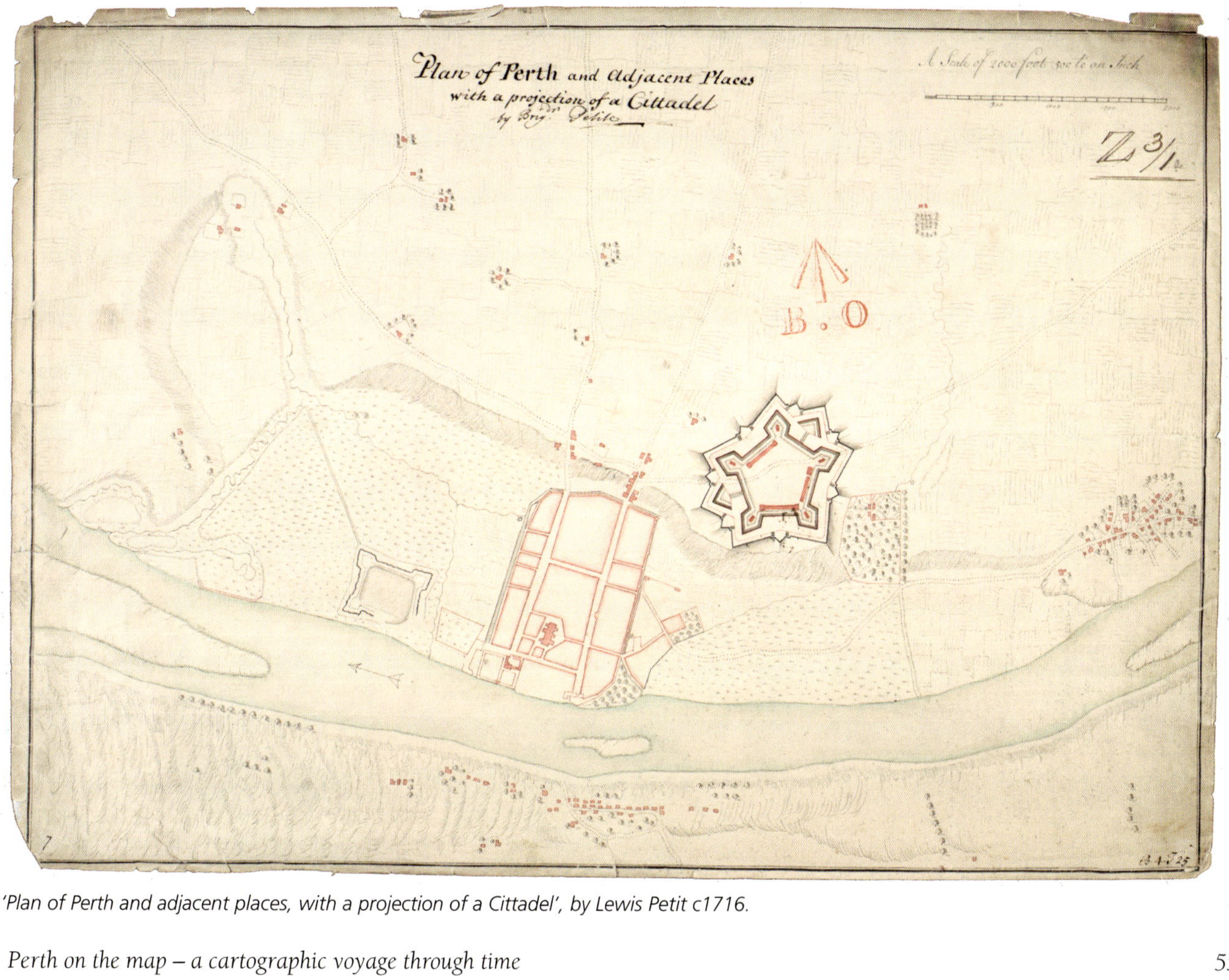

'Plan of Perth and adjacent places, with a projection of a Cittadel', by Lewis Petit c1716.

most strongly illustrates Petit's extension of European military theory in fortification and cartography into Scotland. The projected new fort was based on a pentagon with bastions at each corner, on higher ground to the north-west of Perth, and would be significantly less vulnerable to newer mobile cannon fire than the South Inch. The new fort would also be protected from the artillery fire by extensive outworks, including triangular ravelins and revetments. This is an imagined cartography, never realised, and we can only assume that lack of funds, and a priority given to the network of forts further north in Scotland, prevented this scheme from development.[10] Whilst space does not allow their consideration here, the Board of Ordnance engineers also composed fine plans and profiles of buildings under their control in Perth, including Gowrie House, scene of the Gowrie Conspiracy, and later gifted to the Duke of Cumberland.[11]

As the main work of military engineers was very focused on forts, battles and roads, general topographic mapping was very limited, and during the 1745 Rebellion the British army commanders 'found themselves greatly embarrassed through want of a proper survey of the country'.[12] Soon after the defeat of the Jacobites at Culloden in May 1746, the British King (George II) was petitioned to support a Military Survey of Scotland and the primary practical responsibility for this was delegated to the Assistant Quartermaster in the Board of Ordnance, William Roy. Roy's Military Survey of Scotland is one of the most attractive and detailed maps of eighteenth century Scotland, and has been well-researched.[13] Although the survey was not based upon accurate triangulation, but rather a set of measured traverses along selected important landscape features using theodolites and chains, it nevertheless marked a significant cartographic breakthrough. Roy was characteristically modest about the results, describing it 'as a magnificent military sketch, than a very accurate map of the country',[14] and it is often helpful to interpret the map as a work of military reconnaissance, selecting features in the landscape of interest to an army commander. The depiction of relief and use of colour reflects broader military traditions in cartography. One of the chief draughtsmen employed on the Survey was Paul Sandby, who went on to become a celebrated watercolourist, but he trained as a military engineer. The survey was conducted in two parts, first the Highlands to 1752, and then the Lowlands to 1755, before the outbreak of the Seven Years War in Europe led to engineers being recalled from Scotland. The Roy depiction of Perth can therefore be dated to before 1752, and shows a similarly compact Perth, slightly expanded to the west, with a large wood covering the burgh muir.[15] The pacification of Scotland that it encouraged led to new maps with a very different purpose and aesthetic.

Enlightenment and improvement mapping

From the 1760s the face of the rural landscape around Perth was transformed through drainage, enclosure, consolidation of holdings, new crop rotations, techniques, rural industries and roads. This agricultural improvement was driven particularly by landowners, who employed estate surveyors and factors as their agents. These land surveyors were often also called upon to map urban areas and their hinterlands – for feuing land, enclosing burgh muirs, or in planning new mills and communications. From 1759, the Society of Arts gave financial inducements to these land surveyors to create maps of whole counties, if they used trigonometry and the one-inch to the mile scale. There were important links between these developments. Perth's expansion, fuelled partly by the growth in trade through agricultural development and its location at the centre of this broad and productive rural hinterland, was recorded by the very estate surveyors who were driving the process on landed estates. The private financing of these new maps was driven too by civic and other patrons, and by subscribers and buyers within emerging urban centres such as Perth.

James Stobie was estate factor to the 4th Duke of Atholl for over two decades from 1780 to 1804. Through his estate mapping work for the duke, and the patronage and connections of the duke's brother in law, Thomas Graham of Balgowan, Lord Lynedoch, Stobie was able to survey and publish one of the finest county maps in Scotland, of Perth and Clackmannan in 1783. The 4th Duke effectively financed widespread mapping of large parts of Perthshire, through his large estates, planting, agricultural improvement and the sale and purchase of land. Stobie's map was an important statement of the power of landed aristocracy – attractive vignettes of their houses adorn the perimeter of the map – and provides an appropriate backdrop to the mapping of Perth at this time. Stobie includes a fine view of Perth from the north, and an inset town plan in its lower left corner. Stobie's map is also good for showing the mill lades and mills within the city and the new roads and routeways into the city, growing in importance at this time.[16]

Stobie's county map was so fine, and the costs of resurveying the county were so great, that it was still being used fifty years later as a county map. When the Edinburgh publisher John Thomson compiled county maps for his *Atlas of Scotland* published in 1832 – a project that ruined him financially – the land surveyor William Johnson effectively made a copy of Stobie's map and inset in 1827. The post 1780s developments are shown in a very sketchy way, with the old letters of the legend still not hammered out from the old copper plate.

In eighteenth century Scotland, an emerging print culture in cities also provided new opportunities for publishing maps. An expanding group of students, the middle-classes, and members of learned and civic societies, all had need of maps: in geographic and scientific books, in travel accounts, to picture what their towns and cities looked like, and to encourage travel between them. In Perth, the founding of the Academy in 1760 with its classes in geometry, geography and natural history under John Mair,[17] the founding of the Literary and Antiquarian Society in 1784 with its public lectures, and the growth of bookselling, printing and publishing within the city provide illustrations of this new demand for maps. Robert Morison, Postmaster in Perth from 1745, founded a circulating library in 1752, and with his sons as printers, went on to publish James Cant's edition of *The Muses Threnodie* in 1774 (with its important map of Perth by Archibald Rutherford – see below), the *Encyclopaedia Perthensis* (1796–1806), and *Perth Courier* (from 1809). Instrument makers, such as James Kirkwood, who was licensed as a clock and watchmaker in Perth in 1771, turned their hands to engraving maps and globes.

The many professional and practical linkages that drove map-making within this urban world are well-illustrated by Archibald Rutherford (1743–1779). Rutherford was born in Jedburgh into a family of saddlers and lorimers, and trained as a land surveyor under Archibald Jerdon before acting as factor to William Elliot of Wells. Rutherford then worked as the Drawing Master in Perth Academy, supplementing his income through freelance land surveying. He worked for the Perth Bridge Commissioners in planning the approach roads to Smeaton's new bridge across the Tay, opened in 1771. Through James Cant's encouragement, the Town Council paid £10 to Rutherford to survey Perth, resulting in his fine plan of 1774, engraved by James Kirkwood; it was the

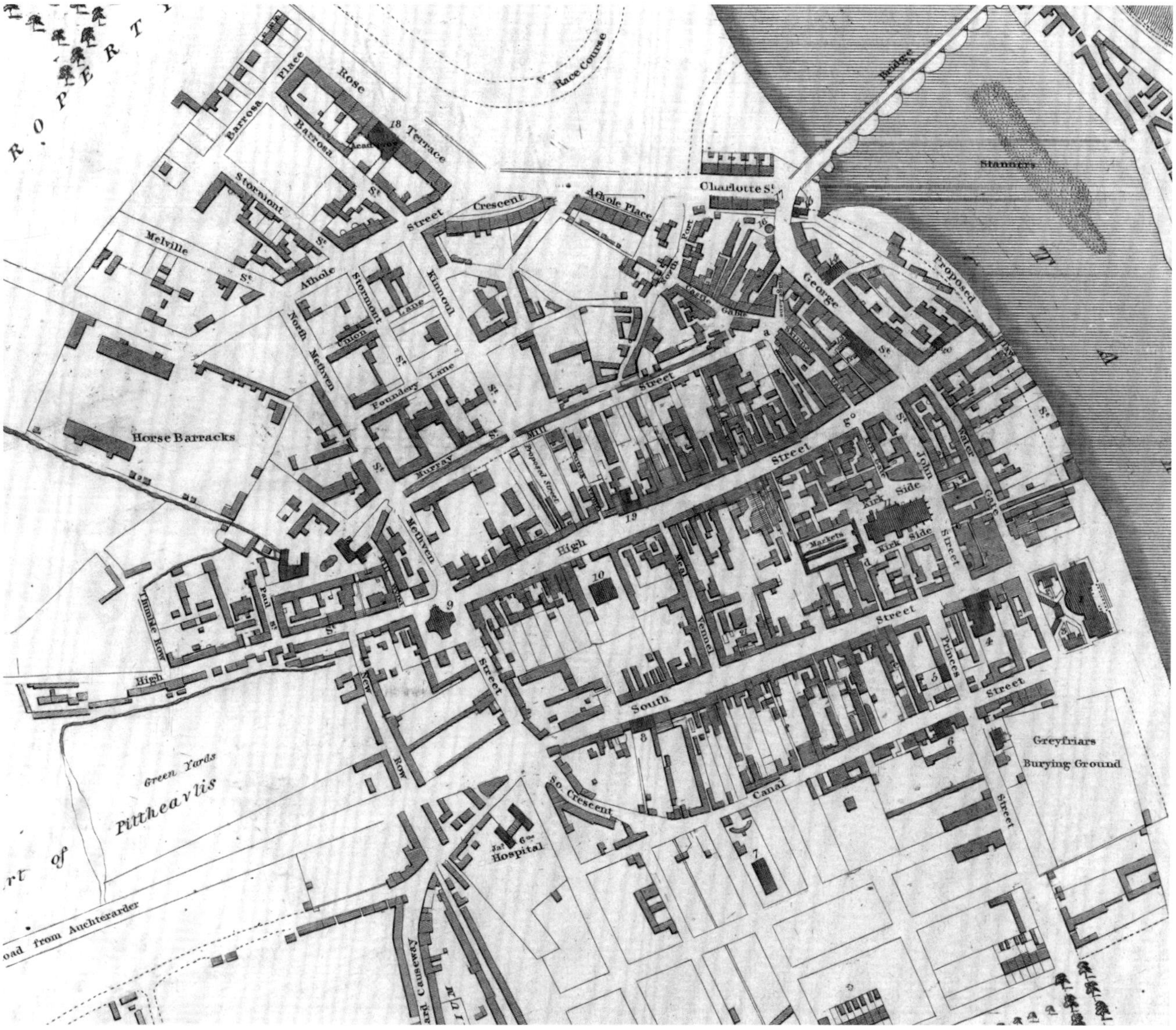

'Plan of the City of Perth from actual survey, by John Wood' 1823.

first engraved plan of Perth. It is of interest too to note the social and religious connections between those involved: Robert Morison and James Cant as publishers, Rutherford and Kirkwood were all members of the Glasite congregation in Perth.[18]

As Perth steadily grew in size, with new streets, industries, civic buildings and thoroughfares, map-makers were often called upon in the planning of new developments. The architect Robert Reid's work in Perth was particularly at the instigation of Thomas Hay Marshall, Provost of Perth, for planning the Georgian New Town expansion. In 1801, Reid was appointed architect of Marshall Place and Rose Terrace in Perth, and he was also responsible for Atholl Place and Crescent, King's Place and King James' Place. Reid was commissioned by the Town Council to draft a very detailed plan of 1809, the largest scale plan of the city before the Ordnance Survey. As well as proposing designs for the County Buildings in Perth (1812–14), Reid played a significant role in the architectural and practical development in several other Scottish cities, becoming King's Architect and Surveyor in Scotland, as well as 'His Majesty's Architect in Scotland' (1821).

In the face of rapid urban change, other map-makers often tried to anticipate new developments, not always correctly, or found their accurate maps were quickly outdated by other developments on the ground. William MacFarlane's map of 1792, for example, shows some expansion of the city since Stobie and Rutherford's map, but anticipates several developments that were then only at the planning stage: the new turnpike road to Dunkeld, the New Town in the area of Barossa Place, Barrack Street, Atholl Street and Rose Terrace, along with a second New Town on the South Inch.[19] *The Plan of Perth with The Intended Additions And Improvements* (1806), and those maps based upon it in the Guide to the City and County of Perth from 1810 onwards, anticipate an open-ended High Street at its eastern end, at least two decades before the eventual demolition of the Council House.

The most significant private surveyor of Scottish towns in the early 19th century in terms of the quality of his work and the number of maps he produced was John Wood. Originally from Yorkshire, Wood settled in Edinburgh from 1813, and published fifty plans of Scottish towns between 1818 and 1826. Wood's original survey of Perth shows excellent detail of the city at this time, including the new road from Auchterarder being built to link with South Street, the new gas works to the south of Canal Street, and the new County Buildings, then known as the Sheriff Court, with the county jail behind it. The proposed Tay Street is shown, half a century before completion, but clearly marked as such, and there is a detailed list of public buildings, churches and inns with names of proprietors. Wood's maps were published separately, but also forty-eight plans were brought together in his *Town Atlas of*

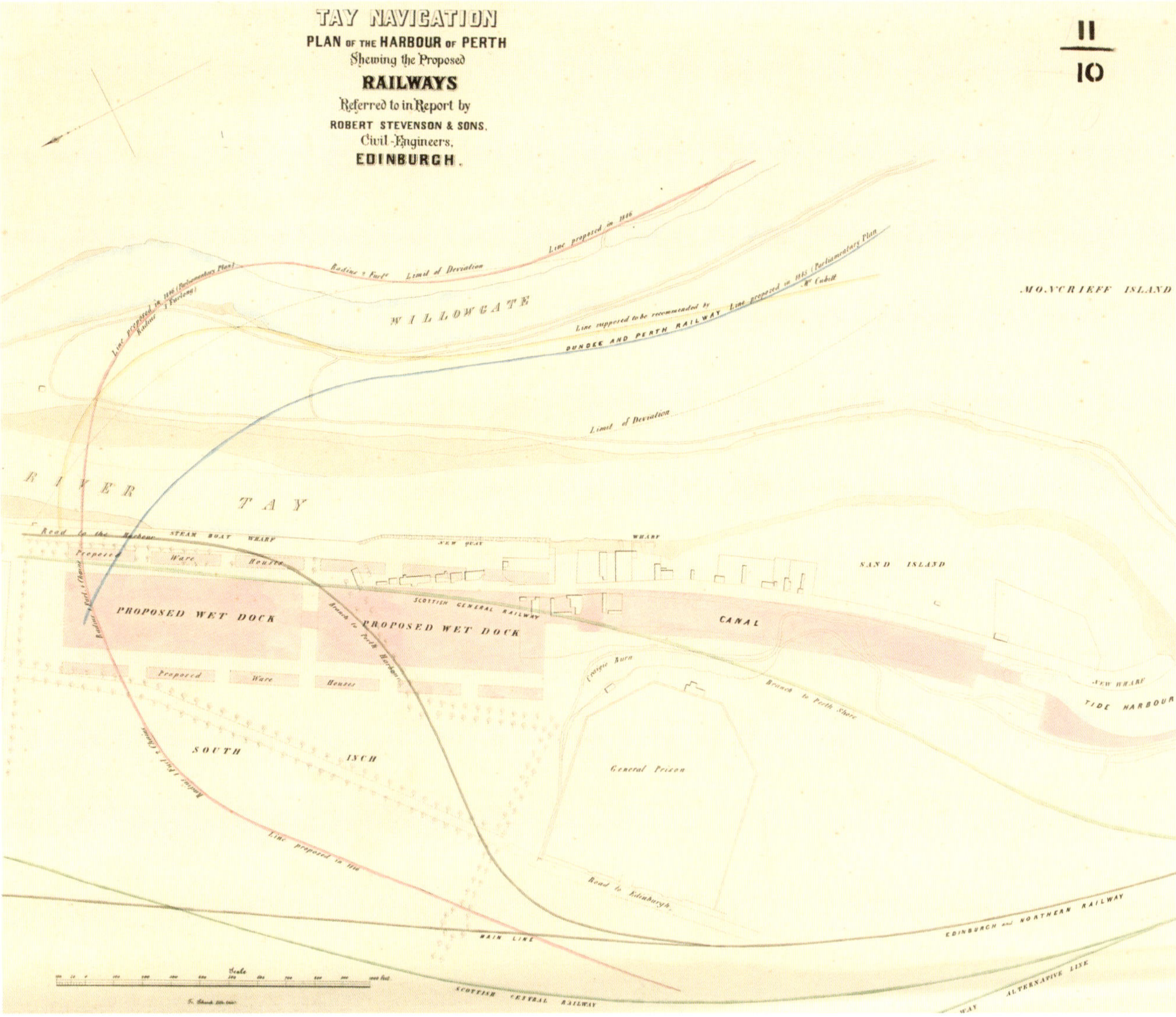

Tay Navigation: 'Plan of the Harbour of Perth Shewing the Proposed Railways', 1846.

Scotland (1828). This atlas was accompanied by Wood's *Descriptive Account of the Principal Towns in Scotland,* published as a separate volume in the same year.

New maps were also required for constructing docks and routes for railways and trams. The National Library of Scotland was fortunate in receiving the principal archives of the Stevenson firm of civil engineers, including detailed infrastructure plans and drawings of harbours, railways, bridges and roads. Amongst several nineteenth century plans of the harbour and railways around Perth is their *Tay Navigation: Plan of the Harbour of Perth Shewing the Proposed Railways* (1846). This captures Perth at an interesting stage between traditional sea transport and new rail communication. In spite of a new tidal basin completed in 1845, and schemes to increase the tidal scour of the channel, the harbour steadily declined in importance as the size of ships increased and freight moved to the railways. The plan shows several new wet docks that were being considered at this time, none of which was completed, and a spaghetti-like network of new railways that were proposed. Within the next four years, the Dundee & Perth Railway, opening in 1847, the Scottish Central Railway (later to be absorbed by the Caledonian), opening in 1848, and the Edinburgh & Northern and Scottish Midland Junction Railway, all converged on Perth. Perth's location made it a key railway centre, and the expansion of the station and city as a result of this are well recorded on maps from this time.

Civic and institutional state mapping

State-funded mapping, particularly through the work of Ordnance Survey, provided new content and purposes on maps, for example, in recording the expanding urban franchise, or for improving sanitation and urban infrastructure. The need for new parliamentary boundaries in implementing the Reform Act of 1832 led to new surveys and plans of seventy-five towns in Scotland, including Perth.[20] The First, or 'Great', Reform Act of that year granted extra seats in the House of Commons to those larger towns and cities whose population had expanded during the Industrial Revolution, and took away parliamentary seats from those towns with a small or declining population. Each burgh was visited by two commissioners, Mr William Murray and Captain J.W. Pringle of the Royal Engineers, and under their direction, plans were drawn up to illustrate the verbal descriptions of the new boundaries. In this work, the urban map based on first-hand information was used to delimit the new political geography of Scotland's cities. The *Reports Upon The Boundaries Of The Several Cities, Burghs, And Towns In Scotland In Respect To The Election Of Members To Serve In Parliament* (1832) also contains information on trade, manufactures and the general circumstances of the individual burgh, its population and number of residential houses, its assessed taxes, together with a detailed description of the proposed new boundary.

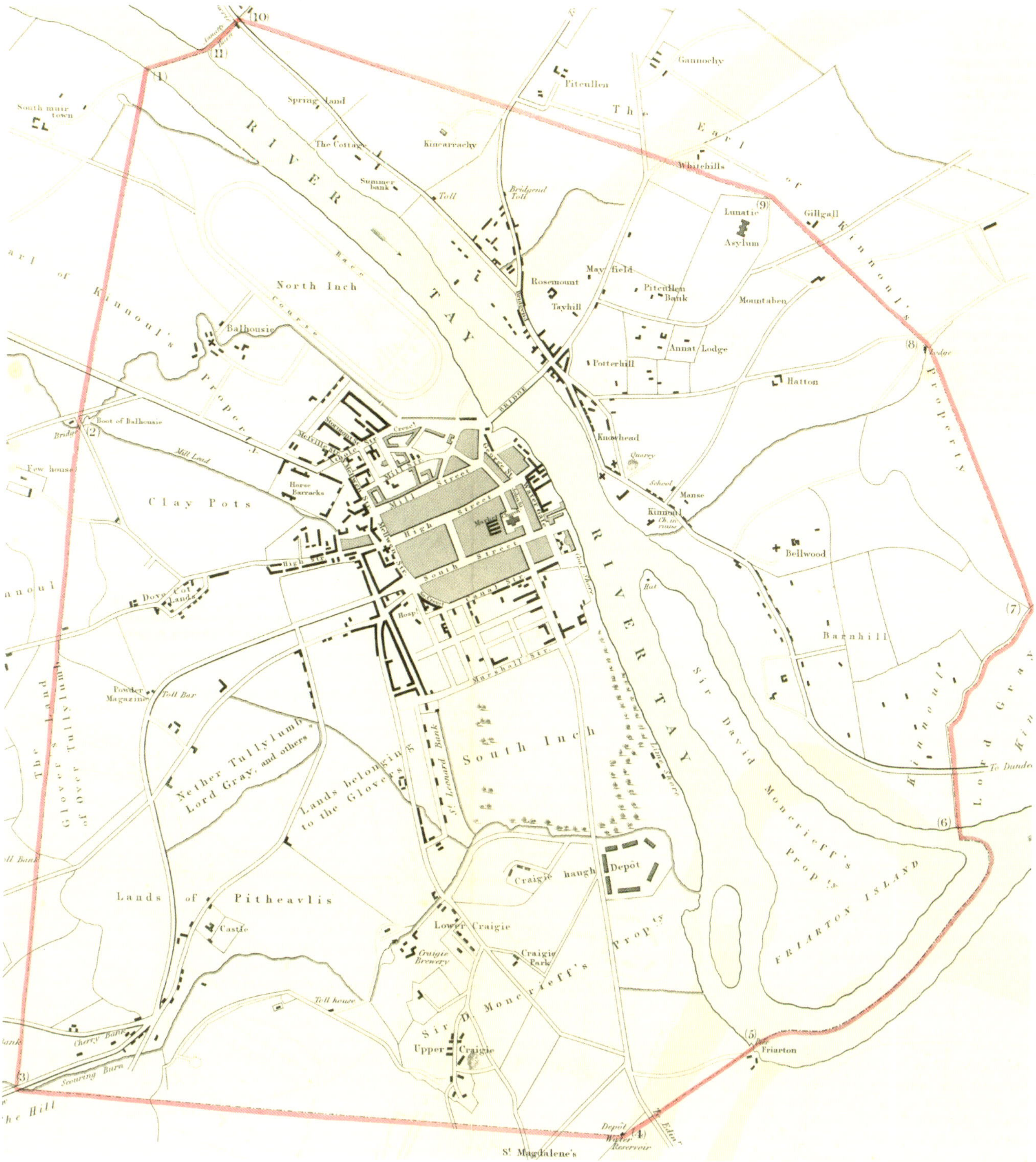

Perth from 'Reports upon the Boundaries of the several Cities, Burghs, and Towns in Scotland in respect to the election of members to serve in Parliament', 1832.

Ordnance Survey began mapping Scotland in the south-west of the country from 1843, proceeding generally in a north-easterly direction, county by county. This was by far the most comprehensive depiction of Perth, with new levels of detail and accuracy, as well as being the first mapping to accurately show contours. Fifty-nine towns (defined as all settlements with over 4,000 residents) were mapped between 1847 (Stranraer) and 1874 (Wick), as part of the initial county map surveys; Perth was first surveyed in 1860, with maps published in 1863, benefiting from the decision in 1855, to survey towns at the uniquely large scale of 126 inches to one mile or 1:500. Perth was covered in twenty-five A0 (double-elephant) sized sheets. The broader motive for this was primarily to improve urban sanitation, as well as clear slums and improve lighting and gas supply. There had been outbreaks of cholera in Perth as recently as 1832 and 1849. Interiors of public buildings were mapped, seating in churches, and even the positions of drying poles and trees in back gardens. Ordnance Survey returned to map Perth again in 1900, 1924 and in the 1960s; from this time, Perth was revised 'continuously' by Ordnance Survey, with new paper maps or more recently, new vector lines in a digital database, whenever significant change occurs on the ground.

Ordnance Survey maps often provided an essential basis for a wide range of other 'derived' maps by other commercial publishers, including the famous Scottish firms of Bartholomew, Gall & Inglis, and W. & A.K. Johnston. Developments in printing and lithography allowed large print runs of maps in colour at low cost, as well as easy updating. These included street maps for visitors, tramway maps, cycling and motoring maps, and maps within Post Office and other trade directories. The Perth Directory was

Detail from the Ordnance Survey 1:10,560 mapping of Perth (Perthshire sheet XCVIII), surveyed 1860, published 1866.

first published in 1837–8, and continued in a similar format until 1939. Many of these directories included a map, and due to the frequency of revision, are very useful for tracking detailed change on the ground. Maps by Ordnance Survey and other publishers also allowed local authorities to use these as a base layer for overlays as planning maps, categorising urban zones and new developments up to the present day.

In the twentieth century, mapping has been revolutionised by aerial reconnaissance, and air photos also provide another visual insight into Perth. After the Second World War, the need for rapid reconnaissance information for post-War planning, and availability of flight crew led to a massive aerial photographic survey of Great Britain (1944–1950), called Operation Revue. The air photos were flown by the Royal Air Force, mainly using wartime Spitfire and Mosquito aircraft, and Ordnance Survey published selected mosaics covering the more built-up parts of Scotland. With Ordnance Survey mapping at least two decades earlier or later than this time for Perth, these air photos are very useful as a topographic record of the city at the end of the Second World War.

Within the last two decades, digital street mapping on computers, mobile devices, or on the dashboard has provided a new and increasingly predominant view of urban spaces such as Perth. This mapping changes rapidly – in content, perspective and quality – and it can also be integrated with a wide range of other information to create new maps. Digital street maps of Perth may seem to offer a very different way of representing the city, but in fact they have close links with earlier maps, in terms of aesthetics, and their multiple perspectives on the city. The largest providers of mapping – Google, Microsoft and Yahoo – provide map content primarily built on detailed street network mapping and so a relatively restricted range of urban features are shown. The multinational corporations that fund, control and sustain these digital map databases promote a standard, globally homogenised rendering of urban spaces compared to earlier maps. In their basis and production, their flexibility of presentation, their instant electronic availability and updating, as well as their limitations, these maps are perhaps as much a window into our current values and society as into the urban landscape of Perth today.

End Notes

1 J. Duncan, 'Early maps of Perth', *Journal of the Perthshire Society of Natural Science* XVIII (2010), pp.10-54.
2 T. McLaren. 'Early plans of Perth', *Transactions of the Perthshire Society of Natural Science* 10 (1938-42), pp. 1-22
3 The maps by Matthew Paris, thirteenth century monk who lived and worked at St Albans, illustrated his *Chronica Majora,* a world history from the Creation down to his own time. They are held in the British Library, and can be viewed online on the *Unveiling of Britain* website (http://www.bl.uk/onlinegallery/onlineex/unvbrit/)
4 The Gough map, named after Richard Gough, the eighteenth century antiquarian who discovered it, is held in the Bodleian Library, Oxford (http://www.goughmap.org/)
5 E.P. Dennison, 'Timothy Pont's portrayal of towns', in Ian C. Cunningham (ed) *The Nation Survey'd: essays on late sixteenth-century Scotland as depicted by Timothy Pont* (East Linton, 2001), pp. 125-138.
6 NLS, MS.1647 Z.03/01d – http://maps.nls.uk/military/record.cfm?id=209
7 Although there are good contemporary plans of the Cromwellian fortifications at Leith, Ayr and Inverness in the 1650s, sadly none survive for Perth, in spite of the enormity of the construction project, with over 140 houses demolished (AA Tait, 'The Protectorate Citadels of Scotland', *Architectural History* 8 (1965), pp. 9-24).
8 NLS, MS.1647 Z.03/02a-c - http://maps.nls.uk/military/placename.cfm?keyword=Perth
9 *Plan of Perth & adjacent places, with a projection of a Cittadel* (NLS, MS.1647 Z.03/01a and b, http://maps.nls.uk/military/record.cfm?id=206)
10 C. Fleet, 'Lewis Petit and his Plans of Scottish Fortifications and Towns, 1714-16', *Cartographic Journal* 44(4), 2007, 329-341.
11 Plan & section of the Kings House & Garden at Perth (1723), NLS, MS.1647 Z.03/03a and b, http://maps.nls.uk/military/record.cfm?id=213; Plans and elevation of the Earl of Gowrie's House, Perth, NLS, Acc.10497 Wade.581 http://maps.nls.uk/military/15.html;
12 Memorial from John Watson, brother of General David Watson to the Treasury, c1770, quoted in full in D.G. Moir, *The Early Maps of Scotland to 1850,* Vol. 1 (Edinburgh, 1973), pp. 105-6
13 Y. O'Donoghue, *William Roy 1726–1790: Pioneer of the Ordnance Survey.* (London, 1977); G. Whittington & A.J.S. Gibson, *The Military Survey of Scotland 1747–1755: A Critique.* Historical Geography Research Series, Number 18 (Norwich, 1986); *The Great Map: the Military Survey of Scotland 1747–55,* with introductory essays by Yolande Hodson, Chris Tabraham and Charles W.J. Withers (Edinburgh, 2007).
14 W. Roy, 'An Account of the Measurement of a Base on Hounslow Heath', *Philosophical Transactions of the Royal Society* LXXV (1785), p. 386
15 The Roy Military Survey of Scotland can be viewed online at http://maps.nls.uk/roy/index.html. The Roy detail of Perth also appears in Duncan, *Early Maps of Perth,* p. 18
16 C. Fleet, 'James Stobie and his surveying of the Perthshire landscape, 1780–1804', *History Scotland,* 5(4), July-August 2005, p.40-47.
17 C. W. J. Withers, *Geography, Science and National Identity: Scotland since 1520* (Cambridge, 2001), p.137.
18 C.D. Waterston, 'Archibald Rutherford (1743–c.1779) parts 1-3', *The Scottish Genealogist* (2010), part 1 LVII (June 2010), 55-63; part 2 LVII(3), 112-125; and part 3 LVII(4), 170-175.
19 D. Graham-Campbell, *Perth: the fair city* (Edinburgh, 1994).
20 Online image of map and accompanying report at: http://maps.nls.uk/towns/reform/page.cfm?id=2619

Ordnance Survey air photo mosaic of Perth, 1948.

The Anglification of Perth?

Charles McKean

Slezer's view of Perth from the north-east c1678. This view (angle corrected) shows a large unwalled town dominated by St John's steeple. The Blackfriars is straight ahead, and the Upper Shore or harbour is visible centre left. Bottom left is the Gowrie Lodging and Monk's Tower (author).

An English county town?

During the nineteenth century, and despite the enormous railway encroachment along its west side, Perth became perhaps the nearest Scotland had to an English county town. Its shops, crafts and facilities such as hotels and auction houses appeared designed for the custom of the regional gentry. In short, it exuded class. It was not a large step, therefore, to assume that the attraction of the Quality to Perth had been a deliberate agenda. That being so, it was entirely reasonable to set up a research project to compare Worcester to Perth in the later eighteenth century.[1] After all, they were both British county towns with the same population, in a comparable geographic relationship to the capital city, both controlling a major bridge joining the heart of the country to the badlands beyond. It was a great surprise, therefore, that the report that came back concluded that the similarities between the Scottish and the English county town were far outweighed by their differences. Perhaps Perth's smiling neo-classical façade, as represented by Rose Terrace and Marshall Place, was misleading.

Perth from the south-east in the 1840s. This peaceful picture represents Perth's county town image, nestling in a bend of the Tay, with the Highland hills in the background and a Highlander in the foreground. Calm and order is underlined by the prominence of the prison in the foreground (author).

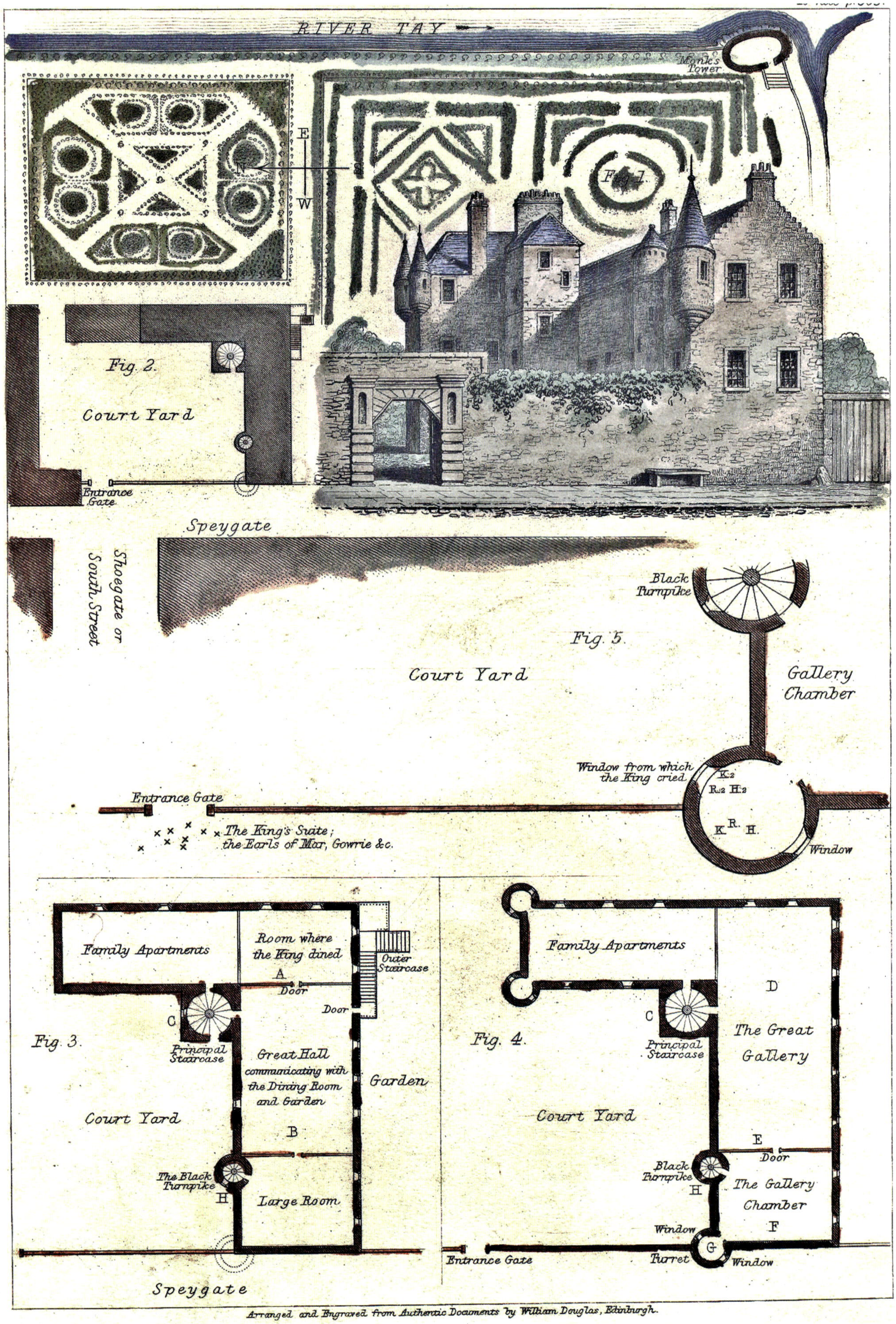

Gowrie Lodging. An early nineteenth century reconstruction of the Gowrie Lodging and its garden, prepared for a book on the Gowrie conspiracy. It gives a good idea of the extent and layout of the garden overlooking the Tay with the Monk's Tower. Gifted to the duke of Cumberland before Culloden in 1746, it remained an artillery barracks until the new one was built. (author).

The nature of Perth beyond the myth

Surprisingly little research has been undertaken on Old Perth, and much has been based upon endless repetitions of the same history: namely that the burgh had been walled and moated, and comprised two streets – High Street and South Street. For a certain period – possibly between 1650 and 1770 – Perth was indeed partly walled in its north-west corner, but to judge from Jean de Beauge's scornful dismissal of its defencelessness in 1547 – when he had suggested the demolition of St John's Kirk and its replacement by a citadel[2] – it shared with all other Scots burghs the characteristic of being fundamentally undefended. Indeed, from the absence of walls in John Slezer's 1680s engraving, it is at least possible that the walls were thrown up in 1715 when the 'rebels' threw up fortifications around its west side. The much vaunted 'moat' was the lade taken from the river Almond which still flows along the north, west and south sides of the town – albeit now mostly underground and no longer servicing industry.

Perhaps Perth had indeed been laid out with two equal streets in its early days, but that was certainly not the case by the early eighteenth century. The heart of the town was the market place, which lay at the east end of the northern street, where it widened as it abutted the upper harbour at North Shore. At the western end of that market place, marked by the mercat cross at the junction of Skinnergate, the street re-orientated itself north of west, to lead out through the town's gate or Turret Port to the road to Glasgow. Until the later eighteenth century, this main road westwards was called North Street; afterwards High Street. The visitor from Edinburgh, however, would enter the town past the substantial remains of Oliver's Fort on the South Inch, through the Spey Port (by the Gowrie Lodging), pass up the Watergate into the market place, left then right into Skinnergate, and then out through Castle Gable Port to the Dunkeld Road. It seems quite clear that the southern street (now South Street) was not only always industrial, but only partially occupied. The name of its gate – Soutargate (or shoemakers') Port – confirms that, as does the presence of Shuttle Row on its south side. Industry tended to follow water, and one part of the lade ran along the back of South Street in what was called the Spey Stank. It is also quite likely that Perth, like Inverness and Dundee, had suffered urban contraction in the seventeenth century, for in the early eighteenth century the Council was petitioned to permit the erection of a Fish Cross and fishmarket in South Street since it was so decayed it needed the regeneration that a fish market would bring. It was still not fully occupied in 1774. Throughout most of the eighteenth century, South Street attracted neither public buildings nor high-ranking occupants; just the Grammar School up a close.

South Street was superseded as the first working district of the burgh in the mid eighteenth century with the growth of the burgh's new industrial suburb lying just outside the burgh boundary to the north and north-west. Here were the mills, a weavers' colony, a linen manufactory,[3] the brewery and – later – the new barracks. Just east, alongside the north mill lade were the skinners' yards and the Horse Fair. The skinners' yards were no mean enterprise: in 1800, 20,000 sheep alone were killed and dressed there.[4]

Perth Harbour in 1798 (author).

Oddly however, at South Street's east end, where it abutted Speygate, things were significantly different. Here, and in Watergate, lay the houses and lodgings of the regional nobility and aristocracy: the earls of Errol and Kinnoull, and the great lodging of the earls of Gowrie – which, for most of the period, was in use as an artillery barracks.

It is curious how little of this Perth survives and, paradoxically, how much. The noble town houses have mostly gone, although Watergate still hangs on, sheltering ancient fabric behind later facades. The market place, with its tolbooth, Council House, weighhouse, mercat cross and library has been so obliterated that there is not the slightest surviving vestige of the ancient heart of the burgh, and its location remains unknown to most Perth natives, likewise the harbour at North Shore. Yet North (now High) Street presents a douce and regular largely eighteenth century demeanour on its north side, masking much older fabric and urban patterns in the closes behind.

Perth in the Age of Improvement

In some ways, how Perth's burgh council tackled the processes of improvement over the eighteenth century was very typical of other Scots burghs: but in other ways, quite distinctive. As might be expected, it took action early to remove thatched roofs,[5] deal with derelict sites, crack down on timber-galleried facades (although some – particularly the Kinnoull Lodging in Watergate – survived into the mid twentieth century), and required staircases projecting into the street to be rebuilt at the rear (some of which rebuilding can be seen in, for example, Skinnergate). On the principal streets, this was more or less complete by 1770. Paving and lighting began, naturally, with the market place, and gradually extended westwards toward Turret Port and northwards into Skinnergate and Castle Gable Port; and, as in a number of other burghs, required repaving as different types and strengths of stone were tested.[6] It was initially restricted to the burgh's principal streets, and there was no assumption that it would necessarily apply to all streets or even all closes. The inhabitants of South Street had to make petition after petition for their street to be brought up to the same standard quite a long time later.[7] However, in terms of repair, maintenance and general convenience, Perth was substantially improved by the 1770s, and much of North Street had been refronted or rebuilt with the regular and fashionable new apartments (don't be distracted by the fact that contemporaries used the term 'house' for an apartment) that characterise High Street today. Many Scots burghs had apartments above arcaded merchants' booths and Perth had at least some, at the west end of the market place.[8]

However, as was fairly typical elsewhere, it was the growth in commerce and wheeled traffic that impelled change. Goods landed at North Shore had to get out to the country, and those going north had to negotiate the tight turn into Skinnergate avoiding the mercat cross. So the cross was removed in 1765, and the junction widened.[9]

Where Perth was less typical, however, was in its treatment of its fleshmarket and its tolbooth. By the 1770s, most significant Scots burghs had relocated the fleshmarket from the centre of town out to the periphery, where it would less disturb the noses of the polite. Perth, on the other hand, rebuilt its fleshmarket at the centre of town, on the backlands of College Yards, just to the west of St John's.[10] Equally, a prosperous burgh such as Perth might have been expected to be early in creating a fashionable new town house or assembly rooms, the first wave of which occurred in the 1760–70s. Not so. Perth's tolbooth, set in the north-west corner of the market place, had been fashionably remodelled in the early seventeenth century, and extended about a century later with a baroque Council House above the

Bridge and Monk's Tower by Clerk of Eldin. This 1790s drawing by John Clerk of Eldin shows the dominance of the new bridge. Smaller vessels still enter the harbour immediately downstream of it. The huge oval tower on the left was a summerhouse in the gardens of the Gowrie Lodging and had fine interior decoration (author).

George Street This street, developed between 1770 and 1776, was the principal entry into Perth from the new bridge. It was cut through three long rigs, not entirely regularly, and replaced the Castle Gable Port as the principal entry into the town. It contained the Perth Bank, some inns, and the burgh's principal social venue – the Glovers' Hall (author).

weighhouse, which formed the eastern wall of the market. An inadequate prison building had been added behind on the rigs to the north. Although various improvements were made both to the prison and to the Council House – the latter being ennobled with a raised ceiling and rather grander plasterwork[11] – Perth's Council does simply not appear to be moved to emulate the fine new civic buildings of, say, Dundee, Edinburgh, Glasgow, Inverness, Montrose or Forfar. It was only in the 1790s that the Council became frustrated with their current arrangements; and when they reached that point, their impulse was less to build a more fashionable town house in the ancient location than to abandon that location and begin again elsewhere.

The impact of the bridge

Perth was, and remained, a transport hub, and this factor had the greatest impact upon the Georgian fabric: roads in the eighteenth century and railways in the nineteenth. The impulse began with the 1756 subscription for a new bridge across the Tay, whose foundation stone was laid ten years later, and which opened in 1771. Although the burgh council contributed, the initiative had come from the county, and the lion's share of the finance from the Commission for the Forfeited Estates. The town's principal headache was to provide the necessary new communication between the bridge and the market place now that the old route down through the skinners' yards and up the narrow Skinnergate was deemed inadequate. So a new street was planned along the ridge, and three plots and their rigs were purchased on the north side of the market place. Purchase took place by negotiation, and the fact that it was not yet fully opened into the market place by the time of Rutherford's map in 1774 indicates a slow and not fully planned process. That it was less effective than originally conceived is evident from the fact that the plan had been for the new street to face into a widened Watergate, thus producing a clear north–south route through the burgh.[12] It was blocked by the obdurate owner of the building on the north-west corner of the Watergate who refused to play ball.

The new street, eventually named George Street, was more of a place than a street, swelling out in the centre rather that displaying the geometric rigidities of, say, Edinburgh's New Town. It was feued out as inns and apartments above shops and quickly became fashionable. Here was constructed the Glovers' Hall, for many years the location of Perth's most fashionable assemblies, and the Perth Bank. In essence, this was a central urban street rather than a suburban one. Nonetheless, it took almost twenty years to complete and be fully paved, indicative of a lack of Council resolution or funds. Moreover, once it had debouched into the market place, however, the latter's diminishing sense of enclosure was exploded: and the kink that indicated its junction with North Street was largely smoothed out. From the harbour at North Shore to the Turret or Red Bridge Port, the street was now known as High Street.

It was perhaps inevitable that the approach from the south, from Edinburgh, would be next. The Council had opened a new street between South Street and the Spey Stank in 1769[13] and thereafter there was rapid feuing of the Spey Stank and the Spey Ridge. Called variously Princess or Princes Street, the new road eventually led south to the Long Causeway, and was probably why the ditches of Oliver's Fort were filled in and its ramparts removed (thus causing the relocation of the town's stables). Since it was laid out on an axis with St John's steeple, and Kirkgate and Skinnergate to the north, the new street could not be carried straight through the town, leaving the traveller to have to turn right, and then left again into the narrow Watergate. The initial intention was to widen Watergate since it would then face directly up George Street; but owners still proving difficult, it was eventually decided to construct an entirely new street on the line of Salt Vennel, which brought it along the eastern edge of the parish kirk. Again, built in sections and laid out relatively ad hoc over the next fifteen years – the consequence of the vagaries of negotiation rather than having sought powers of compulsory purchase – the street attracted great criticism for its humdrum nature. This new street of mixed commercial and residential finally carried the name of St John's Street. If anything, however, St John's Street confirmed the north-eastern end of Perth as its elite area.[14]

By the 1790s, therefore, Perth remained a fundamentally Scottish burgh with its public buildings in their ancient locations, its now square whinstone-paved (or cobbled) streets improved by the removal of projecting stairs, galleries and other obstructions and regularised street frontages, with much wider new streets feeding the traffic through. South Street and Spey Stank remained largely workaday – a linen manufactory, a stables and a riding school had been added, but Perth's new industries were now deeply embedded to the west and north-west. Moreover, despite the fact that its inhabitants employed four times as many female servants as their equivalents in Dundee,[15] social life in Dundee was, so far as public buildings was concerned, considerably more sophisticated. Whereas Perth residents were dependent either upon the Glovers' Hall or the ballrooms in inns like the Salutation for their assemblies and routs, Dundee's had the choice of the splendid Trades House, or the smart new Seamen's Fraternity Hall by the shore and would soon be adding the Thistle Hall in Union Street, never mind the splendid Guildry chamber in William Adam's Town House or the Ballroom in the New Inn. None of Perth's new streets had shown even the flawed decision-making and control of Dundee's Castle and Tay Streets. The burgh was, in short, falling behind.

Rebranding the burgh

In 1792, however, perhaps inspired by the Council's belated decision to feu out Charlotte Street leading to the bridge, Thomas Anderson sought the Council's agreement to his developing the lands of the Blackfriars, at the north end of town, 'on a proper plan', if the Council would extend the royalty accordingly. This was the first herald of what became called Perth's 'system of improvement', devised by Anderson, his son-in-law Thomas Hay Marshall, and their architect, the Edinburgh architect and property developer Robert Reid,[16] which would encompass the north, east and south of the burgh.

Anderson wanted to begin by building a street of 'good houses fronting the North Inch' and to regularise his design so that it led into Charlotte Street. In return, he wanted to straighten out the mill lade for better effect, the diversion of Dunkeld road, and an assurance from the Council that it would not tolerate construction on the North Inch in all time coming.[17] That being granted, Anderson prepared a scheme for a grid-iron suburb against the west side of the newly improved North Inch, which by the addition of a statue not only became a fashionable racecourse, but was used by the burgh elite as the ***parade*** – the Rotten Row – where people went to take the air and converse. Equally, the passage between this smart new suburb and the High Street, along George Street, all lit by lustre globes, became the town's urban parade.

This view of the High Street shows the regular refronting of older apartment buildings undertaken in the mid eighteenth century, to provide gracious living. This was the centre of the improved burgh until the development of the North Inch (author).

Rose Terrace. The most fully realised part of the plan for improving Perth by Thomas Hay Marshall and the architect Robert Reid. Effectively the eastern wall of the northern 'new town', it comprised dignified terraced houses facing the North Inch with the new Perth Academy at the centre (© PKHT).

The first step in this plan was the construction of Atholl Crescent, whose east-most bookend house contains much older fabric (perhaps from the Blackfriars) behind its Georgian façade; but the cynosure was the classical wall lining the west side of the North Inch, named Rose Terrace after Anderson's flighty daughter. Rose was married to the future lord provost Thomas Hay Marshall, who developed the terrace with, as they said in Edinburgh, 'houses after the English manner' rather than the flatted apartments that had been built in George and High Streets. At the centre of the terrace were the new Seminaries – a building designed in 1802 by Marshall's architect friend Reid[18] to contain two educational institutions: the ancient Grammar School relocated from South Street, and Perth Academy – the more modern scientific institution that had been founded in 1760. Despite this splendid beginning, the grid-iron northern suburb remained incomplete, and the houses behind Rose Terrace were much more quotidian. Although the development reinforced north Perth as the elite end of town, the west-most street in Anderson's plan extended down the west perimeter of the town centre to the South Inch – indicating possible unfinished business.

The Council was now, particularly with Marshall as provost, developing its own agenda which, given the provost's close relationship with Robert Reid, was planned to be realised through him. The lade running down the west side of town was culverted and transformed into Methven Street, and as it turned east along Spey Stank it was likewise covered over in 1801 to become Canal Street.[19] The trustees of the James VI Hospital then decided to feu out their lands facing on to the South Inch at the bottom end of this proposed street. Although they had a relatively exclusive development in mind – they wanted it gated and barred to commercial traffic – their ambition was restricted to a few streets of well-built douce stone cottages focused upon King Street. The real impact upon South Inch, however, lay to the east, toward the river. Here Marshall planned a grandiose development of, originally, four great terraces of houses developed in the round – that is to say houses facing north as well as south. They would frame South Inch in a much more splendiferous way than did Rose Terrace at the North Inch, and present a triumphant façade to all those entering the burgh from Edinburgh. It was, indeed, named after the proposer and inspirer – the provost himself.

There was, however, something seriously aberrational about this notion. First, Marshall Place was a long way – two or three street-blocks – south of the town proper, and left available vacant land between it and the burgh. The new terraces were thus placed at the mercy of whoever built in the gap in between. Secondly, south Perth had always been industrious if not industrial, and the Spey Stank (Canal Street) and Spey Ridge had both been colonised in an ad hoc manner for manufactories, stables etc. Unsurprisingly, this was where the gas works and water works would settle within a few years: not the most choice neighbours for Perth's most expensive street, its equivalent of Edinburgh's stupendous Great King Street – same date, same architecture – if rather grander in scale. Moreover, Reid's first proposal had been for expensive detached houses, which he then modified into the huge palace blocks of terrace houses. Only two south-facing terraces were completed – almost twenty years later – and the northern wing of these city blocks was swiftly dropped. Marshall Place was in the wrong location, and the elite were not prepared to swap north Perth for south Perth. So what brought it there?

Perth's 'system of improvement'

When James Cant, Perth's contemporary historian, described the burgh's urban ambitions as a *system of improvement* in 1805, he was not referring just to the two 'new towns' north and south, but to the buckle proposed to tie them together – namely an urban parade running along the riverbank with a civic megastructure half way up, and a social centre at its head. For two things had changed in the Perth of the 1790s which lead the Council – inspired by the visionary Marshall – to contemplate significant urban restructuring. The first was that the condition of the prison had become insupportable,[20] and during its quest for a new site, the County gentlemen indicated that they would go halves since they also had an increasing demand for a prison.[21] There the matter lay for a decade, until one of the gentry revived the proposal under the terms of jointly building a bridewell[22] and apparently invited the architect James Gillespie, son of the sheriff depute, to design one. (As Gillespie Graham, Gillespie was later to design Cupar's equivalent county hall and Edinburgh's outstanding Moray Place).

Gillespie's great proposal, costed at £10,000,[23] remained abortive, but it stimulated the Council to broader ambition: a new street running along the riverbank to the rear of the Watergate rigs, between the bridge and the Coal Shore (South Shore), with the new civic complex located upon it. With the erection of the new barracks to the north-west of town, the old artillery barracks – namely the Earl of Gowrie's great lodging, that had been originally granted to the Duke of Cumberland before Culloden – had now become available and with its gardens, it occupied the premier position on the banks of the Tay. The civic project, however, had in the meantime swelled. In addition to the bridewell, it was also to contain courtrooms and *all necessary apartments* – implying that the Council was thinking of moving the administration from its old tolbooth and Council Chamber.[24]

Two months on, Robert Reid reinforced his position as Perth's architect by presenting his first plans for Marshall Place; so when the larger civic project was revived three years later, Reid (and presumably his patron Marshall) had little difficulty in seeing off the challenge from James Gillespie and presented plans of his own – ironically at the same Council meeting when the feuars of Marshall Place petitioned for the change of design from individual houses to terraces because they were too costly (not an unusual outcome for Reid).[25] In 1805, however, the year that Cant first referred to Perth's 'system of improvement', the Council set out its urban ambition. At the top end, where the bridge, George Street and the new street all met, there was to be a Coffee Room on the Tontine model below a new town hall, which Marshall naturally asked Reid to design.[26] Cant also recorded that in addition to the Coffee House, the Council planned a new Assembly Rooms adjacent, presumably to replace the Glovers' Hall. A new riparian street would be opened as an urban parade, which would lead down to the other civic buildings for burgh and County on the Gowrie site. Two months later, the Council awarded Marshall a plate worth 200 guineas 'for promoting plans beneficial to the Revenue & highly ornamental to the city and neighbourhood'.[27] In the meantime, materials from the demolishing Gowrie House were being used to pave lesser streets – first Princes Street, then Skinnergate, Castle Gable and finally South Street – in that order.[28]

The joint County/Burgh civic complex stalled in 1808 – perhaps because the town now expected their civic needs to be met by the proposed Tontine at the north end (ignoring the fact that most Tontine projects ended in abject failure). In any case, the burgh council made the extraordinary decision to withdraw and relinquish its share in the Gowrie site civic centre and make it over to the Perth Theatre – provided that the latter conformed with the elevation provided by Robert Reid.[29] That assumed that Reid's presumably classical town hall façade would have made an equally appropriate theatre façade. Those with a mordant view of local politics might well have concurred. But what on earth would the County have made of this cheapening of their grand project? Not long afterwards the County called the burgh to a reckoning, forcing it to grant sufficient space on the Gowrie site

Marshall Place. Developed from 1804, Marshall Place was intended to line South Inch similar to the way Rose Terrace lines North Inch. However, being too far from the town's elite northern corner, only two blocks of a far larger scheme were realised, and it took some 20 years to do so (author).

for 'County buildings to be built and furnished without any claim on the town, the judiciary hall or court room'. By one of these delicious ironies with which Perth was so well endowed, at the same Council meeting that the burgh opted out of its great civic project, David Wedderburn from London offered fifty Guineas to support the Council's intention 'to erect a Monument to the Memory of the late Provost Marshall', as he wished to contribute to the accomplishment of 'an object which is so interesting to the Corporation & to the City & combining ornament & utility in the Execution of so laudable a plan'. It was his

> ardent wish to embrace every opportunity of promoting any measures which the Corporation may adopt as conductive to the welfare & improvement of the Town, & nothing can be better calculated for these purposes than the plan now in agitation, which will do honor to the dead, be an ornament to the City, & tend to keep up that Public Spirit which has so long & so eminently distinguished those who have been entrusted with the Management of your Public concerns.[30]

It is clear, however, that with Marshall's death, the public spirit and burning desire to ornament the city had come to a halt.

The year that the Seminaries finally opened (1809) was also the year that the Council finally decided to close down its Tontine project[31] and, presumably, remain behind in their old civic buildings – as they did until mid century when a new civic building was constructed in place of the fleshmarket in College Yards. Contemporary plans show that the street along the Tay riverbank as constructed, but although the records imply that some action was taken thereto,[32] the plans were before their time. John Wood's 1822 plan shows the riverside without Tay Street, and still inhibited by the gardens, walls and buildings extending east from Watergate.

The County, however, was not as inhibited as the burgh, and pressed ahead with its plans. Reid's designs proving too expensive (and his patron/friend Marshall dead), the County eventually employed Sir Robert Smirke, the celebrated neo-classical London architect who was then rebuilding Kinfauns Castle, to design a courthouse, office and prison, and work began on the river façade in 1817. Marshall Place never managed to earn the *cachet* of north Perth – even though it represented the grander ambition – and it remained terminally tainted by the commercial and industrial uses that engulfed it. These were underscored by the arrival of the railway, when the Dundee and Perth railway ran its viaduct along Spey Ridge to give it the height to cross the Tay, effectively at the north end of Marshall Place's gardens at the level of their piano nobile. Indeed, the amenity of South Inch itself was only protected from being the site of several competing railway stations by the Council having to plead its case before both Parliament and the Board of Trade.

It seems clear that until the late 1790s, Perth had followed the steady improvement pattern largely typical of Scotland – save in its lack of interest in urban grandeur and its refusal to make the most of the opportunities that arose from, for example, the creation of new streets. By contrast with Montrose, it was largely uninterested in new public buildings but deeply encouraging to anything to do with manufacture. Indeed, it appears to have had less interaction with its regional gentry than Montrose – until, that is, the County began to agitate for a prison or bridewell in the 1790s. It appears that Perth regarded itself fundamentally as a working – if not industrial – town. That all changed with Anderson, his son-in-law Marshall, and the small coterie of burgesses who supported him – pre-eminently the mason Bailie John McEwan, contractor of St Paul's church, who attempted to rescue Marshall Place by purchasing multiple plots.

Perth Shore in the 1820s. This view from the east bank shows the completed Sheriff Court by Sir Robert Smirke on the Gowrie site with the embankment for Tay Street in front of it. The rest of the street remains unbuilt (author).

Cant's term 'system of improvement' had referred to a coherent plan for the systematic rebuilding of civic Perth under the hand of a single designer – Robert Reid – which comprised flanking terraces to north and south, and the entire reconstruction of the eastern side of the burgh, with a County complex to the south, on the Gowrie land, and a civic complex to the north, by the bridge, joined together by a spacious new parade called Tay Street. Such ambition was staggering. What Perth planned was not much more, in terms of content, than Ayr was contemplating at about the same time. The difference was the grandeur of a single unified architectural concept extending from one end of the town to the other in the area of highest value – namely the waterside. Only Rose Terrace and Marshall Place were built: the only two parts of the scheme, in short, dependent upon the private rather than the public purse. When the County decided to go it alone on the Gowrie site, it was no longer participating in the broader scheme, and ditched Reid for the Earl of Kinnoull's own architect, Sir Robert Smirke, thus forfeiting the overall sense of urban coherence. Tay Street itself was not completed until the 1870s.

It is surely significant that Perth rarely chose to represent itself to outsiders in the early nineteenth century by images either of Marshall Place, or even of the old town centre and St John's. Instead, the preferred vision was of the only part of the burgh that had achieved the necessary image of coherent and extensive high-quality modernity – namely of smart, modern north Perth, framed by the bridge and Rose Terrace. Occasionally there would be a view from the south-east across the river, showing the river frontage, Smirke's magnificent courthouse and Adam Anderson's extraordinarily classical water works (now the J. D. Fergusson Art Gallery): neo-classical court, neo-classical temple, and regular palace-fronted neo-classical terraces. Thus was the image of neo-classical 'English' county town shaped, adopted and fostered.

But it was a fiction – a veneer. Both Rose Terrace and Marshall Place were elegant facades that concealed thriving and growing industry behind; and as the century wore on, those favoured neo-classical scenes became subverted by industrial smokestacks rising behind.

End Notes

1 S. Mee 'Perth and Worcester: How similar were two British towns in the late eighteenth century?' Dundee University M Litt Dissertation 2007.
2 J. De Beaugué, in Hume Brown, *Early Travellers in Scotland* (new ed, Edinburgh, 1973).
3 Perth and Kinross Council Archive (PKCA) Town Council Minutes (TCM) 15.11.1762
4 T. Garnett, *Observations of a Tour Through the Highlands* (London, 1800), Vol 11, p. 98.
5 Frequently condemned but finally totally banned on 10 November 1781 (TCM)
6 PKCA TCM 6.5.1771
7 PKCA TCM 2.4.1792
8 PKCA TCM 15.11.1762
9 PKCA TCM 1.4.1765
10 PKCA TCM 5.3.1764
11 PKCA TCM 4.4.1776
12 PKCA TCM 7.11.1769
13 PKCA TCM 18.12.1769
14 PKCA TCM 13.12.1799
15 B. Harris, 'Towns, improvement and Cultural Change in Georgian Scotland' in Urban History 32 (2006), p.199.
16 PKCA TCM 4.1.1802
17 PKCA TCM 15.3.1792
18 PKCA TCM 4.1.1802
19 PKCA TCM 2.3.1801
20 PKCA TCM 5.11.1792
21 PKCA TCM 7.10.1793
22 PKCA TCM 1.2.1802
23 PKCA TCM 1.3.1802
24 That is was indeed the intention becomes clear from the later minute of 6 June 1808 when the Council decided to relinquish that part of the new civic complex on the Gowrie site and make it over to the theatre. PKCA TCM 6.6.1808.
25 PKCA TCM 4.11.1805
26 PKCA TCM 2.6.1806, 7.7.1806.
27 PKCA TCM 29.9.1806
28 PKCA TCM 2.2.1807
29 PKCA TCM 6.6.1808
30 PKCA TCM 5.9.1808
31 PKCA TCM 5.6.1809
32 PKCA TCM 5.2.1810

Dr Adam Anderson and Sir Robert Pullar: benefactors of Perth[1]

Rhoda Fothergill

Introduction

Perth, in early times a small settlement at the strategic lowest bridging point of the River Tay, played its part over the centuries in Scottish history. After the religious troubles of the sixteenth and seventeenth centuries, and the political Jacobite Risings of the eighteenth century, textile manufacturing flourished in more settled times and trade developed thanks to the completion of the Perth Bridge in 1772. The French Revolution followed by the Napoleonic Wars interrupted trade, and in the 1860s the supply of cotton to this country was interrupted by the Civil War in America. There was a significant downturn in the economy in the early decades of the nineteenth century. Weavers' wages dropped from thirty shillings to seven or six shillings per week. With low wages and unemployment the weavers became fractious and radical, influenced by the ideals of liberty and equality of the French and the writings of Thomas Paine in *The Rights of Man*. The clamour for Parliamentary Reform grew louder and more insistent, leading to the Reform Act of 1832 and enfranchisement. With the advent of the railways, rail networks were gradually formed. The General Terminus at Perth opened in 1848. Towns and villages in Scotland, England and Wales were linked. By the mid-nineteenth century trade was expanding at home and abroad and the Great Exhibition of 1851 was the showcase for the prosperity and success of Great Britain and her colonies.

Dr Adam Anderson

At the beginning of the nineteenth century the Perth Grammar School in St Ann's Lane, founded in the twelfth century, and the Academy of Literature and Science established in 1761 at the north-west of St John's Kirk lacked suitable and sufficient accommodation. Provost Thomas Hay Marshall gifted a site in Rose Terrace for a fine new building, which was designed by Edinburgh architect Robert Reid. Completed in 1807 it housed the two schools, each retaining its own Rector and curriculum. In 1809 the Magistrates appointed Mr Adam Anderson to the post of Master of the Academy of Perth.

Born in Tulliallan parish on 29 June 1780, Anderson was the son of a Kincardine shipmaster. His mother, Ann Moon, belonged to Errol. In 1797 young Mr Anderson matriculated at St Andrews University where he studied Greek, Latin, natural philosophy, mathematics and divinity. He was an enthusiastic student and a quick learner and, on completing his course, he accepted a post as tutor to the three sons of Mr Greenhill of Fern in Angus. To their father's delight and approval the boys made excellent progress. Adam Anderson continued as tutor and became guardian of his pupils during their studies in Edinburgh. He took the opportunity there of furthering his own studies, attending courses in science, particularly in chemistry, a forefront discipline in the nineteenth century. An excellent communicator with extensive knowledge of mathematical and scientific subjects he had patience, commitment and a good rapport with his pupils. Already are seen the qualities of his character which later brought him to the notice of the Perth Town Council as a trusted diplomat and reliable advisor, arbitrator and mediator in difficult situations and an excellent lecturer and communicator as he committed himself to the modernisation of Perth in the first half of the nineteenth century.

Perth Town Council Minute of 9 August 1809 records Mr Adam Anderson's appointment, which clearly reflects the Council's desire to advance its reputation for promoting a scientific-based education in the town. The Town Council retained Adam Anderson's salary to provide his predecessor, Alexander Gibson, with a pension, Anderson having his teaching fees as an income. However, in 1811 he was granted an annuity of £50 until on the

Dr Adam Anderson (1783-1846) by John MacLaren Barclay dated 1847 (courtesy of Perth Museum and Art Gallery).

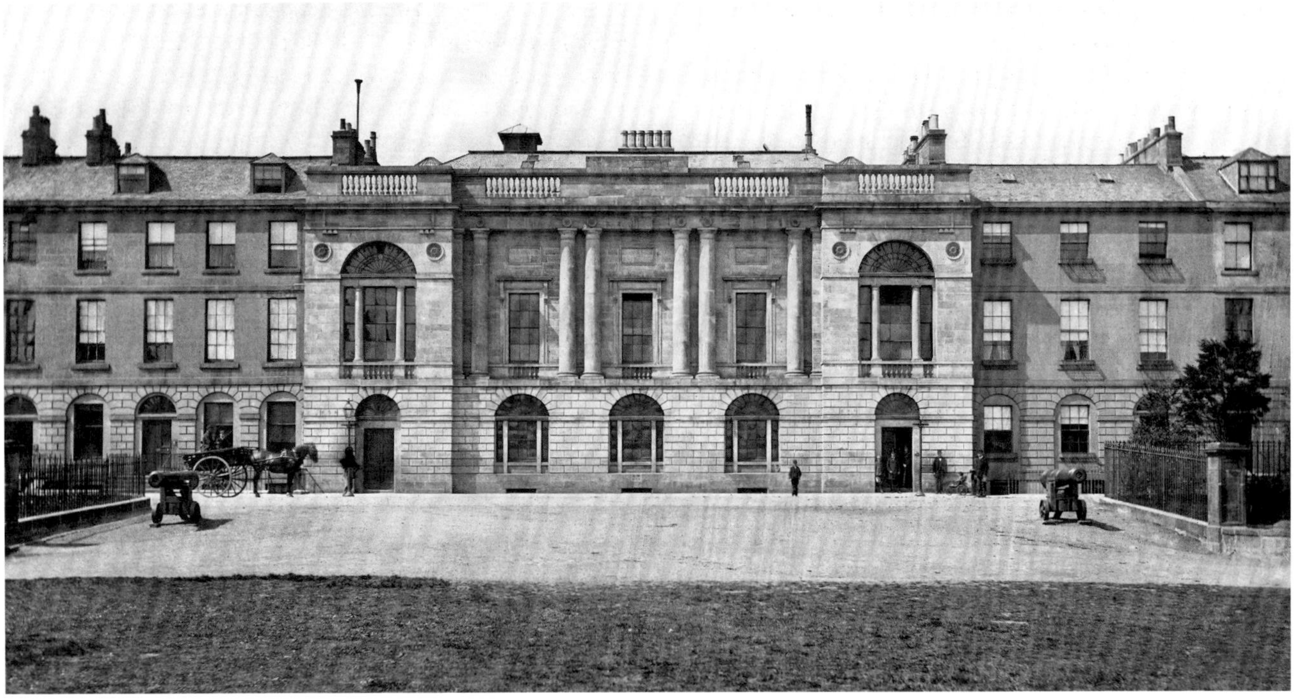

The Academy of Perth, Rose Terrace, opened 1807 moved 1932 (courtesy of Perth Museum and Art Gallery).

death of Alexander Gibson in 1814 he received his full salary of £100. In October 1809 the newly appointed Rector illuminated the front of the Academy by means of variegated lamps to mark the fiftieth anniversary of the King's accession to the throne. The display included a festoon and crown with a medallion below showing the date of the accession – 1760. There were also two diamonds and an illuminated picture of George III with the Latin Motto PATER PATRIAE at the foot of the display.

Perth Courier *Thursday, September 14, 1809*

THE ACADEMY OF PERTH

Will commence its annual Course the 2d of October.
The following branches of Science, will be taught by Mr. Anderson.
Mathematics, comprehending the theory and practice of Arithmetic: Algebra: the theory of Plane Geometry, and its application to the measurement of Heights and Distances; the mensuration and division of Plane Surfaces; Land-surveying, &c.: the theory of Solid Geometry, and its application to the mensuration of Solids; the measurement of Wood, Stone, &c.; and Gauging: the Projection of Solid Bodies, and their Sections or Planes; Perspective: Conic Sections: Fortification: Spherical Trigonometry; Geography; Navigation. &c.
Mechanical Philosophy, comprehending Dynamics: Descriptive and Physical Astronomy: Projectiles, and its application to gunnery: Mechanics: Hydrostatics; Levelling; Hydraulics: Pneumatics; Acoustics; Aerostatics, Meteorology: Magnetism: Electricity: Galvanism: Optics.
Chemistry, and its application to the Arts.
In the practical department of the above branches, to which particular attention will be paid, Mr. Anderson will be assisted by Mr. Wright, who will also teach Book-keeping, and Accounts in all their varieties.
Writing, and Practical Arithmetic, by Mr. Ashmore.
Drawing, and Painting, by Mr. Junor.
Modern Languages, by Mr. Whitehead.
Mr. W. will open a Class for beginners in the French Language, from 4 to 5: and another for those who are more advanced, from 5 to 6 afternoon. He will also give private lessons in German, and Italian; and open a public class for Spanish, to be conducted, as much as possible, through the medium of the French.

The newly appointed Rector threw himself wholeheartedly into his task of increasing the numbers attending the Academy though that took a little longer than he had anticipated. His request for a considerable amount of scientific and mathematical equipment – maps, celestial and terrestrial globes and books for the library as well as scientific apparatus and chemical substances with cupboards to hold the latter – raised the eyebrows of an acquiescent Town Council! The request granted, the Magistrates soon appreciated the increase in the number of scholars and the rising reputation of their Rector and the Academy. Pupils from his classes in mathematics on passing into the mathematics course at St Andrews University were able to join the second year of that course. His method of teaching was always to study the theory with many practical applications of it in demonstrations and experiments.

Adam Anderson was a member of the East Church of St John's Kirk to which charge Rev James Esdaile was appointed in 1810. They became firm friends and both were members of Perth Literary and Antiquarian Society. Adam Anderson, also a member of the Royal Society of Edinburgh, was awarded a Fellowship of that Society in 1820. On coming to Perth he joined the Perth Literary and Antiquarian Society in December 1809, soon becoming superintendent of its natural history department and with his scientific acquirements undertook the classification of mineralogical and natural history specimens of the Society's museum collection.

Rev Esdaile wrote prolifically on religious matters, particularly against voluntaryism in the 1820s. In 1821, when holding office as Treasurer in the Perthshire Bible Society, Adam Anderson addressed a meeting on 'The Duty of Christians of contributing to the Dissemination of the Scriptures'. This address was published. Both men remained loyal to the Established Church at the period of the Disruption of 1843.

However, it was Adam Anderson's many articles detailing his researches, experiments and discoveries on a wide range of mathematical and scientific subjects which became extensively known when published in the *Edinburgh Philosophical Journal,* in the papers of the Royal Society of Edinburgh and by his contributions to the *Edinburgh Encyclopaedia* and to the *Encyclopaedia Britannica* in which his subject was gas lighting.

By the late eighteenth century Perth's dim streets and dimmer vennels were lit by cruise lamps and Greenland whale oil, which gave poor illumination. From 1780 onwards attempts, with limited success, were made to solve the problem and street lighting was remitted to the Police Commission on its formation in 1811. However, the financial position of Perth Town Council and the Police Commission did not permit either to undertake a costly scheme of gas lighting as in Glasgow and Edinburgh so it became a private enterprise. In 1822 Perth Gas Light Company – a joint stock venture – was formed and £10,000 in £25 shares was raised. Undoubtedly paramount to the venture's success was the inclusion of Adam Anderson, chemist and engineer, in the Board of Directors. Always public-spirited here was opportunity to benefit his fellow citizens by using his scientific knowledge. Cattle market ground at Canal Street was acquired, a very convenient site for the proposed gas works beside the south branch of the Town's lade, the water of which was used for cooling in the production of coal gas. The necessary coal was landed at the Coal Shore lying at the entry of the lade into the River Tay.

A simple plan of the gas works is shown on an early map of Perth with the proposed positions of the street lamps. The half moon of horizontal retorts, the gas house and other buildings are marked. In the yard was a tar well. Requests to bury the tar on the South Inch received a firm and speedy response in the negative from the Town Council. One use of interest was during the cholera epidemic in 1832 when several tar barrels were burnt in the Watergate to fumigate the area where so many deaths had occurred during the outbreak. Tar, at this period, was known as a preservative for wood and rope but its future in the aniline dye industry had not then been discovered.

Adam Anderson was always duly attentive to public opinion and to encourage local support and allay fears of the residents who considered gas to be dangerous he undertook to give a course of lectures on coal gas, illustrated by experiments and demonstrations. These, with the encouragement of the Town Council, were well attended and ended in May 1824. The gas works were in operation with gas pipes laid causing great upheaval of mud and dust in Perth streets. Main streets were lit, as were churches, halls, public buildings and the Salutation Inn! Twenty gas burners beautifully illuminated Smeaton's Bridge. Winter evening services and meetings could be held. As for the handloom weavers they could work on in the dark evenings, gas jets, at a cost of ten shillings, being fixed to their looms. By 1828 eight lamps were installed in Greyfriars Burial Ground to deter the body-snatchers of that period – though many declared that they only provided light for them to see the work they were at and lighten their dark deeds.

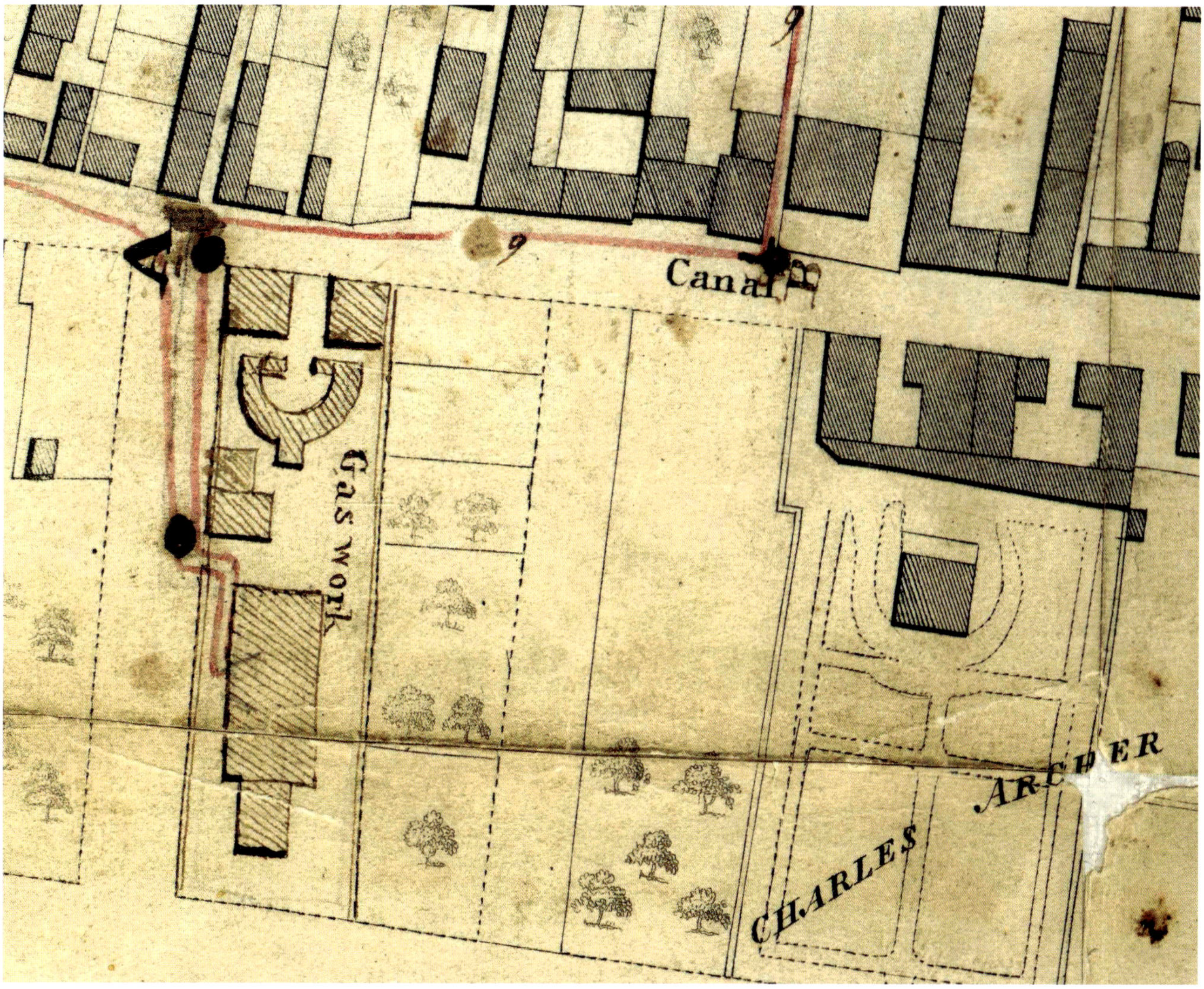

Canal Street on Reid's map of 1809 annotated to show the gasworks and gas-pipes supplying street lighting (AK Bell Library, Local Studies).

The residents of Perth were delighted and all remarked on the clear brilliance of the light provided by Anderson's gas supply. For this public service and modernisation of Perth's street lighting the grateful Gas Company presented Anderson with silver plate to the value of three hundred guineas.

To show his confidence in gas lighting for houses Rector Anderson installed it in his own home in 1825 in St Leonard's Bank to which he had recently removed with his family from Rose Terrace near the Academy. On 31 July 1815 he had married Agnes Ramsay, daughter of ex-Provost James Ramsay, merchant, of Croft. The death of Adam Anderson's wife, on 22 April 1826, left the four children Eliza, Andrew, Amelia Agnes and Jemima in the care of their father. It was just two years before the death of Professor Anderson that the family suffered the loss of Amelia Agnes who died of consumption at the home of her grandmother Mrs Ramsay of Croft.

On 15 July 1830 there is an interesting report in the *Perthshire Courier* of an exhibition of the progress of musical pupils of Samson Duncan and his son, teachers of pianoforte and violin. The abilities of the pupils, their delicacy of fingering, their feeling for the music played are praised and among those listed for mention are the Misses Anderson, St Leonard's Bank and the Misses Duncan, Athole Place. In November the following year, the world-famous violinist, Paganini performed in the Theatre Royal, Kinnoull Street. Would Dr Anderson and his young family have attended that event?

In 1824 the Act for the Standardisation of Weights and Measures was passed and new Imperial measures were required by law to be introduced.[2] In a Town Council Minute of 1 December 1806 there is mentioned the Parsonage Tiends of the Parish which consisted of three hundred Bolls of Victual which was divided between the two ministers of St John's Kirk as part of their stipends. One hundred and sixty Bolls, three Firlots, two Pecks, two Lippies and two-thirds of a Lippie of meal and one hundred and thirty-nine Bolls, one Peck, one Lippie and one third of a Lippie of Bear to be paid equally as before to Rev Mr James Scott and James Moodie during their respective encumbrances of the East and Middle Churches. This is an example of the rather cumbersome old weights and measures.

At the request of Duncan Macneill, Sheriff-Depute of the County of Perth, Rector Anderson with his assistant, Mr Forbes, compiled a report indicating the complications and implications of converting Scots/Scotch measures of Bolls, Firlots and Ells into Imperial pints and quarts, feet and yards. There had been some standardisation of Scottish measures since the seventeenth century but now there was to be complete uniformity in Great Britain. Initially, and after some delay, Rector Anderson and his assistant obtained a set of old measures, a set of new Imperial weights and measures and a set of balances capable of measuring weights from a grain to a hundredweight. The report of 1826 with an appendix of 1827 giving rules and tables of conversion was published in Perth by R. Morrison in 1827.[3]

Not all were in favour of the new Imperial measures and the mathematical conversions required and yet again Dr Anderson saw the need for convincing the public that uniformity would do much to reduce fraud in trading and was to everyone's benefit. He considered it a necessary modernisation for Perth. As before in the case of gas lighting, he offered a series of free lectures on the subject which, with the encouragement of the Town Council and the inclusion of practical demonstrations of the process of the conversions using his own apparatus, were well attended. In recognition of his work, a public dinner in his honour was arranged in August 1828 by the gentlemen of the County when all present agreed with Lord Provost Robert Ross that Dr Anderson used his skills 'more for the public good than his own aggrandizement'.

After his successful completion of the Perth Gas Works, and his mathematical marathon on the new Imperial weights and measures, Adam Anderson was awarded the degree of LL.D. by St Andrews University in 1827. As Rector of the Perth Academy he gave continuous encouragement to extend the provision of education for the working classes. The Manufacturers' School, established in 1810 in King James VI Hospital, gave basic reading, writing and arithmetic to the sons of their employees. Stewart's Free School, established in 1814 by the Trade Incorporations with a bequest from William Stewart, a native of Perth and a London merchant, educated boys from the age of seven to fourteen years 'of poor and honest parents'. In 1835 two national schools were established by the Town Council, with Government aid, to supply elementary education to children of working classes at a very cheap rate of 3d per month! The three parish churches of St John's Kirk by the late 1830s had established parish schools, recalling the ideal of the early Reformers of 'a school in every parish'. Some of the eager young scholars were occasionally offered free places at the Perth Academy by Rector Anderson who may well have helped collect data for the education survey by the Town Council in 1834 which revealed forty-one per cent of children of five to fourteen years attended no school!

Adult education was also promoted by Anderson, who was a leader in the founding of the Mechanics Institute in 1830. To a large public audience he explained the principles of a Mechanics Institute offering to give a series of lectures on arithmetic, geometry and chemistry. Thomas Bruce, Anderson's assistant, took over the mathematics and Anderson extended his scientific lectures. Three hundred students enrolled at 6/- per annum and, with donations, a Mechanics Library was set up. By 1834 support for the Institute, which met in the Academy, had waned and eventually lapsed.

As the passing of the Reform Bill approached Dr Anderson planned to celebrate the King's birthday with a display of 'waterworks'. The apparatus he devised was of an interesting and curious shape and as it was to be costly the report in the *Perthshire Courier* of 3 May 1832 announces that a subscription will be raised. The apparatus was to show in an ornamental way the uses to which the new supply of water could be put. So many subscribed that the surplus funds provided a firework display carried out by Dr Anderson himself. On Reform Jubilee Day, 9 August 1832, the splendid 'waterworks' stood again in the High Street at the junction of Watergate and George Street. Water flowed through all day. Supported by anchors, four dolphins, six feet high, spouted jets of water from their mouths, which turned a number of small wheels on the exhibit. All admired it, though it made passage in the High Street rather uncomfortable and crowded.

Reform Jubilee Day had begun with a gathering of Town Council, High Constables and Navigation Commissioners at the North Inch who walked to Princes Street and Shore Road where, with full Masonic honours, the foundation stone of the new harbour was laid.

The management of the River Tay was vested in the Town Council. By its charter of 'Free Port, Harbour and Navigation' it had an obligation to maintain the navigation of the river but not to the detriment of other interests, particularly those of the salmon fishings, which were of paramount importance to the economy of the town. By the eighteenth century vessels sailed upriver to Perth from the Mediterranean, wine and fruit from Spain, with European goods via Hamburg and Rotterdam, from the Baltic and Scandinavian countries and with flax and hemp from Russia. In 1807 John Rennie, civil engineer, advised forming a wet dock where ships would berth rather than lying at the old quays at the South Inch dangerously close to the rapid currents of the Tay. Over time sandbanks and fords had built up and without clear regulation piers, cairns or landing places and extended jetties had been erected by proprietors on each bank of the river. Dr Anderson, recalling his shipmaster father and his own memories of shipping on the River Forth, took great interest in the improvement of the shipping fairway of the Tay. He was called upon as advisor, arbitrator and as an independent, unbiased mediator by the Town Council. In December 1829 a letter from Sir David Moncreiffe, who had been making alterations to the Weel Ford adjacent to his property at Friarton, stated that he did not wish to interfere with river navigation and would be pleased to abide by the decision of Dr Anderson and Mr Douglas on this matter. Dr Anderson had, two years earlier, also been delegated to inspect the site of a new cairn for hauling in nets proposed by John S. Richardson of Pitfour.

Two Navigation Acts of 1830[4] and 1834[5] set up a Harbour/ Navigation Commission with limited powers to borrow money and to supervise the improvements. In the Town Council Minutes of 7 May 1832 a report of an inspection of the river is signed by Dr Anderson and Mr James Jardine, civil engineer. The suggestion is that Sleepless Island, Derry Island and Balhepburn Island, all lying close to the riverbank, be connected to it by filling in the narrow channels of water with the materials being dredged from the river bed. This would divert the water of these channels into the main river and increase the scour. Due to costs, operations were spaced out through the 1830s with dredging and the mechanical removal of large stones, one weighing fifty tons!

During the outbreak of cholera in the 1830s Dr Anderson served on a voluntary 'board of health' helping to distribute soup and bread to poor families who were particularly victims of the disease. There was little hospital accommodation in Perth and an old spinning mill in Mill Street served as a temporary hospital. To establish a purpose-built hospital a subscription list was set up. Dr Anderson was on the Committee of Subscribers and a site to the west of the town in York Place was acquired. On 5 October 1836 the foundation stone of the new building was laid by Lord Kinnaird with full Masonic honours. At five o'clock a public dinner was held to celebrate the achievement. The Earl of Breadalbane referred to the New City and County Infirmary, expressing the hope that it might lead to the formation of a medical school at Perth. Perth already had its Academy 'approaching in eminence to a university'. Lord Kinnaird remarked that the grand procession was the largest ever seen in the town and the most outstanding in order and regularity. Dr Anderson, as organiser and marshal, was thanked by the assembled company. His services were practical as well as scientific!

Professor Anderson was appointed to the Chair of Natural Philosophy at St Andrews University and formally inducted in August 1837. A few weeks later in October he attended a public dinner in his honour with two hundred City and County gentlemen. The officials on that occasion were former pupils – the Chairman Sir John S. Richardson of Pitfour and Croupiers Bailie Sidey of Perth and William S. Turnbull of Huntingtower.

During term time Professor Anderson lodged in St Andrews but with a tenant in his home in St Leonards Bank, he spent his vacations with his relatives at Croft House. In 1846 on the last day that he was in Perth before going to begin the university term at St Andrews he visited the waterworks examining it minutely, as always giving his greatest attention to that undertaking, which probably gave him the greatest pleasure. He called for steps and with a piece of chalk printed in beautiful capitals 'AQUAM IGNE et AQUA HAURIO' (by fire and water I draw out water). These letters were later placed permanently above the entrance.

Ten years after arriving in Perth Rector Adam Anderson had been requested by the Town Council to submit a chemical analysis of the spring at Clathymore as a possible supply of water for the town. Dr Anderson and Mr James Jardine, civil engineer, in 1828 were still searching for a chemically suitable and sufficient supply of water. Dr Anderson as chemist finally decided on an intake of River Tay water at the north end of Moncreiffe Island. After the passing of the Perth Water Act 1829[6] Dr Anderson, now chemist and supervising engineer, presented his completed plan to the Town Council and Water Commissioners in December of that year.

Operations began immediately and by May 1832 a water supply was being piped through the town and in use for Dr Anderson's 'waterworks' exhibit in the High Street. Over that period the *Perthshire Courier* updated the townspeople on progress, which gives a diary of the project.

January 1830 The original site of the building on the west bank of the river adjacent to Greyfriars burial ground was abandoned due to fears that water seepage from the burial ground might infiltrate and pollute the water pipes close by. The Town Council purchased part of Hepburn's Woodyard, which lay to the south. The building would be a fitting termination to the long projected street at the riverside (Tay Street – finally formed in 1883!).

February 1830 Dr Anderson had designed a building for the new site which showed great elegance with also regard for economy and utility. The building was round, hence the elegance and Anderson may well have been influenced by the construction of the Rotunda in George Street, completed in 1824 as a memorial to the late Provost Thomas Hay Marshall.

June 1830 There was comment that the site of the intake of water was down river from the outflow of the town's sewers and lades!

August 1830 While working on the foundations of the building two men were injured when a large stone, being lowered, slipped. Each was paid two pounds for bruising suffered.

October 1830 Almost insurmountable difficulties with the excavation work were overcome. The filter bed was finished and the excavation of the riverbed to a depth of about three feet for holding the great water pipe was in progress.

November 1830 The water pipe was laid half way across but rain, swells in the river and floods into the excavated channel interrupted the work. Every opportunity was seized when the storm abated, the men working by torchlight till ten o'clock. In the Water Act the time allowed for laying the pipe across the river was limited by the close season for salmon.

April 1831 Workmen had commenced laying the water pipes of cast iron in Princes Street. The final length laid being about five miles.

September 1831 The building was nearly finished, a classic design by Dr Anderson carried out by the local masons, Cameron and Galletly, the contractors. There was assurance that the cost was so moderate, about £13,000, that to cover the cost and the upkeep the

Anderson's waterworks and the first railway bridge in Perth, constructed in laminated wood c1860 (courtesy of Perth Museum and Art Gallery).

rate of assessment on houses would be ninepence in the pound and on places of business tuppence farthing.

And finally, **5 August 1832**, water from the new waterworks had been flowing for some days. Quantity and quality were good. In five hours the reservoir tank covered by the splendid dome of the building was filled – seven hundred gallons – and the receiving wells were kept full from the filter bed. Of interest perhaps was a test in George Street when a fire plug was opened and the water shot out, its own force taking it up to the height of the roofs of the highest houses and over the top of some of the lower ones.[7]

The striking appearance of the gleaming white building of Longannet stone belied its industrial interior. Several trees were cut down in the avenue at the South Inch to give a clear view of the waterworks to steamer passengers arriving at Perth.
Professor Adam Anderson died at his lodgings in St Andrews on 5 December 1846. There was a great depth of sorrow felt in Perth. They lamented the loss of a gentleman, eminent in talent, modest in demeanour, generous, patient and amiable at all times.

Members of the Town Council agreed to honour Adam Anderson in a public funeral. Ten days after his death, professors, teachers and students, public bodies and friends escorted his hearse to the Swilken Burn on the outskirts of the town where the journey began for interment in Greyfriars Burial Ground. The hearse was met just before two o'clock on its approach to the South Inch, by the Lord Provost, Magistrates and Councillors, Ministers of the Presbytery of Perth, the Sheriff, Fiscal of the Society of Procurators, Rector Miller and teachers of the Seminaries, the National Schools and others with a large number of scholars of Perth. Also present were the Water Commissioners and very many citizens and friends. Formed in order and led by the Town Sergeants with their halbert heads muffled in black crêpe, the procession moved forward. A snow shower was falling but cleared as the solemn and silent crowd walked on to the burial ground. From his graveside the tall chimney of his waterworks was visible, as it is to this day.

Anderson's grave in Greyfriars burial ground, Perth (© PKHT).

Lord Provost John Pullar of Perth by John MacLaren Barclay in 1875 (courtesy of Perth Museum and Art Gallery).

Sir Robert Pullar

Shortly before his death Professor Anderson and his fellow proprietors in St Leonard's Bank and Marshall Place petitioned against the proposal of a rail terminus on the South Inch. The advent of the railways and the opening of the General Terminus in 1848 immediately to the west resulted in better trade facilities with increasing prosperity for Perth and more employment opportunities. In that year too Robert Pullar, having served his seven-year apprenticeship in his father's dyeing and cleaning business, became a partner – John Pullar and Son.

John Pullar had founded the business in 1824 within premises at Burt's Close, Mill Street and on the opening of the waterworks in 1832 the still comparatively small industry requested a supply of 670 gallons of water daily. The water of the town's lade was also used. With manufacturing at a low ebb John Pullar had diversified, undertaking dyeing of yarns and piece work. Plant dyes were used, many brought by ship to Perth Harbour – boxwood, indigo and madder, the latter producing a bright turkey red.

Dyers worked six days a week with long hours from six o'clock in the morning. The heat from the vats and the strong odours of the dyes made work in the dye-house unpleasant. Children as young as eight years of age were to be found working in these conditions but the Bleaching and Dyeing Bill of 1856 ruled that 'no female or young person work more than sixty hours per week and no child be employed at bleaching, dyeing or finishing'.

In 1824 John Pullar had a workforce of himself and two trained dyers with four apprentices. In 1848 Robert Pullar, as his father's partner, set about expanding the business by establishing agencies, at first in local towns and later through Scotland, England and Wales, using the rail link. He took advantage of a cheaper parcel rate to London, which increased the volume of goods. He used advertising in newspapers and all their horse drawn carts carried the message – Pullars of Perth. The firm exhibited with other Perth businesses at the Great Exhibition of 1851 and received the Royal Warrant 'Dyers to her Majesty the Queen' the following year.

Chemistry was still an important discipline and it was clear that coal tar had undiscovered uses. William Henry Perkin, a student at the Royal School of Chemistry, experimenting in his own laboratory with coal tar produced a good mauve or magenta dye, an aniline or synthetic purple dye. Perkin came to Robert Pullar, the practical dyer, to seek help in finding a fixative for the dye on silk, cotton and wool. This accomplished, he took out a patent on 26 August 1856. Although London and Glasgow dyers were hesitant Robert Pullar used aniline dyes with a tremendous growth in business.

James Ferguson Pullar joined his brother as a partner in 1865 and the following year dry cleaning was introduced. By this time the workforce had increased to 500 workers. No water was used but it involved unstable cleaning agents such as benzine in the factory in a built-up, residential area. In 1882 Messrs Pullars – the North British Dyeworks – purchased one hundred and twelve acres of Tulloch Bleachworks, building a new factory and establishing a new suburb with housing, a school and a community/sports hall. Each factory had a Pullar's Fire Brigade.

With characteristic enterprise electricity by steam engine was introduced in 1878 with the purchase of electric machines and lighting and the first telephone number 01 in 1880. John Pullar died in December 1878. The founder of the business had also served his town as a Water Commissioner, as a Councillor and a Lord Provost. Holding that office he had pushed for the widening of Perth Bridge, which was carried out in 1869, and for the completion of Tay Street promenade. The new Municipal Buildings at the foot of the High Street were nearing completion when he died.

Pullars of Perth provided sports equipment and facilities for their employees. James Ferguson Pullar, a music lover, instituted Pullars Silver Band providing fine instruments for members and for Perth Silver Band and Fechney School Band. He also gifted organs to Kinnoull Church and to St Andrews Church. John Pullar had always wished to see an organ installed in Perth City Hall (opened in 1844). In 1887, Queen Victoria's Golden Jubilee year, Robert and James F. Pullar gifted to the town a fine organ by Mr Miller of Perth and Dundee, organ builder, which was installed in the hall. A banquet was arranged. Praise was given to the commercial enterprise of the Pullar family, which gave employment to the citizens of Perth and they were thanked for sharing their good fortune in material benefits.

In 1886 a committee chaired by Robert Pullar raised subscriptions which, with donations from Perth professional and business men, enabled the committee to build Perth Swimming Baths in Dunkeld Road. It was eventually handed over to the Town Council. In 1896 at the opening session of the swimming baths Sir Robert Pullar explained that Perth was now recognised by the Scottish Amateur Swimming Association as a centre in its own right – not, as formerly, linked to Dundee. There were five clubs in Perth, one being Pullars Club.

In 1895 Queen Victoria conferred a knighthood on Robert Pullar. Congratulations flooded in and the people of Perth were delighted. In April 1896 at a large gathering in the City Hall Lord Provost Dewar presented to Sir Robert Pullar his portrait in oils by Sir John Everett Millais who said that he was delighted to paint the portrait of one who had done so much for Perth and its citizens.

The presentation of the Freedom of Perth to Lord Rosebery in 1898. The organ was gifted to Perth by Sir Robert Pullar and his brother and was used until around 2000. It was shipped in 2006 to Melbourne, Australia to be used in a ladies college (AK Bell Library, Local Studies).

Towards the end of the Victorian era Perth was in great need of a second road bridge to ease traffic congestion, although having planned a new gas works and an electricity station, the Town Council's finances were low. Sir Robert Pullar and his brother James each gave £5,000 towards the cost. Sir Robert and Lady Pullar performed the opening ceremony in October 1900, naming it the Victoria Bridge. About ten weeks later Queen Victoria died in January 1901.

Robert's two sons, Rufus and Albert ran the business but times were changing. The trade unions were more vociferous and demanding. Members of the Dyers' Union, Dundee picketed the factory gates in Mill Street. Germany produced three quarters of the world's dyes and Rufus Pullar, President of the Dyers and Colourists Association, failed to convince British dyers to produce more of their own dyes.

Sir Robert Pullar died in 1912, having attended in 1911 the opening of the new City Hall in King Edward Street at which he was presented with the Freedom of Perth. Rufus Pullar died suddenly in 1917 from strain and overwork.

On the death of Rufus Pullar the personal direction of the firm by three generations of the Pullar family ended after ninety-three years. It was in general a time of great social change. Eastman and Son Ltd Acton Vale, a family firm of cleaners and dyers, took over the management of Pullars of Perth. Frank Eastman, now managing director, granted union membership, introduced a pension scheme and holidays with pay. Pullars and Eastman made a public share flotation under the name of Associated Dyers and Cleaners (A.D.C.).[8] By 1930 it included Stevenson Brothers and Inverness Premier Laundry. In 1938 Johnson Brothers took over A.D.C. After the Second World War Tulloch Works were sold and an extension built on the east end of Mill Street factories, all of which in 1989 was offered for sale. Pullars of Perth was looking to the future. A new factory, with modern equipment for specialised cleaning of clothing used in electronic and pharmaceutical industries, was built at Inveralmond Estate. The new £3.4million factory was opened by Princess Alexandra in 1991 – Apparelmaster UK of Pullars of Perth.

End Notes

1 I would like to express my appreciation of the generous assistance of the staff of the Local Studies Department, A.K. Bell Library and the Perth and Kinross Council Archive. I have used primary sources as below and have also consulted local newspapers, *Perth Courier, Perthshire Advertiser* and *Perthshire Constitutional* for the period 1809–1912, along with the Statistical Accounts for Perth and Perthshire. I would also like to acknowledge Harding, A.W. 1991 *Pullars of Perth*. Perth and Kinross District Libraries and Cameron, K.J. 2007 *The Schoolmaster Engineer, Adam Anderson of Perth and St Andrews*. Tayport Printers.

2 Act V. Georgii IV., Cap LXXIV *An Act for ascertaining and establishing Uniformity of Weights and Measures.* (17th June 1824).

3 Anderson, A 1826 *Report on the Weight and Measures of Perthshire* and 1827 Appendix to the Report. Perth.

4 *An Act for Enlarging, improving and maintaining the Port and Harbour of Perth; for improving the Navigation of the River Tay to the said City; and for the purposes therewith connected.* (Royal Assent 17th June 1830).

5 *An Act to alter and amend an Act passed in the Eleventh year of the Reign of his late majesty and First Year of the Reign of his present Majesty, intituled An Act for enlarging, improving and maintaining the Port and Harbour of Perth; for improving the Navigation of the River Tay to the City, and for other Purposes therewith connected.* (Royal Assent 27th June 1834).

6 Act Georgii IV. Regis. Cap.CIII. for supplying the City of Perth and the Suburbs and Vicinity thereof with Water. (1st June 1829).

7 Anderson, A 1837 *Report to the Commissioners for supplying the City of Perth with Water, on the means employed for carrying into effect that Measure.* Perth.

8 Hudson, J 1989 *Branching Out: The Story of Philip Bollom and The Johnson Group.* White Tree Books.

The History and Legacy of Arthur Bell & Sons

Alia Campbell

Today the Bell's brand is part of Diageo Plc and the records of Arthur Bell & Sons Ltd are one of the most prominent collections on the shelves at the Diageo Archive,[1] indeed it is the very first collection on the shelves: 'AB' – Arthur Bell & Sons Ltd. The Bell's collection includes just over 8,000 records and bottles dating from 1837 to the present, and is very much a business collection comprising mostly of minute books, correspondence, legal papers, sales and financial ledgers, adverts and packaging. Using these records, as well as selected secondary sources, this paper will tell the story of Arthur Bell & Sons, one of Perth's greatest Scotch whisky houses, as well as the legacy of Bell's in Perth and in the whisky industry.

The History of Arthur Bell & Sons

The story of Arthur Bell & Sons starts with the well-known phrase that appears on every bottle of Bell's, 'Established in Perth 1825'. Arthur Bell was born on 30 November 1825 in Surrey Square in London. He was the seventh of fifteen children born to Hannah Bruce and Robert Fitzroy Bell, a general agent. Unfortunately, nothing is known about Arthur Bell's early life and how and when he came to live in Perth, a town that would eventually offer him great opportunities.

In the early days of the whisky industry, Perth and the surrounding area was home to no fewer than twenty-three small stills by the end of the eighteenth century; however, the whisky industry in Perth seems to have really taken off, just as it did across the rest of Scotland, during the last few decades of the nineteenth century. By this point, Perth had been associated with the whisky trade for generations because it was situated perfectly at the entrance to the highlands as well as being very central.

In 1825, many decades before the trade in whisky in Scotland really took off, Thomas Sandeman set up shop on the south side of the historic church of St John in the Kirkgate in Perth. He traded in whisky, wines, beers and tea, and together with other Perth merchants he bought the old granary at the Speygate and converted it into a warehouse. Only one original document survives from this early period, a letter book dating from 1837. The ink is very faded, but it is still very valuable for the archive to have letters written in Thomas Sandeman's own hand, and an idea of the general running of Sandeman's shop.

Thomas Sandeman died in 1837 leaving a business with an annual profit of more than £900 to his clerk James Roy who continued the business with his partner Alex Miller.[2] A few years later, in 1845, Roy and Miller employed the then twenty year old Arthur J. Bell as a traveller. The company's trade at this time was mainly local and retail but some wholesale trade was done with publicans and hoteliers. Arthur Bell's duties were to extend sales beyond Perth and each spring he toured the highlands seeking orders and collecting payments.

Six years later Miller retired and Arthur Bell became James Roy's new partner. They continued to trade from the Kirkgate, and it is likely that it was around this time, once he had become a partner in the firm, that Arthur Bell began to experiment with whiskies and develop his blending skills. The business continued as Roy & Bell until 1862, when James Roy retired, and for the next few years, Arthur Bell was in partnership with his nephew Thomas R. Sandeman.

The mid 1860s were important years for Arthur Bell. In 1864 he married Isabella Warden Duff, the daughter of a merchant, but his business was making a meagre profit for two partners and Arthur Bell had eleven relatives to support, eight of whom were female, which caused him a great deal of anxiety.

In 1865 Arthur Bell and Thomas R. Sandeman had a disagreement over expenses that Sandeman had incurred on personal business but charged to the partnership and his lax attitude towards the business. Arthur Bell was saddled with various expenses such as Sandeman's bill for a horse and gig, and he struggled to bear the injustice he felt at the hands of his younger partner, who had been the best man at his wedding. Later that year, Arthur and Isabella Bell had their first child, Mary Louisa (Louie). Arthur Kinmond (A.K.) followed in 1868, as well as Robert Duff (R.D.), who was born in 1871 and Mabel Caroline who was born in 1874.

In resolving his quarrel with Sandeman, Arthur Bell showed himself to be a very principled man with strong opinions. Honesty and decency in all walks of life were of the upmost importance to him and after having to replace Sandeman's capital with a loan from the Central bank when the partnership broke down, Arthur Bell denied himself a profit at the end of the year and vowed never to borrow money from the bank ever again. From this point on Arthur Bell was the sole owner of the business and the first thing he did was change the name to Arthur Bell Wine Merchants.

THE Copartnery of BELL & SANDEMAN, Wine and Spirit Merchants in Perth, of which the Subscribers were the sole Partners, was this day DISSOLVED by mutual consent.

The Subscriber, Arthur Bell, who continues to carry on the business on his own account, is authorised to receive and pay all debts due to and by the late Company.

ARTHUR BELL.
THOMAS R. SANDEMAN.

Excerpt from the Edinburgh Gazette, 19 May 1865, announcing that Arthur Bell plans to continue the business under his own name after the dissolution of Bell & Sandeman.

The next few decades did not run particularly smoothly for Arthur Bell. Although he had started well ahead of the rest of the trade in trying to sell his whisky to the English as far back as 1855, he had not had very much success, and the assimilation of English and Scottish excise duties in 1856 did not help matters. It is said that he appointed the first Scotch whisky agent in London in 1862. Arthur Bell felt that if the Scots liked his whisky, Londoners should too. His first agent, a Mr Young, reported back that the people of London found Bell's whisky to have too heavy a taste. Arthur Bell was astonished that anyone would be more concerned with strength than with quality. Despite going through four agents, there was little success in London and Arthur Bell decided to give up his attempt to capture some of the London market in 1871, and decided to concentrate on his Scottish orders and exploring the export trade. He did not test the English market again until the mid 1880s, by which time Scotch whisky was already becoming quite popular with English consumers.[3]

Arthur Bell, like many great whisky blenders of his time, took great pride in the quality of his products, as an excerpt from one of his letter books reveals:

> That several fine whiskies blended together please the palates of a greater number of people than one whisky unmixed, consequently I have long adopted that practice, and never found it necessary to send out show cards but just allowed the quality of my goods to speak for themselves.[4]

Arthur Bell was so confident that the quality of his goods would speak for themselves that he did not even put his name on them. His whiskies had no brand names, his casks had no titles, his bottles had no labels and he owned no trademarks. His justification for this was that all of these things cost money and he preferred to spend all of his on making sure his whisky was of the highest quality. There can be no doubt that his business was slower to grow than it might have been if he had allocated part of his budget to some kind of branding and marketing. As a result of the lack of branding on early Bell's bottles, they are very difficult for even a trained eye to identify as having anything to do with Arthur Bell Wine Merchants as it was then, and the archive has never been able to actively collect anything other than sample bottles from this period, as they at least have hand written labels featuring the Bell's name.

Eventually it became clear that Arthur Bell would have to change with the times. In the early 1890s, despite being told by prospective agents in Australia that he ought to think up a suitable brand name, and even after some very suitable examples were suggested to him by his sons, he was still arguing, 'That no exporter can ship a good quality if he is called upon to expend such large sums in advertising, and I have decided not to advertise, but to try what can be done by the quality alone.'[5]

It was in the early 1890s that A.K. Bell and R.D. Bell began to get involved in the business. The next generation of Bell's were keen to make their mark and help develop the company, but in order to modernise the way their father did business they would first need to change his very conservative attitude. A.K. Bell had some contacts in Australia and had managed to get the ball rolling in the search for suitable agents. In 1892, R.D. Bell and

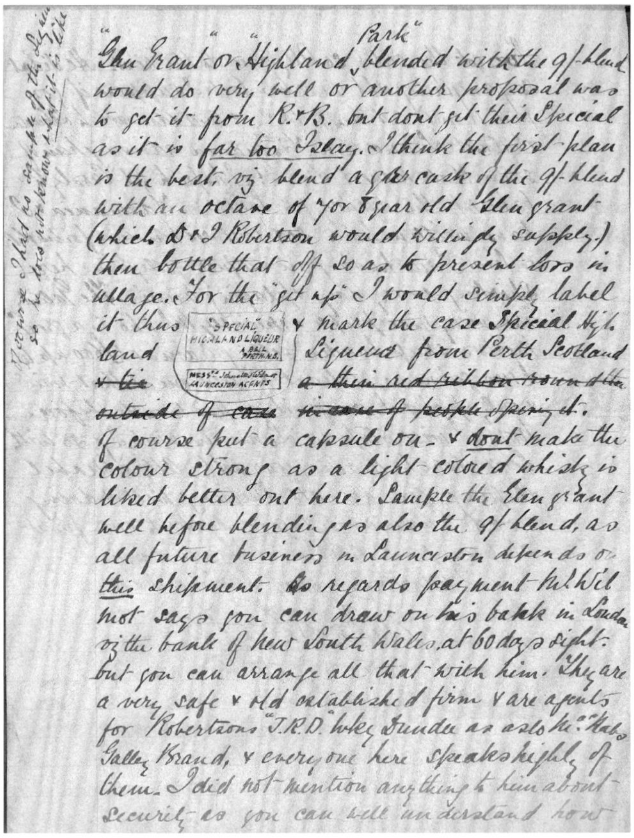
"Glen Grant" or "Highland Park" blended with the 9/- blend would do very well or another proposal was to get it from R & B. but dont get their Special as it is far too Islay. I think the first plan is the best, viz blend a qtr cask of the 9/- blend with an octave of 7 or 8 year old Glen grant (which D & J Robertson would willingly supply.) then bottle that off so as to prevent loss in ullage. For the "get up" I would simply label it thus & mark the case Special Highland Liqueur from Perth Scotland

Of course put a capsule on - & dont make the colour strong as a light colored whisky is liked better out here. Sample the Glen grant well before blending as also the 9/- blend, as all future business in Launceston depends on this shipment. As regards payment Mr Wil[illegible] says you can draw on his bank in London viz the bank of New South Wales, at 60 days sight. but you can arrange all that with him. They are a very safe & old established firm & are agents for Robertsons "J.R.D." whisky Dundee as also [illegible] Galley Brand, & everyone here speaks highly of them. I did not mention anything to him about security as you can well understand how

Part of a letter from Robert Duff Bell to Arthur Bell written during his trip to Australia in 1892, showing a rough sketch of what a Bell's branded label could look like.

his sister Louie were sent on a trip to the southern hemisphere to visit relations and look for opportunities to extend the business. From the correspondence that R.D. sent home, it seems that he was subtly trying to convince his father of the advantages of advertising and that he and A. K. had already discussed and were in agreement on this idea. To his father, R.D. wrote, 'The money that is spent here in advertising must be something enormous and they say nothing can be done here without it.'[6] Meanwhile to his brother he wrote:

> The competition in whisky here is worse than at home and people will have nothing unless a well-known brand – in fact, they are brand mad. Everything is brand, brand, brand. All the fences miles into the bush are plastered over with Claymore whisky, Robertson's J.R.D whisky, Galley Brand Whisky, Buchanan's house of Commons, Dawson's Whisky, etc., etc., too numerous to mention.[7]

The Bell brothers were both keen to work for their father's business and to expand it. They were in agreement that expansion could only be achieved through advertising, and advertising would only work if they adopted appropriate brand names. Arthur Bell was quick to point out to his sons that the company's profits had been £1,713 in 1890, and had risen to £5,726 in 1895, but by this time he must have been confident enough to pass on the reins to the next generation as he made A. K. a junior partner in 1895 and extended the same terms to R.D. just one year later. Arthur Bell Wine Merchants became Arthur Bell & Sons and by this point the company was exporting to Australia, Tasmania, New Zealand, Ceylon, India, Italy and France.

Undated photograph of Arthur Bell.

Undated photograph of Arthur Kinmond (A.K.) Bell.

Undated photograph of Robert Duff Bell.

The archive holds examples of many labels from this period, including those of two of the most popular of Bell's blended Scotch whiskies. The label for 'Scotch Fir Old Scotch Whisky', first issued in 1897, features a highland scene and several thistles and the label for 'Skerryvore Old Scotch Whisky' features an image of rough seas and a lighthouse in the distance. Nowhere on either of these labels do the names 'Bell's' or 'Arthur Bell & Sons' appear.

Arthur Bell died in 1900 leaving the business in the capable hands of his sons. In the five years since A.K. had joined the business profits had doubled to more than £11,000. A.K. had already begun to make a number of changes to the business by the time his father died. More agents were appointed and in 1904, at long last, the Bell's name finally appeared on the label and the first Bell's advert was published. It featured the name of the company, the name of the whisky and an image of a curler in a kilt. One of the oldest photographs in the Arthur Bell & Sons archive collection shows some of the Bell's staff with a framed version of the curler advert, taken in 1904.

Just a few years after this, another big change happened when the company moved from the Kirkgate to Victoria Street in 1908. These changes, along with the successful export of Bell's whisky into the Canadian market, gave a profit of more than £24,000 in 1913. R.D. retired around the same time, happy in the knowledge that the company was safe in the capable hands of his older brother and that he could retire and live comfortably.

Photograph of Bell's staff at the Canal Street premises in 1904. The staff are pictured with the first Bell's advert 'The Curler', which was produced the same year.

When the Great War came in 1914, most of the men employed by Bell's volunteered to join the army and at the same time, the price of whisky rocketed. This meant that Bell's employed women for the first time, and luckily, A.K. had re-invested a substantial proportion of the profits in mature whisky stocks and this helped the firm to survive the Immature Spirits Act of 1915, which stipulated that new make spirit had to be aged in cask for a minimum of three years before it could be legally considered to be Scotch whisky.

Arthur Bell & Sons became a limited company in 1921, with A.K. becoming Governing Director. At this point the company had a respectable capital of £350,000. Despite this, the inter-war period turned out to be a miserable time for Bell's on the whole, just as it did for the rest of the industry. Prohibition in America, which lasted from 1920 until 1933, had a fairly catastrophic effect on many companies within the whisky industry, and Arthur Bell & Sons was no exception.

Having kept their heads above water during the 1920s, the worst year was 1932, when Bell's lost more than £10,000; however, once again their stock enabled them to survive and A. K. was quick to turn things around with the purchase of P. Mackenzie & Co in 1933, which included the Blair Athol distillery in Pitlochry and the Dufftown Glenlivet distillery in Dufftown. A pamphlet produced by Bell's in 1935 describes the whole production process within the company, starting at the Blair Athol and Dufftown Glenlivet distilleries and describing how stock was then held at the Bell's bonded warehouse in Edinburgh, where over half a million gallons of whisky were maturing at the time. There were also bonded warehouses at Blair Athol, at Auchtermuchty and Perth. By this point the company also had their own cooperage in Perth, as well as a bottling warehouse where they handled their own case-making and all aspects of the bottling process.[8] The purchase of Inchgower distillery was successfully negotiated in 1936, and this meant that Bell's were the proud owners of three distilleries and the respective malts from these distilleries all went on to become key components in all of the Bell's famous blends.

At this point, the company is described as having, '…one of the largest stocks of Old Scotch Whisky in existence… and thus in a position to maintain the age of their bottled whiskies, which is a vital point in the success of any Scotch whisky business.'[9]

Despite the difficulties of the early 1930s, several other very positive things came out of the inter-war period none the less. The famous Bell's decanters were first conceived in the 1920s, in a classic whisky decanter shape made of a dark blue glass with 'Bell's Perth whisky' engraved on the front. These glass decanters later evolved into the bell shaped, porcelain decanters that have since been produced to commemorate various royal births and marriages, and more recently as limited edition bottling each Christmas. The company slogan 'Afore Ye Go' was registered in 1925, it went on to appear on many successful advertising campaigns, as well as on the neck label and the bottle closure. Just like the Bell's decanters, the slogan is still an important part of the brand's identity today.

The outbreak of the Second World War came in 1939 and the whisky industry was expected to 'export or die'; this meant there was an immense amount of pressure to export whisky products to bring much needed money into the country, but at the same time, the whisky companies were being deprived of the raw materials they needed to make the whisky. A. K. did not live to see victory in 1945 as he died on a Sunday morning in April 1942 after a short illness. His last annual report announced a profit of more than £100,000. R.D. reluctantly stepped into the shoes of Managing Director after his brother's sudden death, but his involvement was short lived as he died in June 1942. This ended the involvement of the Bell's family in Arthur Bell & Sons Ltd.

The next Managing Director of Bell's was William Govan Farquharson, who had joined as a chartered accountant in 1924. 'Farquie', as he was known, registered a Company Coat of Arms to celebrate the great victory in 1945; it featured a bell and a pair of lions, and has appeared on every bottle of Bell's Scotch whisky since it was granted. Farquharson also took the company public in 1949 to raise money for essential distillery reconstruction work to meet the growing demand for whisky at the time.[10]

In the 1950s, Bell's were exporting to more than 130 markets and large-scale advertising campaigns such as 'As Told by Bell's' were appearing in the press. Premium Bell's brands such as the 12 Year Old Royal Vat De Luxe were doing well in the United States and the standard Bell's decanters were becoming very popular, with many consumers choosing to keep them and treating them as collectables.

In 1963 the company's profits exceeded £1 million for the first time and continued to grow from strength to strength. Between 1970 and 1980 under Managing Director Raymond Miquel profits grew from just over £18 million to £159 million and by 1979 Bell's commanded twenty-five per cent of the home market.

October 1973 saw the company headquarters move from Victoria Street to the newly built Cherrybank building on the outskirts of Perth. In 1979 the Cherrybank Reception Centre was completed which gave Bell's the opportunity to entertain guests in a purpose built area. The Bell's Cherrybank Gardens were opened in 1988 and contained the National Heather Collection. This was converted into a visitor centre in 2000 and finally closed in 2002 when the Cherrybank Gardens and visitor centre were given to the Scotland's Garden Trust. In 1985, Bell's was taken over by Guinness, who merged with Grand Metropolitan in 1997 to form Diageo, and Bell's has been a part of Diageo ever since.

The Legacy of Arthur Bell & Sons

Today, the legacy of Arthur Bell & Sons in Perth is clear to see. If people hear the name 'Bell's' they instantly think of the popular Scotch whisky brand, but it is probably the legacy of good deeds and gifts left by A.K. Bell that has left a bigger mark on the people of Perth. When A. K. died in 1942, the *Perth Advertiser* commented,

> Perth has lost one of its greatest benefactors of all time. Mr Bell's love of his native city found expression in innumerable ways and he leaves behind him such a record of good deeds as is it has been given to few men to perform.
>
> The intimation that he had passed away came as a shock to his closest friends, whose profound sense of loss has been shared by the citizens in general. It was typical of a man of Mr Bell's tremendous vitality that he should be active until the last.

An artist's impression of the Gannochy housing estate, early 1920s.

The first and possibly the greatest of A.K.'s philanthropic deeds was to build the Gannochy housing estate between 1924 and 1932. This was a model housing estate of 150 homes, which provided inexpensive rented accommodation for the people of Perth. This was just one in a long line of projects that A.K. initiated to improve industry, the built and natural environment and the leisure facilities for the people of Perth. At the end of 1937, it was announced that A.K. would receive the freedom of Perth in recognition of his great contributions. This was the same year that he founded the Gannochy Trust, an act that would ensure that others would continue to be inspired by his philanthropy once he was gone.

Today the Gannochy Trust continues to make significant contributions to projects all across the country, but with a preference to Perth & Kinross in respect of A.K. Bell's wishes. A.K.'s legacy can clearly be seen through the work that is still done by The Gannochy Trust to help all the areas of society and the environment that he was passionate about.

Evolution of the Bell's Extra Special bottle, 1930s to the present bottle.

The legacy of Arthur Bell & Sons as a company lives on through the preservation of their records and bottles of all the wonderful products that they have produced. As a company, Diageo takes its history and heritage very seriously as so many of the Diageo brands have their roots in the eighteenth and nineteenth centuries, and it is important that they are represented in a way that respects their heritage. The company uses historical records and bottles to find inspiration for new advertising campaigns and product innovations; old recipes, blending books and stock books are often researched to make sure that contemporary blends are authentic Bell's blends.

Arthur Bell himself has recently been made into a brand icon and has appeared as an illustrated and animated character in the advertising campaign, 'The Spirit of Arthur Bell'. Whether or not the real Arthur Bell would have been quite as cheery as the new illustrated Arthur will never be known, but at least now, after so many years of letting the products speak for themselves and playing down his own achievements, Arthur Bell is the face and the voice of his most successful product, Bell's Blended Scotch whisky.

All images courtesy of the Diageo Archive.

End Notes

1 The Diageo Archive contains records relating to nearly 1,500 historic brands of Scotch whisky, vodka, gin, rum and various other alcoholic beverages, with brands dating back more than four hundred years, and every day there are new additions to the collections from some of the 180 markets that Diageo currently trades in. Apart from the mammoth task of collecting, cataloguing and preserving all of this material to maintain Diageo's corporate memory, it is the job of the archivists to tell the story of these brands through all the company records that Diageo has inherited, dating all the way back to the brand founders in the eighteenth and nineteenth centuries.

2 Roy & Miller, *Ledger 1837–1850*, Diageo Archive.

3 Information from this section is mainly taken from: J. House, *Pride of Perth, The Story of Arthur Bell & Sons Ltd. Scotch Whisky Distillers* (London, 1986 edn.).

4 Arthur Bell Wine Merchants, *Letter book,* 9 December 1879, Diageo Archive.

5 Arthur Bell Wine Merchants, *Letter book,* 16 January 1891, Diageo Archive.

6 Arthur Bell Wine Merchants, R. D. Bell, *Letter to A. Bell,* 1892, Diageo Archive.

7 House, *Pride of Perth,* p.36

8 Arthur Bell & Sons Ltd., *An Old Scotch Whisky House,* (Perth, 1935), p. 14-19.

9 Bell's, *An Old Scotch Whisky House,* p. 20.

10 Information from this section is mainly taken from: House, *Pride of Perth.*

Dewar's Perth Whisky: The origins of a global brand

Jacqui Seargeant

Introduction

The earliest foundations of John Dewar & Sons were forged within the old city of Perth. Although the company is long gone from the area, there is a rich legacy of industrial heritage, of philanthropy and of long cherished memories. The brand was shaped by the historic city that nurtured it and to this day Perth and its people hold many reminders of the Dewar days.

This paper will focus on the history of John Dewar & Sons' years in Perth, including the people who built the brand, the buildings where the business took place and some of the many stories that survive to the present day of a benevolent employer and a fascinating industry. I will draw on the company's own rich archive to illustrate the key stages of this story.

The Foundation: John Dewar

John Dewar and his two sons, John Alexander Dewar and Thomas Robert Dewar, were the great architects of the company, and benefactors to the Fair City, a city to which they were in many ways devoted. However, John Dewar the father was not actually from Perth. He was born in 1805, to humble crofter parents on a small farm in the very heart of Scotland, just a few miles from Aberfeldy. As one of nine children, there was no need for John to remain on the family farm so in 1828 he walked the twenty-five miles to the city of Perth, where he joined his relative, Alex MacDonald, as a cellarman in his wines and spirits business.

John Dewar, founder of the company.

The MacDonald spirits shop was nestled within the heart of historic Perth in the Castle Gable and John initially took charge of the cellars and stores. As one of the lowest lying parts of the city, the street was narrow and liable to flooding. Any cellarage would therefore have been very vulnerable, so the twenty-three year old John no doubt had his work cut out for him. When Alex died in 1830 John continued to work with Mrs MacDonald, and in 1837 they became partners, changing the name of the business to MacDonald and Dewar.

At this time Perth was a thriving market town with a population of about 20,000, which was modest by the standards of other major cities.[1] However, the spirits business was already flourishing and was to become a major industry during the course of the nineteenth century. By the early 1830s there were seventy-four grocer shops selling beer and spirits in Perth – certainly a lot of competition for John Dewar, though equally there was a large customer base.

In 1846 John Dewar dissolved his business partnership with Mrs MacDonald and while she continued in business in the Castle Gable, John set up shop at 111 High Street (which many years later would become the site for Woolworths). It seems perhaps an audacious move in a city already teeming with shops that sold spirits, however John was now forty-one years old and he knew the market and the city well. He chose his new business location wisely. The premises included a shop, a wine cellar, a spirits cellar and a bonded area. John Dewar's shop was to be a wholesale and retail wine and spirits establishment, boasting in the local press of a large and superior stock of wines, foreign and British spirits, porter and ales, including a large cellarage for stocks of yeast or 'barm' for distillers.[2] His focus from the start was on 'quality', at a time when there were many badly distilled, impure and unhealthy spirits on sale. Dewar became a name you could trust.

All of John Dewar's business was carried out at these premises – maturation of whiskies and other spirits; blending of whiskies; bottling of spirits and of course sales. The same building had previously been a 'Tea Wine and Spirit Warehouse' as early as the 1830s so it was already well adapted for use.[3] The Dewar family business was to continue at these premises for fifty-four years, long after John Dewar died, and in the end it was a matter of the practicality of the burgeoning company that brought an end to John Dewar & Sons' presence on the historic High Street.

Coaching Inn painting by J.C. Maggs.

The Development of Blended Whisky

It was the development of blending that was to launch whisky as an international drink, as the mixing of heavier malt whiskies with lighter grain whiskies created a product with much broader appeal. During the nineteenth century individual whiskies varied markedly, in taste and quality, so blending offered the opportunity to create something new to appeal to a wide range of palates, but also something to a secret recipe that could be branded. John was quick to brand his whisky with the family name and that of his adopted city – Dewar's Perth Whisky. In contrast to the blends the company creates today, which typically contain up to forty different whiskies, John's early blends would have contained perhaps five or six relatively local whiskies. Significantly, his focus was on good quality spirits, and it was this reputation that would help to mould the future of the company. John's business expanded on the popularity of his whisky. In 1860 he employed his first traveller, or salesman, to extend the sale of Dewar's Perth Whisky beyond Perth, into hotels and restaurants throughout Scotland. Business was good.

John originally sold his blends to hotels and inns transported in branded ceramic 'pigs', which were large containers often with a wicker surround for protection. But he is particularly famous for having been the first person to introduce a branded blend of his own whisky in labelled glass bottles.

John Dewar's Civic Life

Despite a thriving business to deal with, John still found plenty of time for civic interests. During the 1840s he demonstrated a desire to help and improve the city of Perth that his son John Alexander Dewar would later continue. By 1843 he had become a Town Councillor, and in 1856 entered the Guildry of Perth.

The Perth Guild of Merchants was similar to the Town Council. Composed of a wide cross-section of merchants and craftsmen, the Guild had many functions including control of weights and measures, with interests in the policing, lighting, quality control, and cleaning of the city streets. In addition the Guild had charitable concerns, taking special care over its members who found themselves in hard times. By 1858 John was a councillor on the 4th ward of Perth, and was also serving on the Police Commission. He demonstrated a sound business sense, and his trustworthy nature must have influenced his election as the president or Dean of the organisation. John was elected Dean of Guild in 1862, the first Dean elected by ballot, and the first to be recorded by an artist's sketch. He held the office for the maximum term of three years, during which time he became renowned for his efficiency. He was proud to serve his city, and see through improvements that would benefit those less fortunate than himself. He continued working in the Guildry for a few more years before retiring from office.

In his lifetime, John's whisky business is said to have reached from Inverness to Edinburgh. When he died he left behind an impressive stock of wines and spirits which included: whisky, brandy, rum, gin, sherry, port, wines such as claret and burgundy, as well as other items associated with drinking, like ginger, cigars and lime. It was a thriving Scottish business founded on his reputation as a blender of fine quality whiskies.

His obituary in the *Perthshire Advertiser* summed up the public image of the man himself:

> 'He was in all respects a liberal minded gentleman, and supported his party not only with his advice but with his pecuniary means. In fact, no deserving person ever applied to Mr Dewar for pecuniary assistance but it was cheerfully given. He was a person of great decision of character, and expressed his opinions with much firmness…'[4]

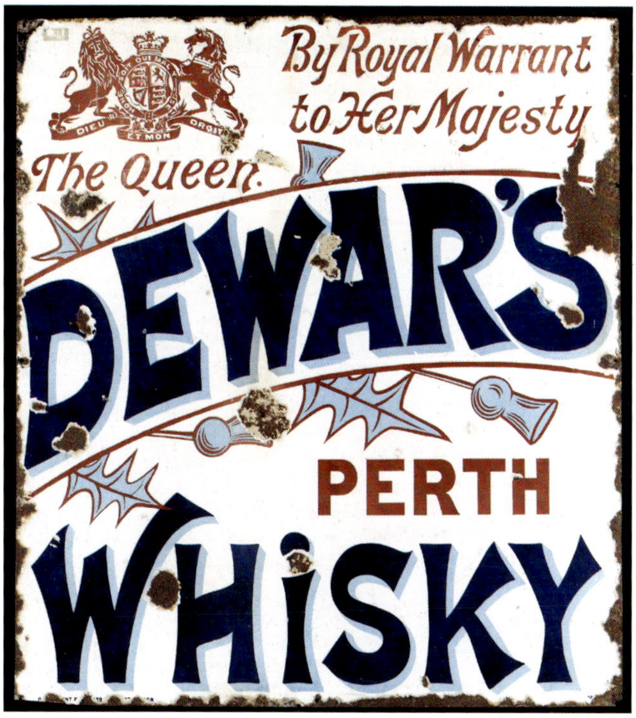

Dewar's advert c1890s.

He left the business in the hands of his son, and his wife Jane. It was John Alexander and his brother, Thomas, who would be instrumental in developing Dewar's Whisky as an international brand of high quality.

The Next Generation: John and Thomas Dewar

Many writers have over the years spoken of the contrasting personalities of John Alexander and Thomas Dewar, the two brothers, who between them made the family firm and Dewar's whisky one of the 'big three' whisky brands of the early twentieth century.[5] When their father died in 1880 John Alexander Dewar took over the business, having already become a partner with his father. Thomas was brought in a few years later and together they proved to be the perfect partnership. John was like his father – the serious business mind with an eye for the finances, and a flair for blending. Thomas was a restless spirit with a big personality – naturally the sales and marketing man.

Marketing Genius

Thomas Dewar's focus was on advertising the company's products and expanding the markets, first in the UK and subsequently globally. He had a natural flair for advertising and deftly steered the brand image into the public gaze using both eye-catching adverts and his appealing personality.

Thomas especially loved to use old paintings to advertise the company's whisky, in order to reflect the quality and authenticity of the spirit. He purchased a number of very famous paintings to use in the company's advertising, including Monarch of the Glen by Landseer and the famous Macnab by Raeburn. He also collected many of the paintings of Coaching Inns by J. C. Maggs *(left)*, some of which were adapted to promote the Dewar's brand.

The Whisky of his Forefather's was the company's longest running advertising campaign and one typical of Thomas Dewar. It was based on a scene from a light operetta by Gilbert and Sullivan – a man is drinking Dewar's whisky in his ancestral home and the paintings of his forefathers come alive in their desire to try the spirit. It was so popular that it was repainted on many occasions over the decades, and still featured on the label of John Dewar & Sons deluxe blend as late as the 1970s. It reflected Thomas Dewar's love of the theatre and his eye for a successful campaign.

Thomas Dewar was also a pioneer of sensational advertising – he wanted to make his advertisements so unusual and eye catching that people talked about it. The Spirit of his Forefather's became the theme for John Dewar & Sons first cinematic advert in 1898, which was the first ever film advert for a drinks product. This was first screened onto the roof of the Pepper building in New York, reputedly bringing traffic to a stop!

The Impact of Global Expansion

With the power of Thomas Dewar's advertising behind it, the company expanded massively between the 1890s and early 1900s. During this time Thomas also travelled extensively, appointing agents across the globe, and thus John Dewar & Sons started exporting on a large scale. It was John Alexander Dewar back in Scotland who was left with the task of making sure he could meet the growing demand. This meant increasing the production of whisky at the same time as maintaining the high standards established by his father John. Thus it became necessary for the company to expand beyond the High Street property.
In 1891 the firm made its first purchase of heritable property in the form of the Speygate Bonded Warehouse. The building, though old and in need of repair, was nevertheless convenient, spacious, and seemed to provide ample accommodation for the ever expanding blending and bottling operations of the firm.

However, the Speygate offered only part of the solution required for the rapidly expanding company. In 1893 John Dewar & Sons started preparations for a new office and bond at 28 Glasgow Road, where a site had been acquired adjacent to the goods station of the North British Railway Company. A private railway siding into the premises was laid down resulting in a smooth link between the company and the rest of the world – aiding both the delivery of whisky stocks and raw materials as well as the export of the finished product throughout the UK and abroad. The company moved into the new premises in 1894.

The Glasgow Road property was across the road from the cattle market. It's a point which perhaps generally wouldn't be worth mentioning, however staff from that time still tell the incredible story of one day during the 1950s when a cow escaped from the cattle market and somehow managed to find the entrance door to

Dewar's advert c1920s.

Dewar's Perth warehouse staff 1897.

Glasgow Road c1930s.

the John Dewar & Sons bottling hall, which just happened to be open. The huge animal ran amok along the bottling lines, sending the largely female workers running for their lives. Fortunately no one was injured and the animal managed to exit by the door at the end of the hall leaving only a shaken workforce and a slight decline in production for the day.

By the time John Dewar & Sons issued shares and became a public company in 1897, they had property at Glasgow Road, a bonded warehouse at Newtown Road and a bonded warehouse, stores and dwelling-house at Speygate and Canal Street. The company's business development had been exceptionally marked during the previous thirteen years, which was essentially since Thomas Dewar moved to London in 1885 and started to make a name for the brand beyond Scotland. The whisky market was also taking off with a greater demand for old and rare whiskies, and John Dewar & Sons were well placed to cater for such tastes.

By the 1890s the shape and scale of the company was beyond all recognition of the small business established by John Dewar – from a single shop in 1880, to premises throughout the UK, including London, Manchester and Bristol, and agencies all over the world, for example in New York, India and Australia to name but three. The company also had a royal warrant to Queen Victoria and more than fifty prizes and awards for the quality of the whisky. When their father died profits had stood at £1,321.[6] By 1900 profits had reached £59,000[7] and were still climbing, with an annual output of one million proof gallons.

By this time the company had also entirely moved out of the High Street into the Glasgow Road premises. In 1912 a large castle-like building was built for extending the blending and warehousing. The new building was vast, partly because John Dewar & Sons didn't just mature their whiskies, they also carried out a complicated vatting and marrying process to make the blends even smoother. This special blending method had been pioneered by the company's first official Master Blender, A. J. Cameron, who started working for the company as an office boy and finished up as a Director. This movement up the ranks, gathering experience and knowledge, as well as an entire life spent working in one company, was typical of the period. It also helped to give the company a family feel.

By 1913 turnover and profits were more than four times those of 1897 and yet still the company continued to expand. There were nearly 300 staff in Perth alone by the 1920s, the majority of whom lived locally. Further building works were required to improve the Glasgow Road premises to meet increasing demand for the whisky and accommodate staff needs. During the 1930s a new bottling warehouse, casemaking shop and welfare block were built on the Glasgow Road site. This bottling warehouse was said to be the most up-to-date of its kind, with natural light and fresh air, which were considered a great benefit to staff. The welfare block provided dining rooms, first-aid rooms and cloakrooms.

White Label is the whisky everyone tends to associate with John Dewar & Sons, because it is the company's most popular product and has been for over 100 years. It was introduced in 1899 and prior to that John Dewar & Sons produced a whole range of different whisky blends, which were aimed at different prices and customers. These included simple whisky blends of younger whiskies for mixing into toddies, and more aged special whiskies for savouring in small quantities. The company was renowned for their stock of very old and fine whiskies.

John Alexander Dewar: The First Whisky Baron

Thomas Dewar has long been celebrated as a big personality, full of energy and amusing anecdotes; indeed he was very much the personality behind the Dewar's brand identity. Contrastingly John has undeservedly been labelled simply as 'dour'. The reality is that this is largely the result of John's own preference to shun the blaze of publicity, content during his lifetime to see his younger brother Thomas basking in the limelight and keeping the Dewar name in the press. John Dewar, or Lord Forteviot as he was to become, was a man greatly admired by his contemporaries. When he died in 1929 the *Perthshire Advertiser* wrote 'In many respects Lord Forteviot was the greatest man that Perth has ever produced…'.[8]

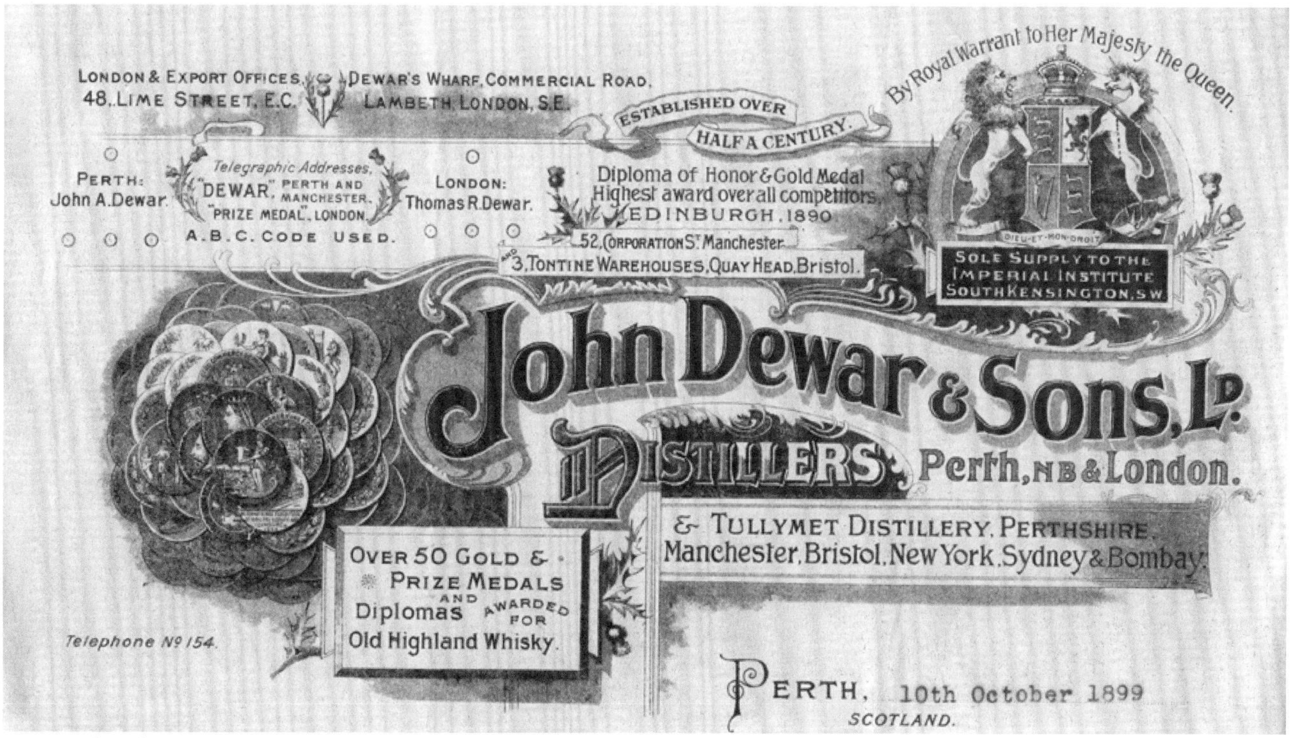

Company letterhead c1900s.

Dewar's bonded warehouse, opened 1913.

Bottling hall c1930s.

John became a prominent Liberal politician, was a landowner and energetic agriculturalist, devoted a great deal of time to serving his home city of Perth, and still found time for a full family life. In 1883 he became one of the youngest members of the Perth Town Council, aged only twenty-seven and with his sound head for figures was elected treasurer five years later. Having completely overhauled the town's finances he was unanimously appointed as Lord Provost in 1893, a position he held for six years.

John had the welfare of the people of Perth in mind when he embarked on a series of city improvements. Under his guidance slum areas were demolished (including Scott Street, Kinnoull Street and King Edward Street), new gas works were erected, and the Victoria Bridge over the River Tay was built. Throughout his life he continued to be a generous benefactor to his native City. He contributed substantial funds for the restoration of the Church of Saint John, and gifted the Maternity Home to the Perth County and City Royal Infirmary. The Forteviot Trust is another of his enduring legacies, established to provide funding for local people.

He also made many smaller, though not insignificant, contributions, which included on a number of occasions, treats for the people living in the Perth poor house. In 1898 he provided a New Year treat in the form of a dinner of meat and potatoes with plum pudding, plus tea, tobacco, sugar and sweets for the children.

In 1900 he was elected Member of Parliament for Invernesshire in the only Liberal victory in Scotland for that election. He won by a slim majority of 301 votes against the Tory candidate, but within six years had proven his worth to the people and won the 1906 election with a majority of thousands. Once again John followed the same pattern he had already established in his native city of Perth, channelling his energies into improving the living standards of the people in his constituency.

In parliament he was extremely active, becoming chairman of various commissions of enquiry, including two investigations into the medical and nursing conditions in the Highlands and Islands. The resulting recommendations, known as the Dewar Report of 1912, brought into the public eye the brutal and often grim reality of the lives of people in the remote areas of Scotland, and spurred the government to make significant grants. This report would later influence the development of the NHS.

John was rewarded a number of times for his lifelong commitment to serving the public. In 1907 he was created a baronet and in 1916 King George V elevated him to the peerage for his services to the state. Thus John became the first of the so-called 'Whisky Barons'[9] (which would later include his brother Thomas Dewar and other key industry players such as James Buchanan, creator of the famous 'Black and White' brand). *The Perthshire Advertiser* reported in 1917 that the peerage had been inevitable, and noted with some humour: 'If the cockneys cannot pronounce "Forteviot" properly, neither can they "Dewar", so that they, at least, are no worse off.'

Dupplin and Forteviot

John had also found the time to develop agricultural interests, continuing his desire for regeneration in his private life. In 1910 he purchased the beautiful estate of Dupplin, four miles west of Perth, from the Earl of Kinnoull. Lord Forteviot immediately put his enormous energy to the task of improvements and was to make Dupplin an impressive estate. He demolished the old farm labourers cottages and despite delays caused by the First World War, rebuilt Forteviot village between 1925 and 1926 in the style of a Dutch township, where he housed the estate workers. A local historian wrote at the time, 'the village was gradually acquiring an appearance of decay.' and that John Alexander Dewar 'determined at once to give the little village a new lease of life.'[10] Forteviot became recognised as one of the model villages of Perthshire and the estate itself was to become the centre for his agricultural interests. In 1927 the new Forteviot Hall was opened by music hall comedian Sir Harry Lauder, a friend of the Dewar family and regular visitor to Dupplin. Dupplin itself became a model dairy farm, and John carried out innovative experiments in cattle feeding and crop growing.

It was not only John Alexander Dewar who demonstrated a commitment to the local area. His son, John Dewar, also became Lord Provost of Perth from 1922 to 1925, continuing the family tradition of civic duties. Thomas Dewar also demonstrated his philanthropic leanings when he gifted Kinnoull Hill to the people

Dupplin Castle.

of Perth in 1923. He said that in his youth he 'capered gaily up and down Kinnoull Hill'. Although he had left his native town, he had never forgotten it and he visited his brother at Dupplin regularly.

It is no wonder then that in 1924 the Perth Town Council unanimously accepted the recommendation of the magistrates to confer the Freedom of the City of Perth upon Lord Forteviot and his brother Thomas. Both modestly declined. John wrote to the Town Clerk that this honour was 'too great', and that 'The pleasure of being allowed to help my native city in any form is in itself sufficient reward.'

Staff Excursions and Sporting Activities

The Dewar family philanthropy was also directed towards its own workforce. With many staff working for the company over a long period of time, there was a family feel to the business of John Dewar & Sons in Perth. Early in the company history numerous benefits were established for staff, including outings, sports and perhaps more importantly, pensions and care for retired staff.

One of the most memorable traditions was the annual staff outing. During the 1890s John Dewar & Sons established a tradition for treating their workers to dinner and an excursion, an annual event that would continue for many decades. The excursions started round about 1895 with a trip to the Small Glen, which included about one hundred employees with everything paid for by the company. Later trips included Comrie, St Fillans and Rumbling Bridge. All participating employees were usually taken to the chosen location by carriages or trains, and on arrival they had lunch, took part in sporting activities or fishing and there was perhaps a beauty contest followed by a dance later in the evening. It was often a full day and evening of activities, weather permitting of course.

Competitive sports were also important to the company and workforce. John Dewar & Sons had a fishing team and cricket team at least as early as 1893, the funds for which were supported by the firm. By the 1920s Dewar's also had a women's football team and later a cricket team. This tradition would continue throughout the company's time in Perth, including other activities such as golf and first aid.

Amalgamation: The Distillery Company Ltd

So far we have traced the early expansion of the company under the firm guidance of the Dewar family. This solid foundation was to prove a great asset to the brand when John Dewar & Sons merged with the Distillers Company Ltd (DCL) in 1925 and though the Dewar family remained involved in the company, it was the start of a series of industry amalgamations which ultimately led to Dewar's becoming part of Guinness during the 1980s. But we are jumping ahead a little bit too fast. As part of the DCL, Dewar's was part of a much larger whisky portfolio which included key competitors such as John Walker & Sons and James Buchanan Ltd. Significantly, they could all share whiskies for blending, and aimed to avoid competing directly with one another and so it was a relatively harmonious solution to a previous period of intense competition. John Alexander Dewar died in 1929 and Thomas Dewar died the following year, but the family continued to guide the company well into the 1980s.

Expansion: Inveralmond

The company continued to flourish following the death of its founders, yet despite significant investment in the Glasgow Road site, by 1957 it was obvious that John Dewar & Sons needed more space, especially for blending and bottling. The company had reached maximum capacity there due to ever increasing sales, and the site itself was ageing. It was time for a significant move.

After careful consideration, the triangular site at Inveralmond on the outskirts of Perth was deemed to be the best location available for expansion and in 1958 John Dewar & Sons purchased land there in order to increase production. The site at Glasgow Road occupied between four and five acres. The new site at Inveralmond was twenty-six acres in size, with an impressive twenty-four extra available to expand into. Inevitably transfer to the new site was a gradual process. In 1959 the company's standard blends became freely available in the home market as the post Second World War quota system was finally abolished, so the need for increased capacity was urgent. The foundation stone at Inveralmond was laid by Lady Forteviot in a short ceremony in 1960. The blending and coopering departments moved into the new accommodation first in 1961 but it wasn't until 1962 that the entire site was ready for occupation. In that same year the old offices on the Glasgow Road were let to the local authority and the property was later sold to Robert Templeton Antiques in 1982.

The Inveralmond site still continued to expand over the next thirty years and by the 1970s about eight hundred people were employed there. It is interesting to trace the growth of the company and changes in technology by examining the development in bottling production. In 1902 John Dewar & Sons had four bottling tables, which were exactly that – long tables where women carried out a great deal of manual work. The women at these tables could comfortably handle an output of 2,000 cases of whisky per day. This is the equivalent of 24,000 bottles per day, or 6,000 per day on one table. In 1973, two new super fast bottling lines were completed at Inveralmond, and the contrast in scale and capacity was truly astonishing. The fastest was capable of handling 10,800 bottles per hour, or 180 bottles per minute, a clear demonstration of the changing scale of the company and the industry.

The involvement of the Dewar family had dwindled over the years, until the relationship ended in the 1980s. John Dewar & Sons remained at Inveralmond until 1994 when the plant was closed down. By the time Bacardi purchased the brand in 1998, John Dewar & Sons no longer had a presence in Perth.

Conclusion

John Dewar & Sons has a rich history in Perth, and a proud foundation, which has in many ways shaped the business that exists today. That heritage is very much bound up with the Dewar family history and continues to be an influencing factor in the brand identity. In Perth itself, a simple walk around the centre of town will reveal old buildings relating to the company and the family, and advertising artefacts of various kinds can still be found in local hotels and pubs. John Dewar & Sons production may have left Perth but history dictates that the brand will always have Perth at its heart.

All images are from the archive of John Dewar & Sons Ltd.

End Notes

1 David Graham-Campbell, Perth – *The Fair City* (Edinburgh 1994), p108.
2 See advert in the *Perthshire Advertiser,* 14 May 1846.
3 See advert in the *Perth Courier*, 1 June 1837.
4 Quote from the *Perthshire Advertiser* 29 January 1880.
5 'The Big Three' included John Dewar & Sons, John Walker & Sons Ltd and James Buchanan & Co Ltd.
6 The approximate equivalent value today would be £63,800.
7 The approximate equivalent value today would be £3,366,000.
8 Quote from the *Perthshire Advertiser* 27 November 1929.
9 This refers to a famous publication about whisky: Allen Andrews, *The Whisky Barons* (Glasgow 2002).
10 Rev Neil Meldrum, *Forteviot – The History of a Strathearn Parish* (Paisley, 1926), p 296.

Risky business: a history of General Accident[1]

Susan Payne

Introduction

This paper charts the history of a company called General Accident. 'GA', as it came to be known, was an insurance and finance company. It had its headquarters in Perth from 1885 until 2001 and became part of the life of the city. Generations of local families worked for GA and many others moved into the area to work for the company. But what was it like to work for General Accident? How did this tiny company in a small city grow worldwide and how did GA eventually lose its name and its headquarters in Perth?

In December 1885 four members of the Highland and Agricultural Society established General Accident. They offered, in return for a payment, insurance against all kinds of accidents. This new company was largely set up because of an Act of Parliament. From 1880 the law stated that employers had to compensate employees who were injured while at work. In agricultural Perthshire, farmers employing many workers using new and dangerous farm machinery were now liable, so GA was established particularly with farmers in mind.

Stanley Norie-Miller in his Black Watch uniform with the ribbon of the Military Cross awarded to him for bravery, 1917 (Courtesy of Perth Museum & Art Gallery, 2001.146.1).

Francis Norie-Miller 'At home', 1914 (Courtesy of Perth Museum & Art Gallery, 2001.195).

The Norrie-Millers

The new company worked from two rooms in Victoria Buildings, Tay Street, Perth. By 1887 one man was already making his mark on the company – Francis Norie-Miller. For eighty years General Accident was dominated by one family – the Norie-Millers, father and son. The father, Francis Norie-Miller, came to work for the company as Secretary in 1887. At the age of twenty-eight he was an arrogant upstart who dared to bargain with his new employers over his pay and conditions. He had lots of energy and charm and a driving ambition. He enjoyed taking risks, using power and keeping tight control. Like all great leaders, Francis had a vision. He saw the GA as an international company and he worked towards that vision relentlessly. During the First World War he crossed the Atlantic no fewer than eight times on company business! In return he expected hard work and loyalty from his staff and he could be a tyrant. Francis also aimed to be a pillar of the community. He encouraged sports and social clubs for his staff and built the Pavilion, in what is now Rodney Gardens, for their use. Among other organisations, he served on the School Board in Perth. He was elected National Liberal MP for Perth when in his seventies. In 1933 he was presented with the Freedom of the City of Perth and in that same year became Chairman and Managing Director of GA. In 1936 he was awarded a baronetcy. In 1938 he became Governor of GA; no longer the dictator, but he was still intensely proud and protective of the company which had developed worldwide under his direction. Ill health finally forced Sir Francis to retire in 1944 but only after he had worked for GA for over fifty years. It was an incredible record.

Francis Norie-Miller's first son, Claud, worked briefly for the company, but died during the First World War. One of the bells in St John's Kirk, Perth was hung as a memorial to him. Francis's second son, Stanley, joined General Accident in 1919. Within four years he had become Deputy General Manager in a clear case of nepotism. Francis wanted Stanley to take over the company after he had gone. This was meant to be a dynasty. Stanley took over as General Manager in 1933, was Managing Director until 1963 and also Chairman from 1951. He was a very different kind of character to his father. He did not enjoy taking risks and he was a careful manager. GA continued to expand, but Stanley was most concerned to keep his father's existing empire together. He controlled board meetings by making sure that any discussion was kept general and even took the minutes himself. He was also very careful with money, new biros were given to staff individually and only after the old one was checked first. But, under Stanley, the company celebrated its seventy-fifth anniversary. Like his father before him he was presented with the Freedom of the City of Perth, in 1961. Stanley was successful in consolidating his father's achievements and he was particularly remembered in his memorial service for his kindness.[2] He resigned in 1968 and ended a staggering eighty years of Norie-Miller family influence on GA.

Life at GA

At the beginning, workers followed a strict regime. By 1904 office hours were set at 9am–5pm Monday to Friday and 9am–1pm on Saturdays. Francis Norie-Miller, manager of the original company, kept tight control of both his business and his staff. Strict rules were laid down for staff behaviour – 'Any unnecessary noise, conversation or laughter… must be immediately checked'.[3] People carried out monotonous jobs and even after the Second World War some still sat on high stools at high desks. In General Buildings, Perth, senior managers only were allowed to use the front door and the lift. The rest came in at the back door and filed past the timekeeper. Staff were not allowed to make tea, but lunch was one and a quarter hours long so that people could go home to eat. There was the chance of every third Saturday off if you worked well. Most staff did work well, serving the whole of their working lives in GA, sometimes generation after generation in one family. Grace Gibbons worked for GA for forty-nine years until she retired in 1968.

The workforce was not always well paid, yet it was loyal and it was hard working. Senior managers were expected to go the extra mile for the company. In 1923 one was told to go to Jamaica for six months on business. He begged not to have to go, saying the heat would kill him and he had a sick wife and mother at home. Francis's reply was cutting, 'I do feel that highly paid officials… should be available at any time… and that is why I am so disappointed'.[4] Even by the 1950s most of the staff continued to carry out routine tasks and whether you were promoted still depended on your being noticed. Staff were required to dress smartly; men wore suits. In the 1960s mini skirts were frowned upon and until the late 1970s women were not allowed to wear trousers. From the 1960s, after the

Interior of General Buildings' Accounts department, Perth, c1910 (Courtesy of Perth Museum & Art Gallery, 2001.572.3).

Norie-Miller years, the strict office rules relaxed. Saturday working ended. The starting and finishing bells were no longer sounded. Now both men and women who worked for twenty-five years were given a gold watch and, after forty years' service, a bonus. Flexible working hours were even introduced from 1974, an idea which would have been unthinkable under Francis Norie-Miller.

Francis Norie-Miller was not a man to be crossed. When some staff wanted to organise a union in 1920 the dispute went on for nine months and the company refused to let an outside body mediate. One hundred and thirty-three staff withdrew their labour and there were two rallies in Westminster. One national journalist in *The Economist* described the GA management action as 'an indefensible act of tyranny'. Publicly, Francis blamed the affair on two women who 'had little to do'.[5] He called it a storm in a teacup and said the publicity was good for the company. Yet he felt it keenly. He announced that no strikers would be re-employed and none of their relatives would ever work for GA. Allegedly, a black book was kept which recorded all their names and then was burned when Francis died. By the 1960s, trade unions were a much stronger force and by the end of 1977 two unions represented GA staff. In 1982, in support of a nationwide pay claim, GA saw its first strike action for sixty years. Unlike the 1920s dispute, this one was settled within a few weeks because GA now urgently needed its staff at work and needed to co-operate with the unions.

GA encouraged staff sports and recreation from the beginning. It was a very enlightened company. Francis Norie-Miller, a keen sportsman himself, invited groups of staff to his home at Cleeve to play tennis and golf. The company built and opened a sports and social club for its staff in 1935. Called the Pavilion, it was built on a scenic piece of land by the River Tay, now known as Rodney Gardens. Staff in GA offices across the UK enjoyed their company outings. Glasgow staff visited the Falls of Clyde for their first ever trip in 1912.

Socially, there was a good atmosphere. Occasions – such as someone leaving, retiring, getting married or being presented with a long-service award – were generally cause for a special event or celebration and the active sports and social life of General Accident was a big bonus for the staff.

The first woman to work for GA began her job in 1894, nine years after the company was first founded. The only woman on the Board was appointed in 1992, one hundred and seven years after the company was founded. The introduction of the typewriter and the effects of the First and Second World Wars were the two factors that really brought large numbers of females into the office. During both world wars women had to be recruited and trained to do men's jobs. The first woman to hold a senior post in a branch was probably a Miss Helen Shand. She became chief clerk in Inverness in 1916, standing in for a man who had left to fight. During the course of the First World War some branches were without ninety-five per cent of their male staff.

General Accident was always a respectable place to work. In 1941, when Lily Turpie joined the company at the age of fourteen, there was a waiting list for jobs. It was easier to get a job if your relatives already worked there – as long as they weren't trouble makers. Lily worked for GA for over forty-five years, working her way up from typist to private secretary to three Chief General Managers.

First and Second World Wars

The First World War stopped General Accident from expanding abroad. Belgium, where it had its biggest investment in Europe, was invaded by Germany so the situation was as bad as it could be. Some GA staff from foreign countries fled to London and parts of the main office in Aldwych were made available for use by the Belgian Consulate. Francis Norie-Miller and his wife even handed over their London house for use by Belgians and the King of the Belgians rewarded them with medals.

Staff volunteered for service and GA promised them their jobs back when they returned. The company even topped up their war service pay and sent them the company magazine *The General's*

Making metal address plates in the Mechanisation Department, Perth, 1950s (Courtesy of Perth Museum & Art Gallery, 2001.307.2).

Review to keep them in touch with home. The war made people at home worry about their property and their families, especially when air raids began and so the insurance naturally increased. In Perth, the *Perthshire Advertiser* newspaper opened a penny fund for the restoration of St John's Kirk as a war memorial. GA topped the list of donors giving 25,336 pennies. Sadly, thirty-nine staff from the Perth office of GA were killed or died in service. At the end of the war, as you might expect from a man like Francis, big claims were lodged by General Accident against Germany for loss of buildings and business!

The Second World War had an even bigger effect on General Accident than the First World War. As in the first war, staff on active service had their service pay made up by the company to that of their normal salaries. But by 1940 this was costing GA £20,000 a year, a vast sum of money. As in the First World War, women took over men's work. There was far more damage at home from air raids than in the first war. GA's own offices suffered badly. Their buildings in London, Plymouth and Portsmouth were destroyed. The Head Office in London was twice affected by bombing and the office in Exeter took a direct hit in 1942. But GA staff, loyal and hardworking as ever, soldiered on. When the first floor ceiling of the Hull office collapsed during an air raid, staff continued to work on the ground floor. Overseas offices were also affected. On the island of Jersey, of course, people rushed to check that their life insurance was still good on the day that Germany invaded. The GA office there came to be neither lit nor heated and staff did their work wrapped in blankets. But the most incredible story of all is surely that of the GA agent in Rangoon, Burma. As the Japanese advanced, he walked eight hundred miles to hand over the company's papers and cash to the GA agent in Calcutta, India! When France fell to Germany in 1940 the Board of General Accident was very worried. Plans were even made for the evacuation of Head Office to Canada. Back in the office, gas mask drills could last for an hour. In 1942 the Ministry of Labour recommended longer working hours because there were fewer workers, so a GA typist might work two nights extra a week for 1s.6d an hour. Some of the Perth staff offered holidays in their homes to fellow staff in London as a respite from the air raids. Head Office in Perth sent parcels and letters to prisoners of war and set up a fund for widows and children at home. After Victory in Europe in May 1945, General Accident awarded a 'victory bonus' to its staff.

Between the wars GA had expanded. As a result Head Office had many more staff at the start of the Second World War but many more died – one hundred and fifty-one compared to thirty-nine during the First World War.

The business

Within a century, General Accident had three different Head Offices in Perth; two were purpose built. The first was in Victoria Buildings, Tay Street, respectable and in a pleasant situation, but much too small for a rapidly growing company. The second, General Buildings, between High Street and Tay Street, opened in 1901, was quite different, prominent, distinctive and imposing with massive marble pillars supporting the second floor. Despite an extension in the 1950s it also became too small. So, in addition, GA also had branch offices and works buildings around the city and, later, the offices called Tayside on Isla Road. Between 1979 and 1983 a new £33 million headquarters was built at Pitheavlis on the edge of the city. It combined departments that had previously been working on nine different sites. The design was very modern. It was like a chest of drawers opening out of the hillside and was described as one of the most exciting and satisfying work environments anywhere. This new Head Office included the main office building, a students and visitors residence, and a sports and social complex. Pitheavlis also provided banking, bus and catering services for its staff. Buchan Marshall, the Chief General Manager, described it as an investment in people.

General Accident was one of the first companies to insure motor vehicles. It became Britain's biggest motor insurer and it was well known in America too. The insurance business really expanded with the introduction of railways and their accidents from the 1840s, but the development of motor cars was to be by far the most important factor. When parliament passed the Locomotives and Highways Act in 1896 and allowed cars to travel faster than walking speed, the potential for accidents and accident insurance suddenly grew. GA saw its chance. In 1903 it had a stand at the first Motor Manufacturers and Traders Show in London and by 1908 it was insuring the cars of the royal family. Britain's first mass-market car, the Austin Seven, was available from 1921. One of GA's board members was William Morris, the motor manufacturer. Between 1924 and 1926 every Morris car was sold with a free GA insurance. GA lost money on the deal but gained huge publicity and built up countless connections with motor dealers. As more cars took to the road there were more accidents. In 1930 the Road Traffic Act made third party insurance compulsory, and instantly increased GA's business. They were really motoring now! During the Second World War the car insurance business was quiet, petrol was rationed and cars were not produced. After the war it took some time before factories could meet the demand for cars. But the first Mini was sold in 1959 for £500 and motorway systems developed from the 1960s. Driving long fast motorway journeys brought more accidents. It

Prospectus for General Accident's Cosmos Utopia insurance policy, 1906 (Courtesy of Perth Museum & Art Gallery, archive 4049).

wasn't until 1983 that front seat belts became compulsory. GA looked for new ways to sell motor insurance. In the past it had conducted its business through agents across the UK, but later, arranging insurance directly over the phone was to become the most important method and 'GA Direct' was set up.

Accidents were everyone's problem. They were what GA insured their policyholders against and what GA had to pay out for. In 1985 the number of deaths and injuries on Britain's roads was 317,524. In the first six months of that year General Accident paid out around £100 million on insurance claims. Insuring people against accidents is a risky business.

Advertising and building up a good reputation was critical for the success of General Accident. As early as 1888 GA was advertising in diaries. The company would pay out £100 if a passenger was killed in a railway accident but only if they were carrying the diary at the time. An impression of strength and confidence was what GA wanted to project. That was the impression that its headquarters at the bottom of the High Street in Perth made on its visitors. The names of early board members were impressive too, including the Hon. C.S. Rolls of Rolls-Royce fame. GA knew where to advertise as well, taking stands at shows. Throughout the twentieth century motor insurance was a particularly good subject for advertisements, portraying terrifying, frustrating, expensive, shocking, funny and annoying experiences. General Accident advertised widely in newspapers, journals, magazines and printed books, on leaflets, posters and billboards. From the 1970s it also advertised on television featuring the actor John Cleese and it also sponsored high profile local, national and international events. In the end, the company came to realise too, that its reputation was not only dependent on advertising but also on the worker on the floor – in fact the person who answered the phone.

Insurance can be a risky business because disasters cannot always be predicted. General Accident was involved with some really big disasters including the loss of the ship Titanic in 1912, the devastation in Australia following cyclones Wanda and Tracy in 1974, and, in the same year in the UK, the explosion at the chemical plant in Flixborough. Flixborough cost GA over £1.5 million – its largest claim ever in Britain. Big claims were also paid out on the loss of two famous racehorses in the 1980s – Shergar and Troy. However, the biggest single loss sustained by GA was caused by Hurricane Gilbert, which hit Jamaica in 1988 and cost the company £30 million. Then, in January 1993, Perthshire itself, the home of General Accident, was hit by flood disaster. Homes, belongings, businesses and livelihoods were all affected. The River Tay and its tributaries flooded the district including 1,500 homes, and within two days GA was dealing with over five hundred insurance claims from local people.

The years since the founding of General Accident have arguably seen more changes in technology than any other period in history. Railways, cars, planes, telegraph machines, telephones, typewriters, satellites, film, television and computers have all changed our way of life. And they made a big impact on GA too. Inside Head Office in Perth we can only imagine the pace of business before the telephone or the typewriter. The year 1892 held great potential. Two managers were sent to Glasgow to see a demonstration of the typewriter. After careful consideration, one machine was bought, but only one. It cost £26.5s, half a year's salary for a clerk. In the same year the Board decided not to have a telephone. It only appeared in 1894 and then only at Head Office in Perth. For decades, Head Office sent messages by the telegraph machine. In 1928 its impressive address was 'Bullion, Perth' but it still only had three phone lines. The Board could never have imagined that direct phone lines would actually become critical for selling insurance quickly and simply! Work was labour intensive with manual record keeping and continuous typing and re-typing. Then, from the 1950s, the pace quickened with the introduction of punched cards, addressing, franking, adding and dictating machines, which all helped to speed up work. A telex machine was installed in Perth and London in 1958 and the first electric typewriter was introduced that year too. But the most important piece of technology was the computer, a machine that could process information quickly. In 1960 General Accident installed an IBM computer, which used punched cards for data input and magnetic tapes for storage. However, this first computer system was not the answer to life, the universe and everything; computers had yet to develop in a way that was most useful for the company. But as more powerful computers were introduced and more information was collected about customers, the company was in a better position to do business. From 1996 a new computer package was introduced which showed all the customer details on one screen. This computer package was the biggest project ever undertaken by the company.

If a company's product can be sold across the world then there is the opportunity for vast numbers of new markets and vast new wealth. By the year 1910 General Accident was already trading in many countries, including America, Ireland, France, Belgium, the Netherlands, Canada, Australia, South Africa, the Argentine, Mexico, Russia, Gibraltar, Spain and India. By 1924 GA was printing its policies in eleven languages and was operating in no fewer than thirty countries. General Accident expanded partly by taking over or merging with other companies, such as the Yorkshire Insurance Company with its business in Brazil, France and Iran. The company's development is legendary. Within a century it expanded into forty countries and employed 17,000 people across the world. In fact, over two-thirds of its premium income came from abroad and Francis Norie-Miller shaped its

Advertising poster from General Accident's 'Keep Motoring' campaign in the 1970s (Courtesy of Perth Museum & Art Gallery, 2001.538.4).

How GA staff felt about computers in 1966. 'Not much is generally known of the men and women who feed and control the computer. There are more of them than you think…' (The General's Review, Vol. LXI, No.2, Autumn 1966, p.41).

rapid development. He personally made thirty-nine transatlantic voyages to establish and monitor overseas business. But, the big question is, why on earth did GA keep its Head Office in the small Scottish city of Perth? The answer is because Francis wanted it here. He argued that it was cheaper to keep offices and staff in Perth than in London, but when Stanley Norie-Miller resigned in 1968 and ended the family involvement, the company began to change. Perth was not necessarily going to continue to be the headquarters and reliable employment and company loyalty were not necessarily going to continue either. The company aimed for the greatest possible and most profitable business across the world, providing services to huge companies as well as to individuals. In 1991, the Chief Executive called a global planning meeting in Perth. Employees from around the world met and shared their experience for the good of the company. GA needed a plan that was strategic and global. Bob Scott, Chief Executive, known as Hurricane Bob, visited GA across the world and came up with ideas for development. Perth had been GA's world headquarters for 113 years but now things were going to move on. The UK investments work was transferred to London in 1996. Only general insurance work was left in Perth. Roseanna Cunningham, the Scottish National Party MP, described it as 'a kick in the teeth for Perth'.[6]

In a global market, size is all-important in the fight for business. New and larger competitors were emerging in the USA and in Europe. GA considered another merger, choosing Commercial Union in 1998. But CGU was to be the name of the new company and local people were inevitably disappointed and sad that the name of General Accident was gone. Employees were worried about their jobs as well. The last GA board meeting was in June 1998. Group headquarters would now be in London, but UK general insurance would have its Head Office at Perth, giving some continuous employment. In reality, Perth had lost Scotland's third largest company and this is where GA's story ends. By 2001, in another merger with Norwich Union, the new company was re-named CGNU and became the seventh largest insurer in the world. New names have arrived since. Most recently, Aviva, still an employer in the town.

Conclusion

For a century, the remarkable General Accident had been an international company with its headquarters in the city of Perth. For many of its employees it had been a family business, with a happy atmosphere and a benevolent parent.

But during its life, the GA changed in character. From having a local identity and being a reliable employer for generations of local families, it became a remote part of a much larger company with a name that was no longer synonymous with Perth.

The last word goes to Francis Norie-Miller, '…men may come and men may go but it [the River Tay] flows on for ever. So, I am convinced, will this great Company continue to be for countless ages of benefit to the peoples of all parts of the world'.[7]

End Notes

1 I particularly wish to acknowledge my great debt to Peter Young, company historian and to Tom Berthon, retired company archivist; other sources include: *Romance of a Business*, (General Accident, 1924) and *The Building of a Business, Quarter Century Memento 1885–1911*, (General Accident Fire & Life Assurance Corporation Ltd, 1911).
2 Programme, memorial service for Sir Stanley Norie-Miller, printed address by Col. Sir James Hutchison, January 1974.
3 Rules and Regulations The General Accident Assurance Corporation Limited, 1904.
4 Young P *A Premium Business*, (Cambridge, 1999), p.101.
5 Young P *A Premium Business*, (Cambridge,1999), p.72.
6 *Perthshire Advertiser* 11 October 1996.
7 I. Gray, *A Business Epic*, (General Accident, 1935), Foreword by F. Norie-Miller.

Index